IMAGES
of Rail

WESTERN CONNECTICUT TROLLEYS

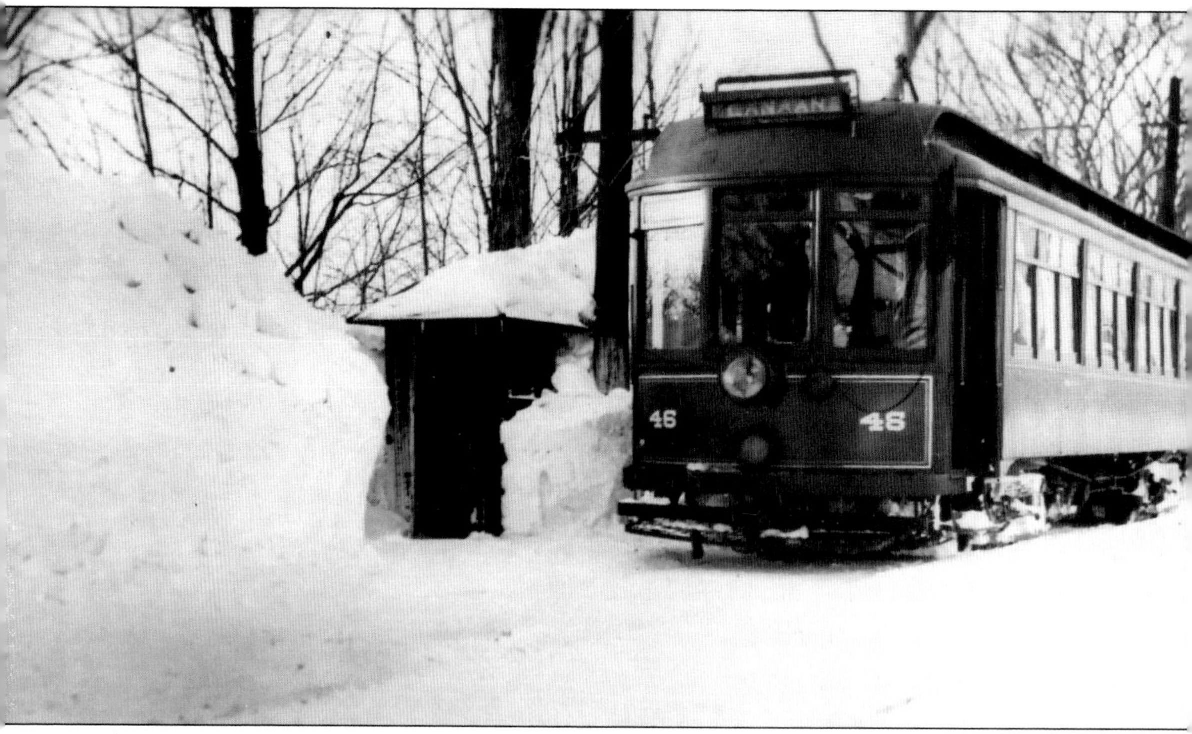

The Berkshire Street Railway was the major streetcar operator in western Massachusetts and, like the Connecticut Company, was a subsidiary of the New Haven Railroad. From 1911 until 1919, the company operated a line from Great Barrington, Massachusetts, to Canaan, Connecticut. Since the Berkshire did not have charter rights in Connecticut, the one-and-a-half-mile track from the state line to the Hotel Canfield, in Canaan, was owned by the New Haven Railroad but operated by the Berkshire. Hourly service was provided, although ridership on the line was quite low. A strike by Berkshire employees shut the system down in 1919. When the grievance was settled, service to Canaan was not resumed. The rail and overhead wire were removed in 1921. Berkshire car No. 46 is shown just north of the Connecticut border during the winter of 1914. Photographs of cars headed to Canaan are extremely rare because the line operated for such a short time. (Courtesy Connecticut Motor Coach Museum Archives.)

On the cover: Please see page 82. (Courtesy Fred Bennett collection.)

IMAGES
of Rail

Western Connecticut Trolleys

Connecticut Motor Coach Museum

ARCADIA
PUBLISHING

ISBN 978-0-7385-4969-9

Published by Arcadia Publishing
Charleston, South Carolina

Printed in the United States of America

Library of Congress Catalog Card Number: 2006935849

For all general information contact Arcadia Publishing at:
Telephone 843-853-2070
Fax 843-853-0044
E-mail sales@arcadiapublishing.com
For customer service and orders:
Toll-Free 1-888-313-2665

Visit us on the Internet at www.arcadiapublishing.com

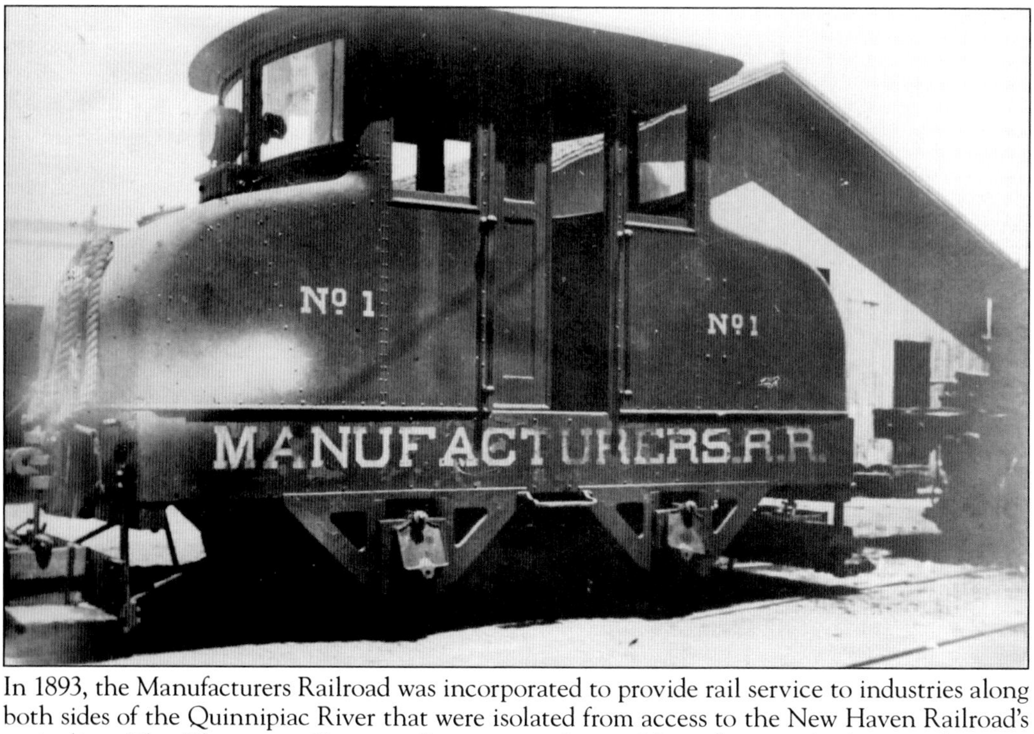

In 1893, the Manufacturers Railroad was incorporated to provide rail service to industries along both sides of the Quinnipiac River that were isolated from access to the New Haven Railroad's main line. The Thompson Houston Company in Lynn, Massachusetts, built Manufacturers car No. 1 in 1893. Prior to delivery, the engine was exhibited at the Columbian Exposition in Chicago and is considered to be the first electric locomotive built in the country. In 1906, the engine was sold to the Joe Cushing Railroad in Fitchburg, Massachusetts, where it was used to move freight cars at a flour mill. It was retired in 1930 and is now on display at the Museum of Transport in St. Louis. (Courtesy Fred Bennett collection.)

Contents

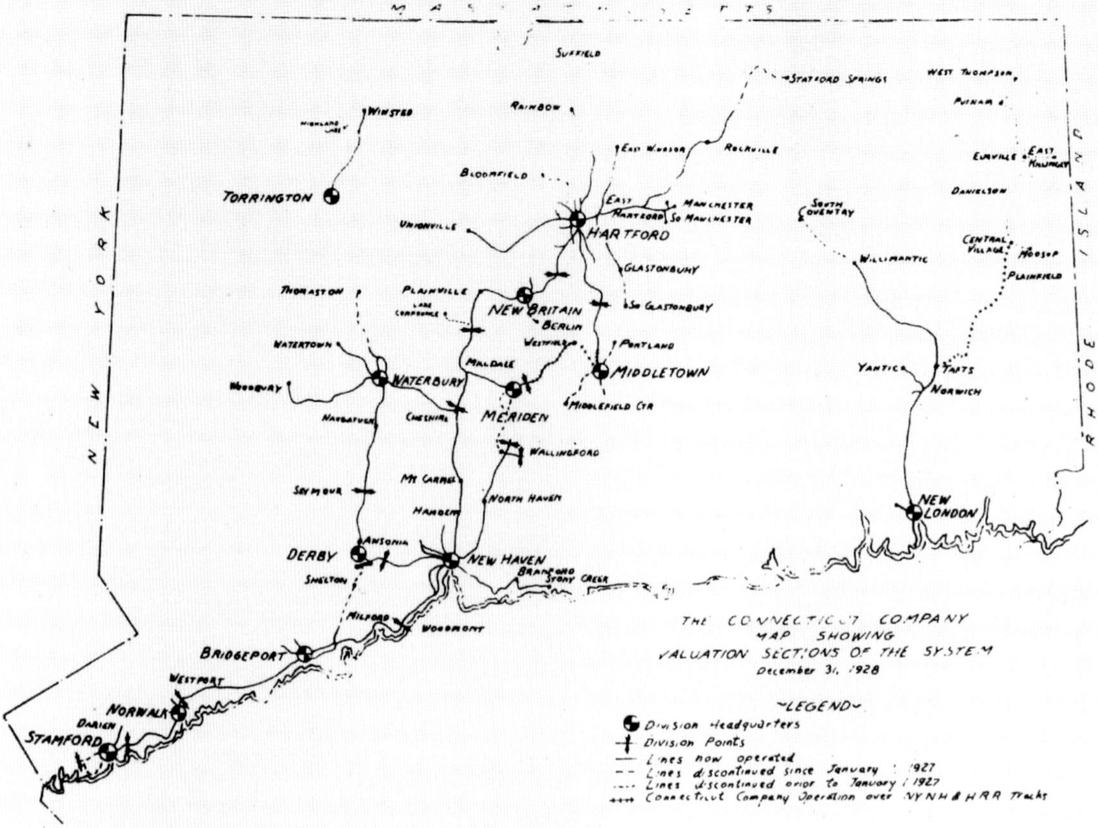

The extent of Connecticut's streetcar system in 1928 is shown in this map. (Courtesy Connecticut Motor Coach Museum Archives.)

INTRODUCTION

Although a small state in area, Connecticut was a giant in commerce, industry, and transportation during the era of the streetcar. The state had an extensive network of over 2,000 miles of railroad and street railway track, which enabled travelers to be transported to virtually any town within its borders. Only a handful of small towns did not have the benefit of some form of transportation using steel wheels on steel rails.

The largest streetcar operator in Connecticut, and one of the largest in the country, the Connecticut Company was formed in 1907 by the New York, New Haven and Hartford Railroad to consolidate the extensive street railway properties that it had acquired over the years. In 1903, Charles S. Mellen, president of the railroad, embarked on a spree of purchasing steamboat lines and street railways in southern New England in order to have a virtual monopoly on transportation in the area. The Connecticut Company controlled the street railways in Bridgeport, Hartford, New London, New Haven, Stamford, Waterbury, and other Connecticut cities. Only Bristol and Danbury had streetcar lines not operated by the company. In the late 1920s, lines were slowly abandoned. Abandonment accelerated over next decade, and by 1940, only Hartford and New Haven had service. Streetcars ran in Hartford until July 1941 and in New Haven until September 1948. In almost all cases, bus service replaced the streetcars, running on the same routes and schedules.

Connecticut's streetcar history has been explored in a number of books. This volume features cities and towns not previously covered, all of which have their own story to tell of the trolley car saga in Connecticut: Bridgeport, Danbury, Meriden, Middletown, Norwalk, and Stamford. Our special thanks go to Fred Bennett of West Granby, who generously provided materials from his extensive collection of streetcar photographs and memorabilia. We would also like to thank Kenneth Rosen and Michael H. Schreiber of the Branford Electric Railway Association and Steve Kellner of the Connecticut Electric Railway Association for allowing the use of images from their archives.

Today one can still ride some of the same streetcars that operated in Hartford, New Haven, and Waterbury at two museums in the state: the Connecticut Trolley Museum, 58 North Road, East Windsor; and the Shore Line Trolley Museum, 17 River Street, East Haven. In addition, visitors to Lake Compounce Park in Bristol can ride a vintage streetcar within the park entrance.

Publication of this book marks an important milestone in the documentation of Connecticut's street railway industry. The histories of all the streetcar lines and companies that operated in the state are now available to the general public in six books.

Alan J. Walker, President
Connecticut Motor Coach Museum
58 North Road
East Windsor, CT 06088
(860) 623-4732

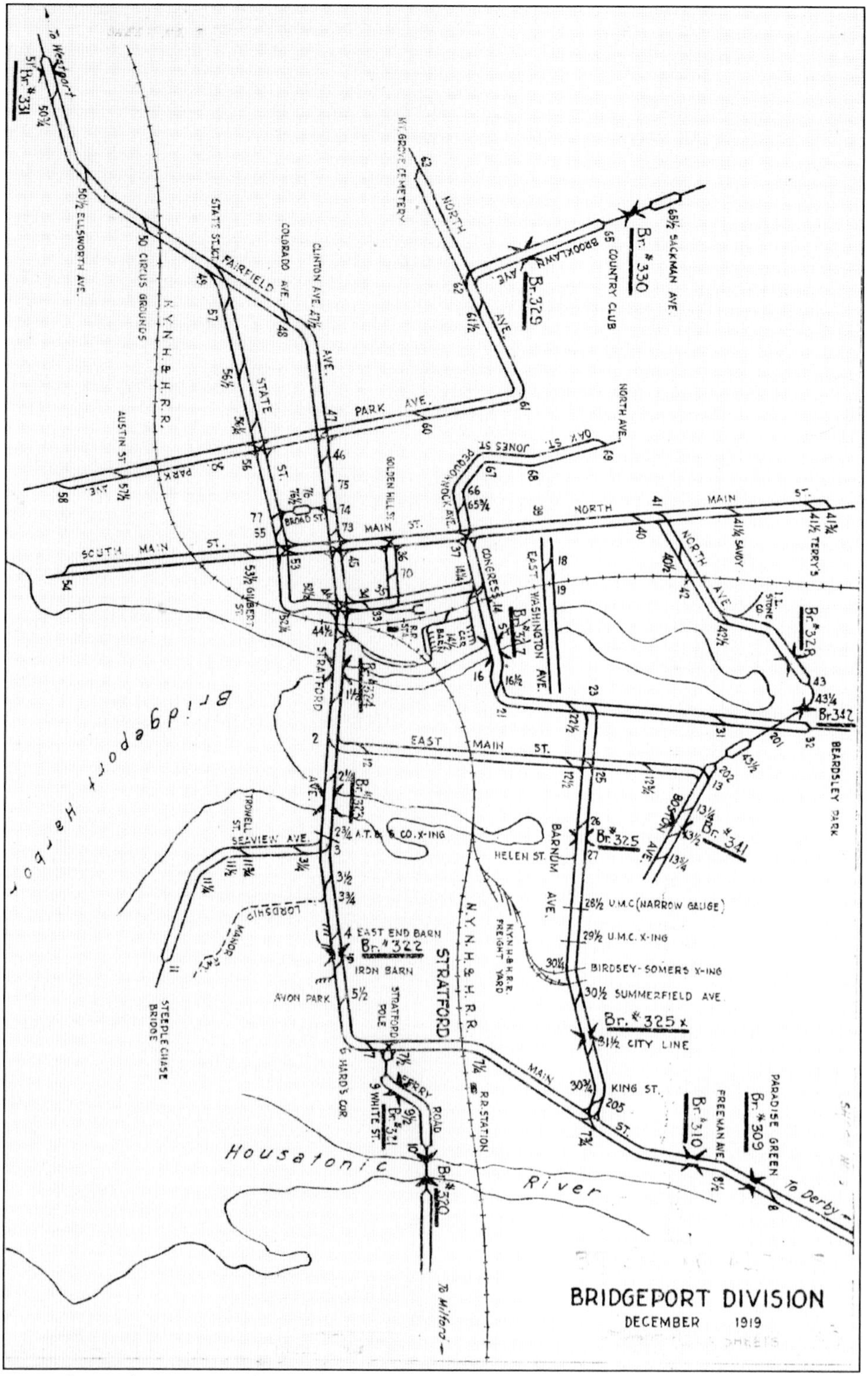

This map shows the streetcar lines in Bridgeport in 1920. (Courtesy Connecticut Motor Coach Museum Archives.)

One

Bridgeport Lines

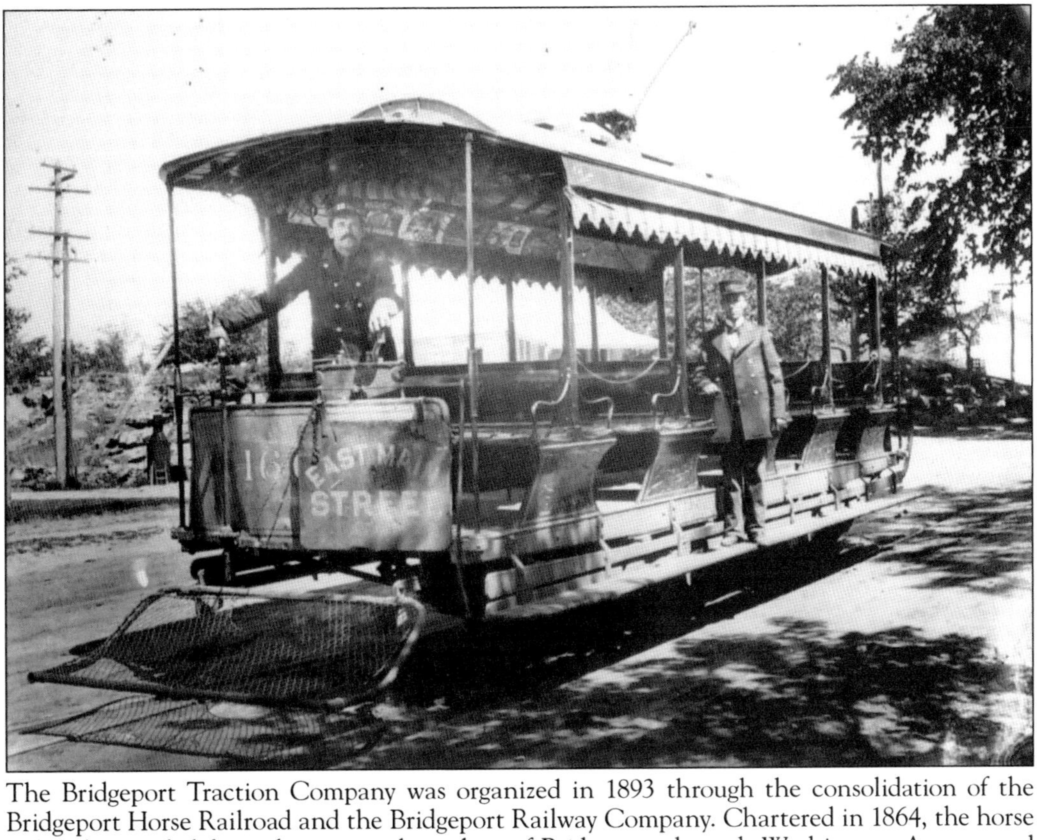

The Bridgeport Traction Company was organized in 1893 through the consolidation of the Bridgeport Horse Railroad and the Bridgeport Railway Company. Chartered in 1864, the horse railroad extended from the eastern boundary of Bridgeport through Washington Avenue and Cedar, Main, and State Streets to Division Street. The company was also authorized to extend a line along Fairfield Avenue to the villages of Fairfield and Southport. Bridgeport Traction Company car No. 16 is pictured with its crew in this 1895 scene. (Courtesy Connecticut Motor Coach Museum Archives.)

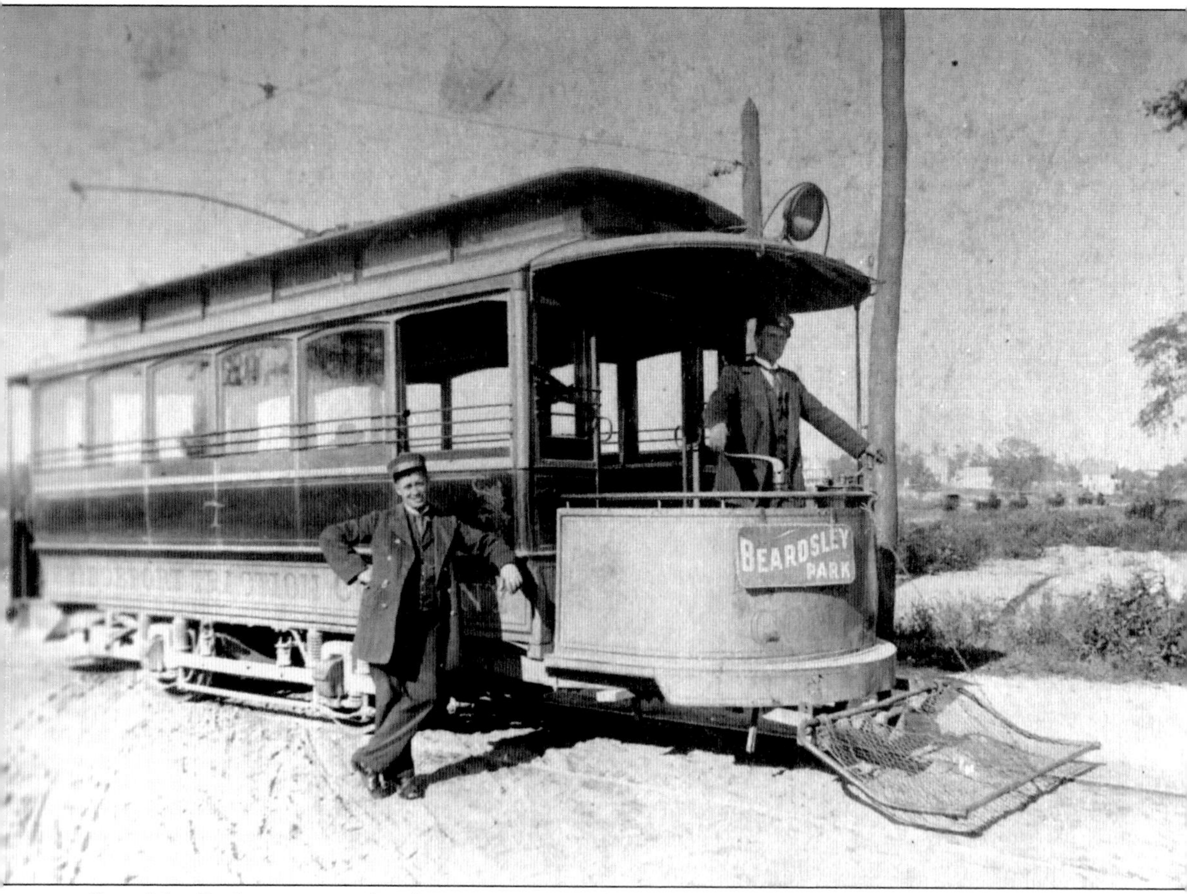

Beardsley Park was a popular destination in Bridgeport's streetcar days, just as it is today. Before the arrival of the television, VCR, and laptop computer, many people simply went "joy riding" on streetcars on their day off during the summer. The 1890s public was so in love with streetcars that it took them both to work and to play. The technology opened up new residential areas all over the country. (Courtesy Connecticut Motor Coach Museum Archives.)

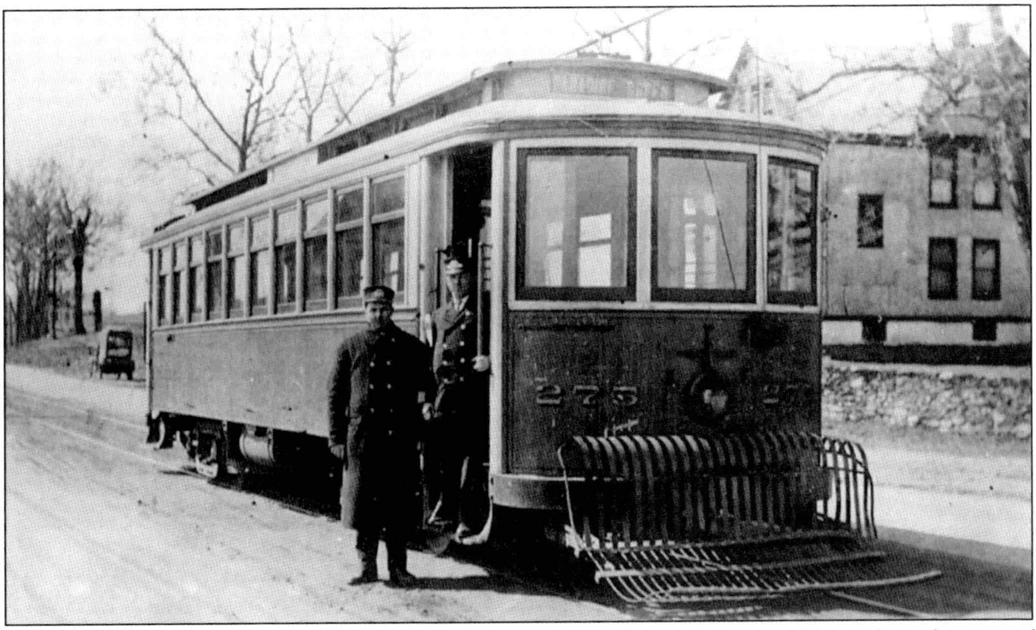

Connecticut Company car No. 275 is shown here in 1914. That year fell within the era of the two-man crew consisting of conductor and motorman. These men worked six 10.5-hour days for $15 a week. While they were paid about half the wages of firefighters and policemen, conductors and motormen liked to feel they were their equals. (Courtesy Connecticut Motor Coach Museum Archives.)

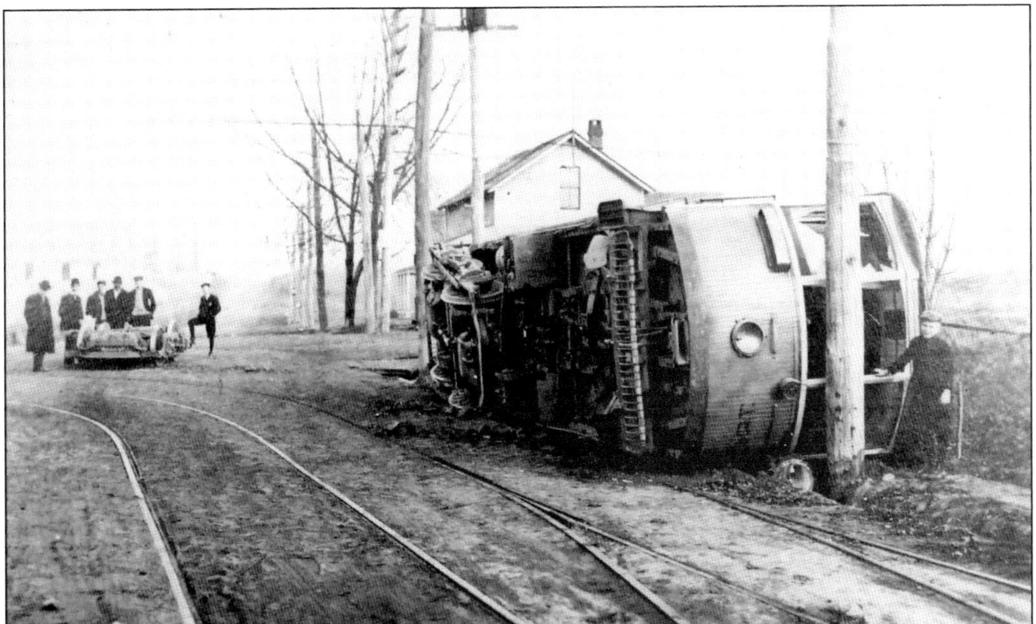

Trolley cars, though for the most part safe transportation, had their own problems, as evidenced in 1910 when Connecticut Company car No. 150 jumped the track in Devon while rounding the corner. The Bridgeport carshop crew no doubt responded with a service car carrying tools and jacks for putting the car back on the track. (Courtesy Fred Bennett collection.)

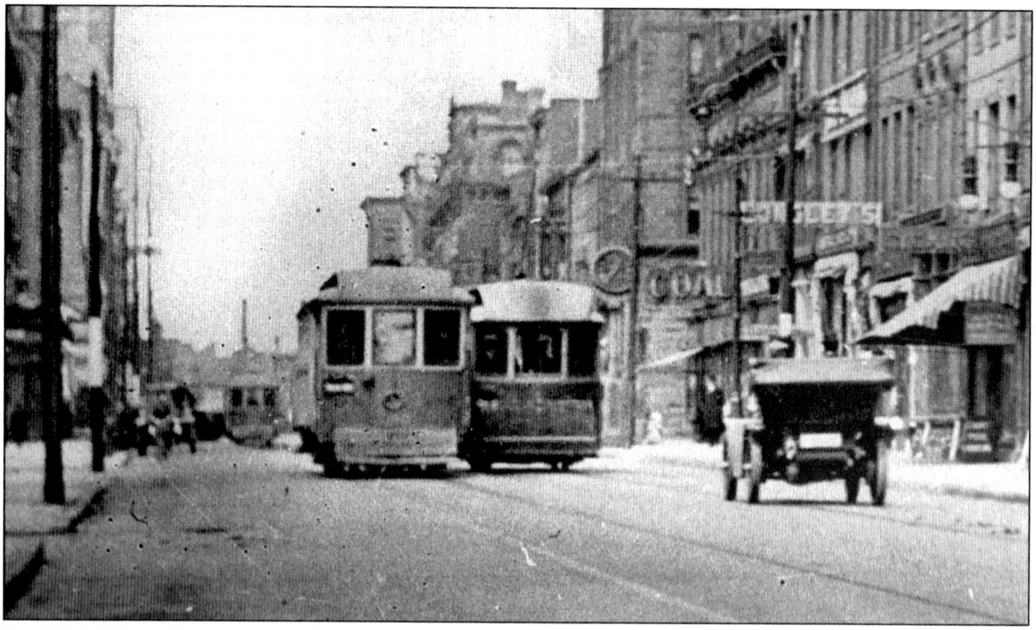

In 1914, Main Street in Bridgeport was still in the era of bicycles and horse-drawn wagons. As time went by, more and more automobiles began to compete with the streetcars. With the end of World War I and the resumption of full automobile production, private automobile ownership took the profitability from the streetcar industry. (Courtesy Connecticut Motor Coach Museum Archives.)

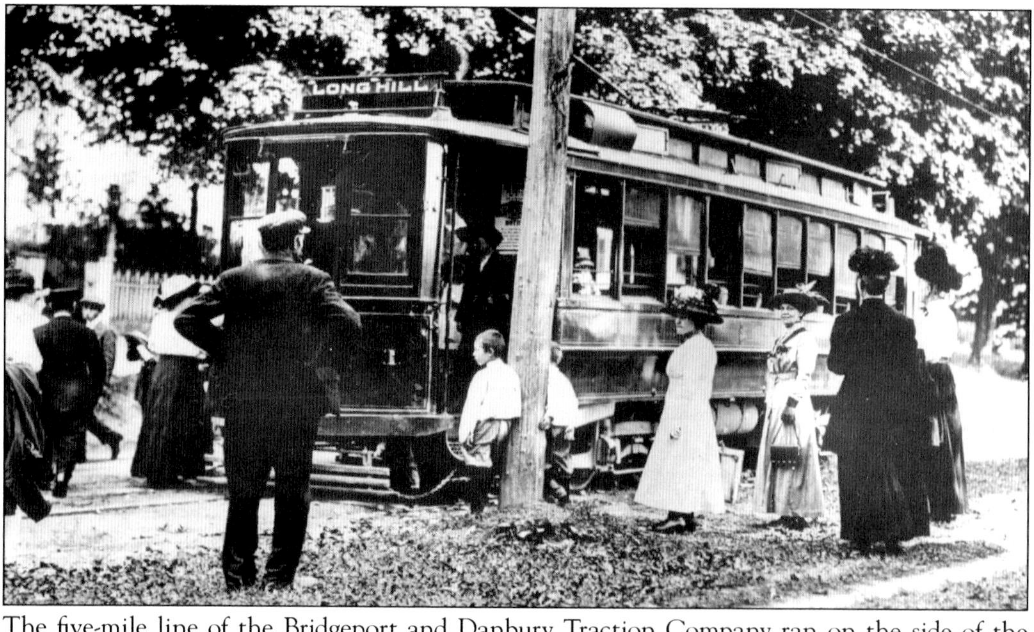

The five-mile line of the Bridgeport and Danbury Traction Company ran on the side of the road and ended at Long Hill with a tree growing in the middle of the track. During its entire history, the line only owned two cars and never made a profit. The cars were painted dark green, prompting people to call them grasshoppers. The line stopped running about 1915. Car No. 1 is pictured in 1914. (Courtesy Connecticut Motor Coach Museum Archives.)

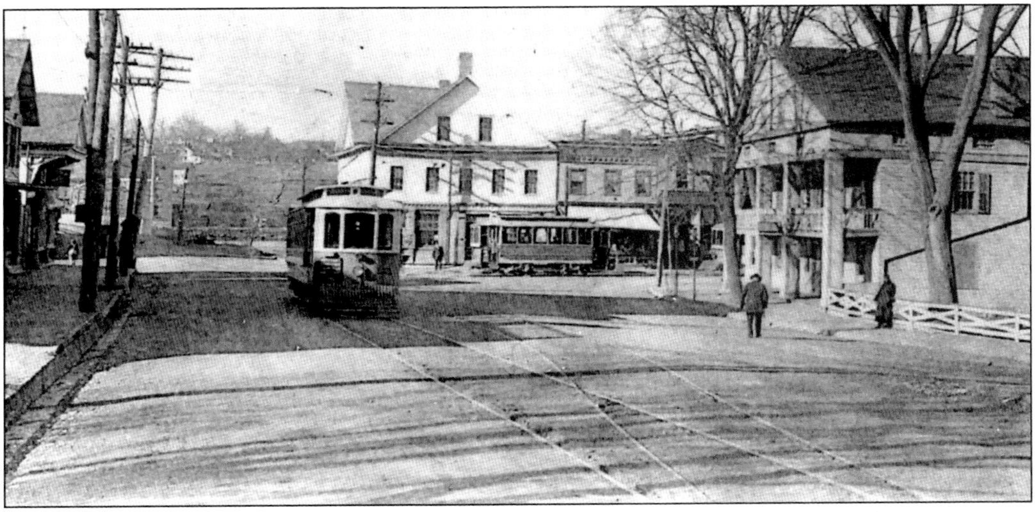

Westport Center is seen in this 1905 view. Without automobile and motor coach competition, ridership grew enormously in the years from 1905 to 1913. Only the financial part of the business was dismal; as riding increased so did cost. The costs of labor, coal, and materials all rose faster than fare increases could mitigate. (Courtesy Connecticut Motor Coach Museum Archives.)

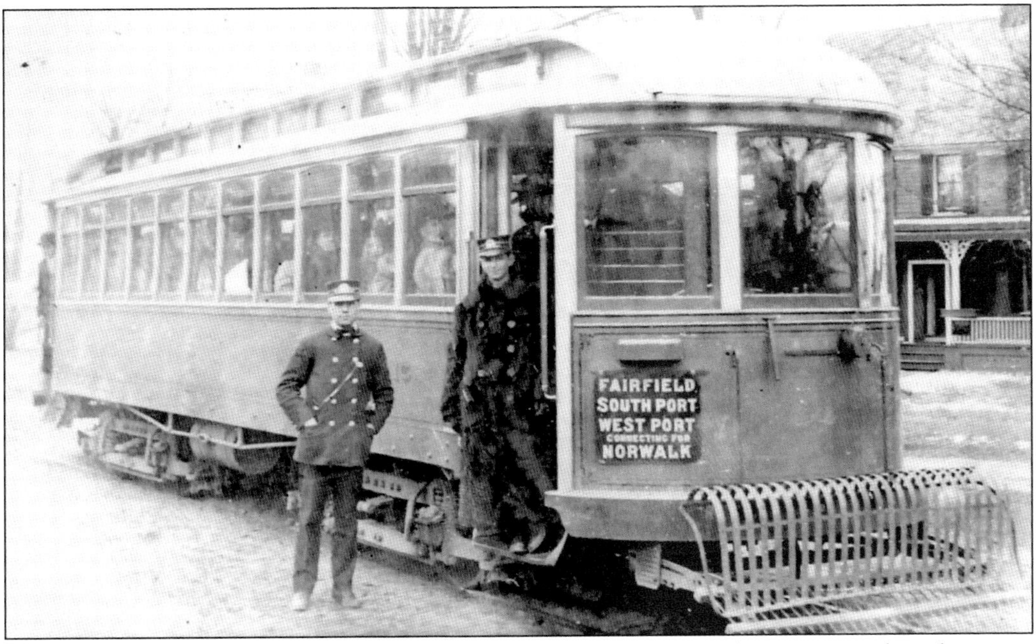

If passengers wanted to travel from Bridgeport to Norwalk by trolley as opposed to the train, which cost twice as much, they could take this car to Westport and then transfer to a Norwalk car. While the Connecticut Company had a very extensive system in Connecticut, passengers had to change cars quite often if they wanted to travel any long distance. (Courtesy Connecticut Motor Coach Museum Archives.)

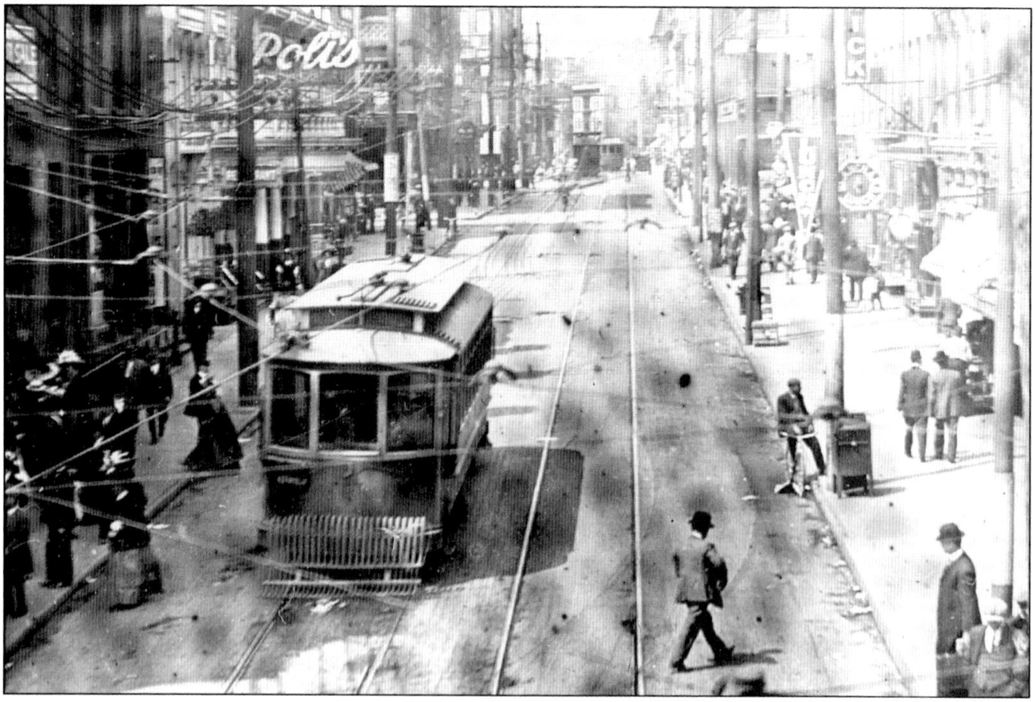

Trolley cars, overhead wires, and pedestrians abound, but there is not an automobile in sight in this 1905 view of downtown Bridgeport. (Courtesy Connecticut Motor Coach Museum Archives.)

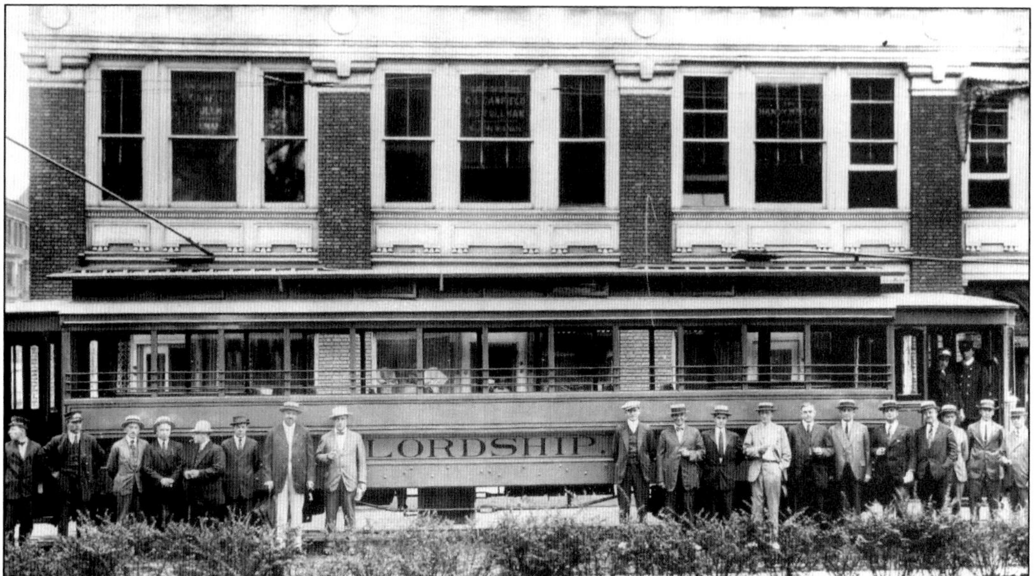

The Lordship Railway was built out to Lordship Beach as part of a real estate development project and operated from 1913 to 1925. The cars ran from the Bridgeport railroad station via Stratford Avenue and then out its own four-mile-long line to the park. Lordship Railway car No. 1 is pictured in 1917 with a very distinguished group of passengers and crew. The Kulman Car Company of Cleveland built this car using the bodies of two obsolete Cleveland Railways single-truck streetcars. (Courtesy Connecticut Motor Coach Museum Archives.)

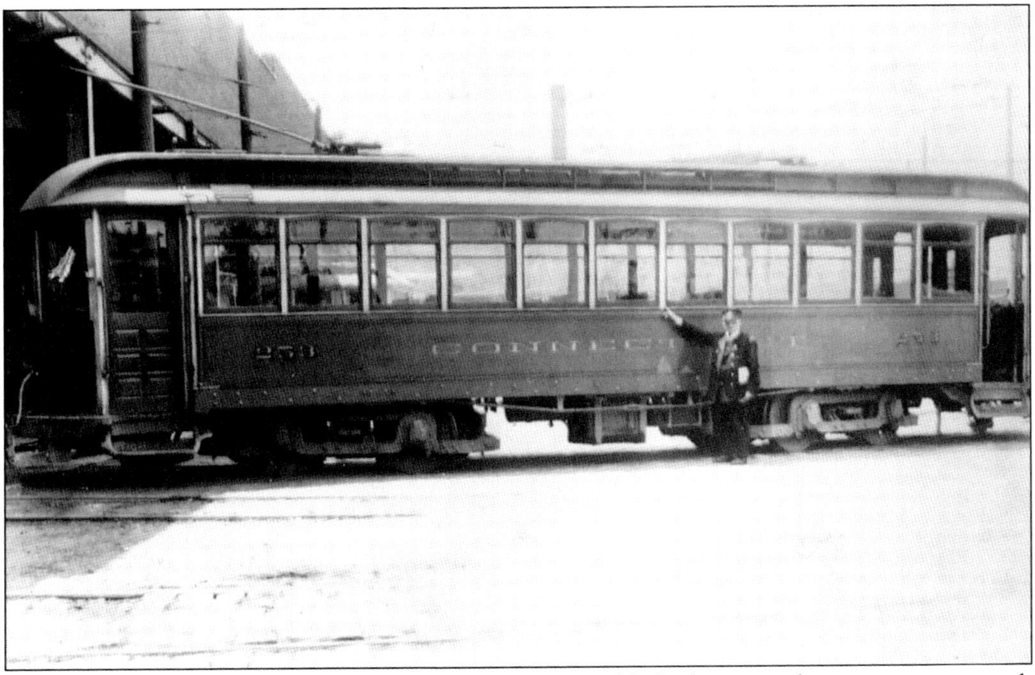

The conductor of Connecticut Company car No. 253 is likely showing where a wagon or truck has hit the car. (Courtesy Connecticut Motor Coach Museum Archives.)

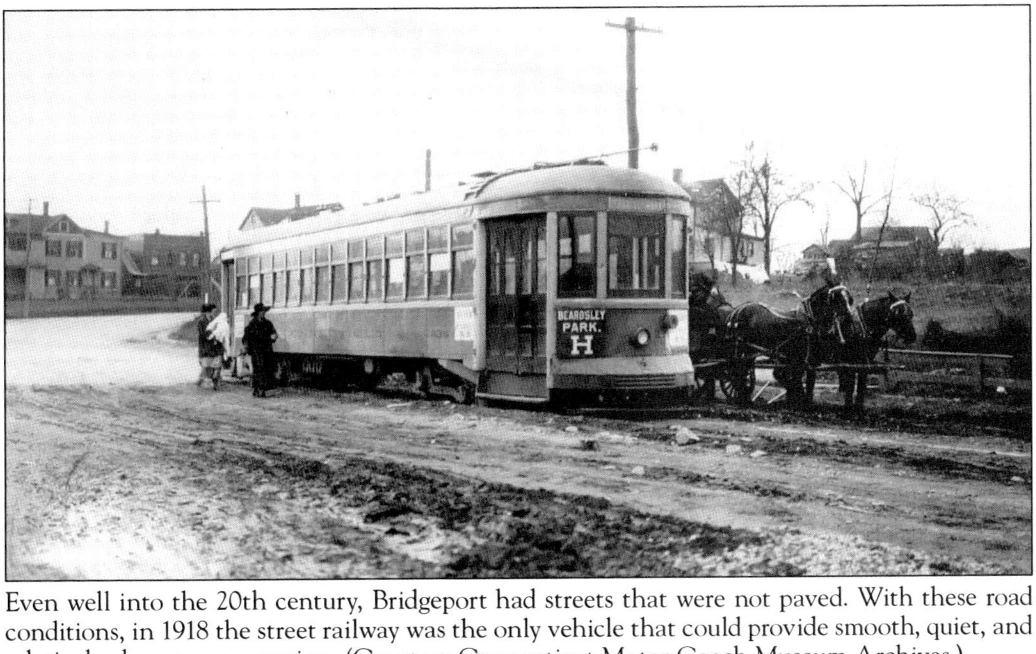

Even well into the 20th century, Bridgeport had streets that were not paved. With these road conditions, in 1918 the street railway was the only vehicle that could provide smooth, quiet, and relatively clean transportation. (Courtesy Connecticut Motor Coach Museum Archives.)

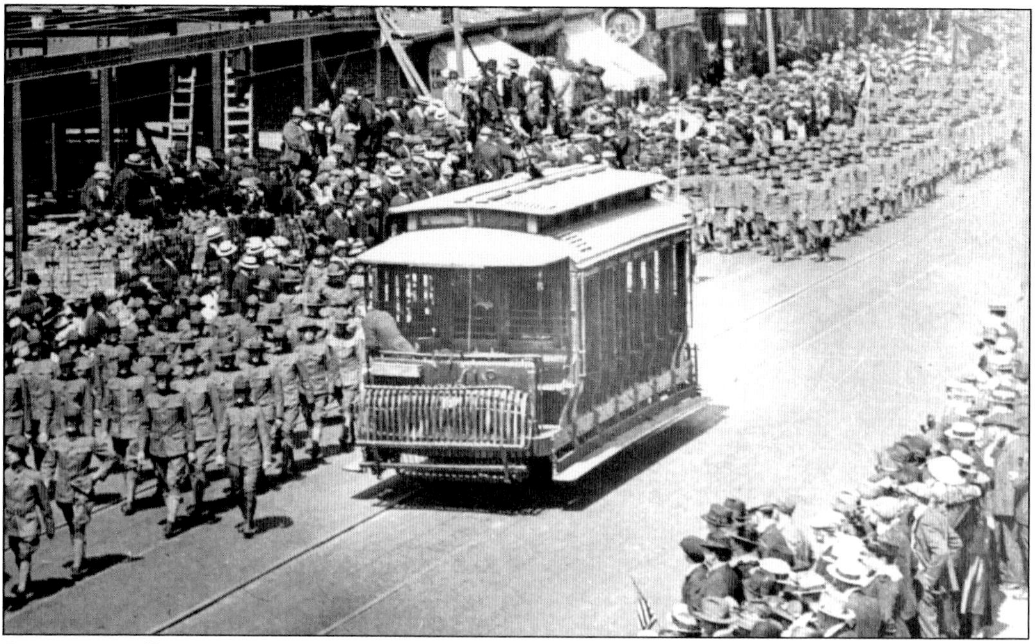

Streetcar traffic was too vital to a city's business community to be shut down even for a short time. During World War I, Main Street in Bridgeport was no different, with a small parade of marching troops squeezing over to let the trolleys pass. (Courtesy Connecticut Motor Coach Museum Archives.)

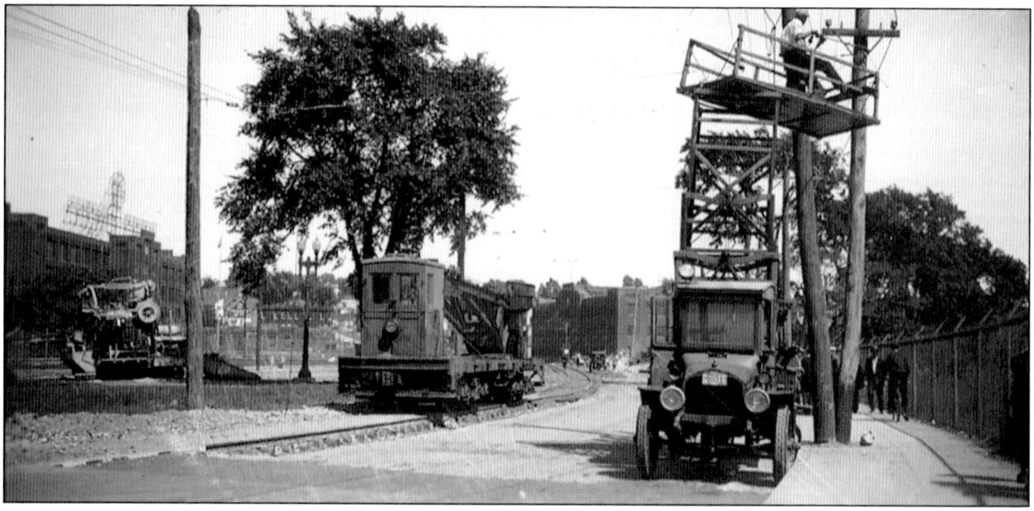

In this 1934 view, road construction is underway on Boston Road in Bridgeport. Despite the fact that streetcar service would end soon, the company was still spending money for improvements. On a line with heavy riding, this expense could be justified, but on lines with only moderate or light riding, street rebuilding projects usually resulted in conversions to bus routes. Emergency calls and maintenance on the overhead wire were performed by the truck on the right. It had a movable tower that could be raised to a convenient height to permit work on the trolley wires. For this reason, it was called a tower wagon. This truck also responded to fires along the streetcar lines, placing "hose jumpers" on the tracks to allow streetcars to pass over the fire department's hose lines. (Courtesy Connecticut Motor Coach Museum Archives.)

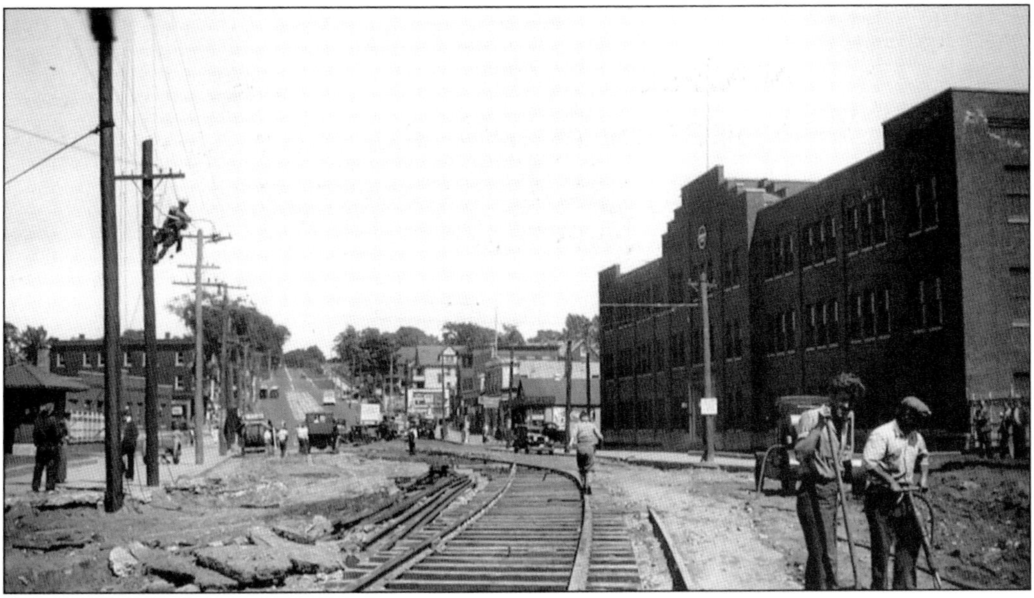

This image provides another view of the construction project on Boston Road in 1934. Certain franchise requirements were quite standard around the country, especially maintenance of the pavement between the rails and for a certain distance on either side. Since track maintenance in pavement was relatively expensive, the streetcar companies used heavier rail and higher quality ties when a line was rebuilt. (Courtesy Connecticut Motor Coach Museum Archives.)

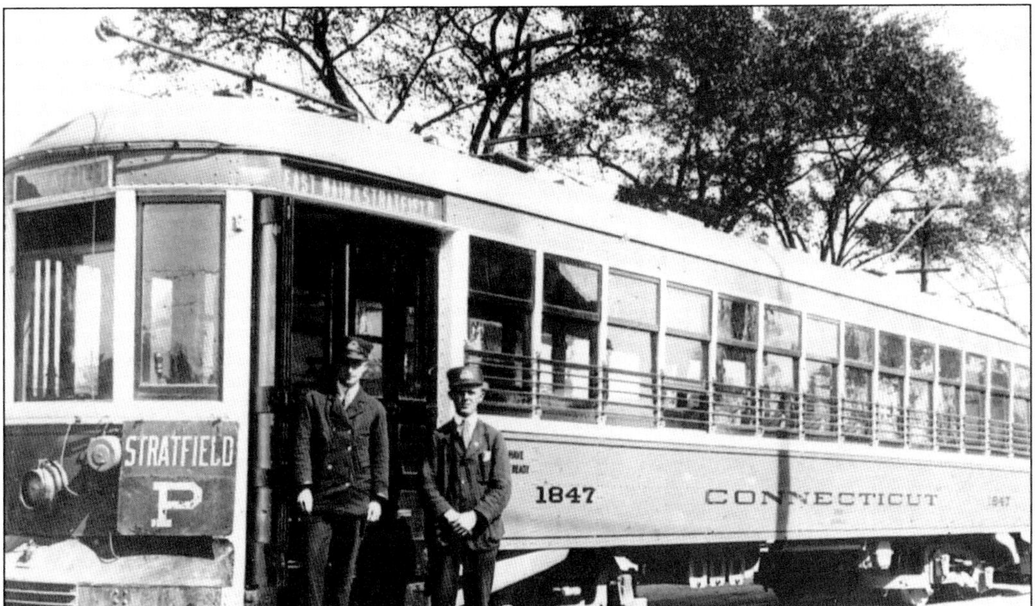

Here are some of the men who ran the streetcars in 1920s Bridgeport. The crew members of car No. 1847 would probably end their careers at the Connecticut Company driving buses—if they were still on the payroll in 1938. (Courtesy Connecticut Motor Coach Museum Archives.)

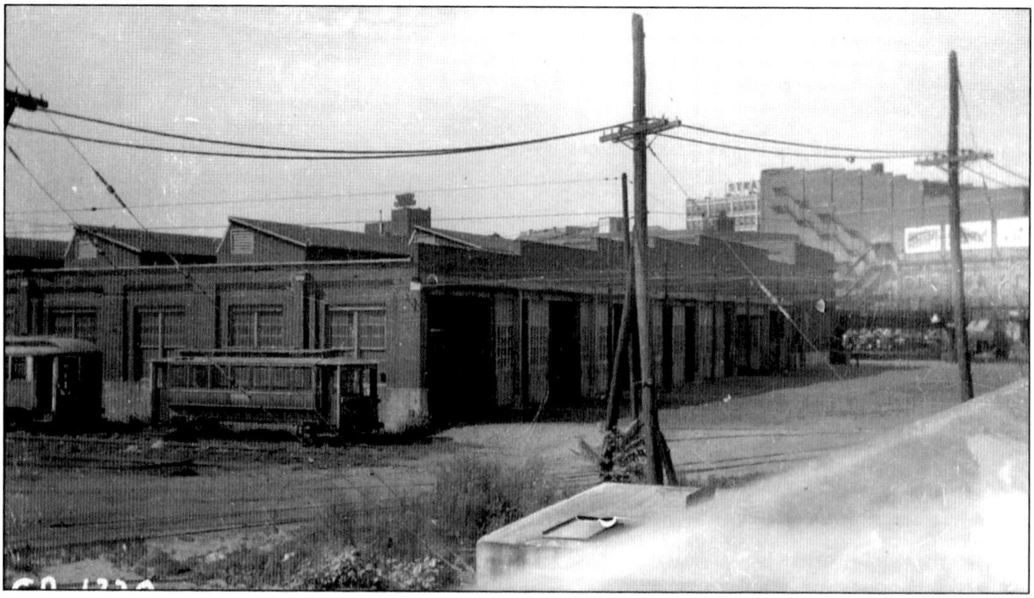

Bridgeport's main carbarn is seen in this 1930s photograph. Note the obsolete wooden car that is being stripped for parts before being sold for scrap. (Courtesy Connecticut Motor Coach Museum Archives.)

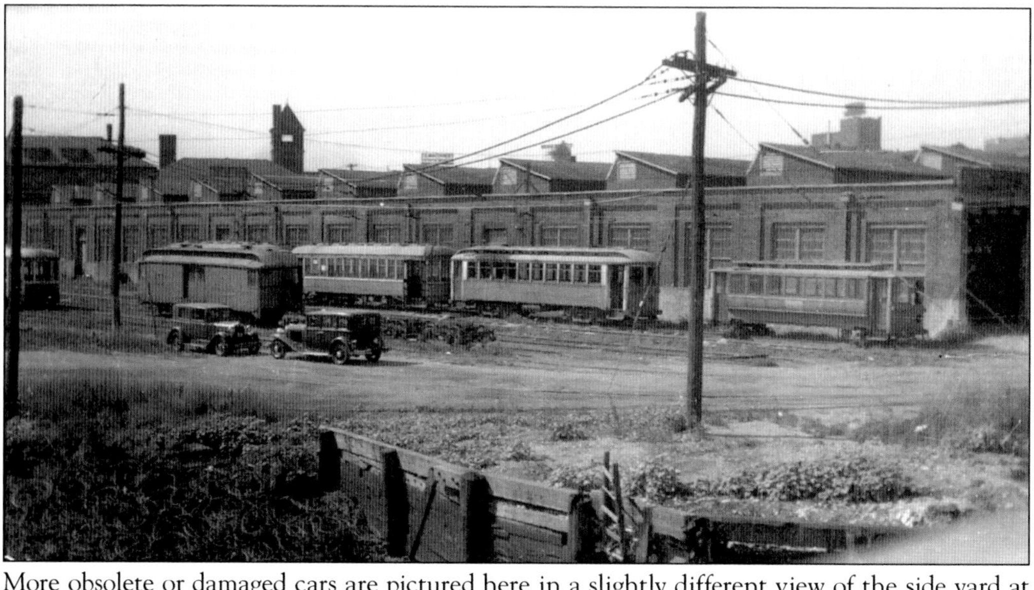

More obsolete or damaged cars are pictured here in a slightly different view of the side yard at the Bridgeport carbarn. (Courtesy Connecticut Motor Coach Museum Archives.)

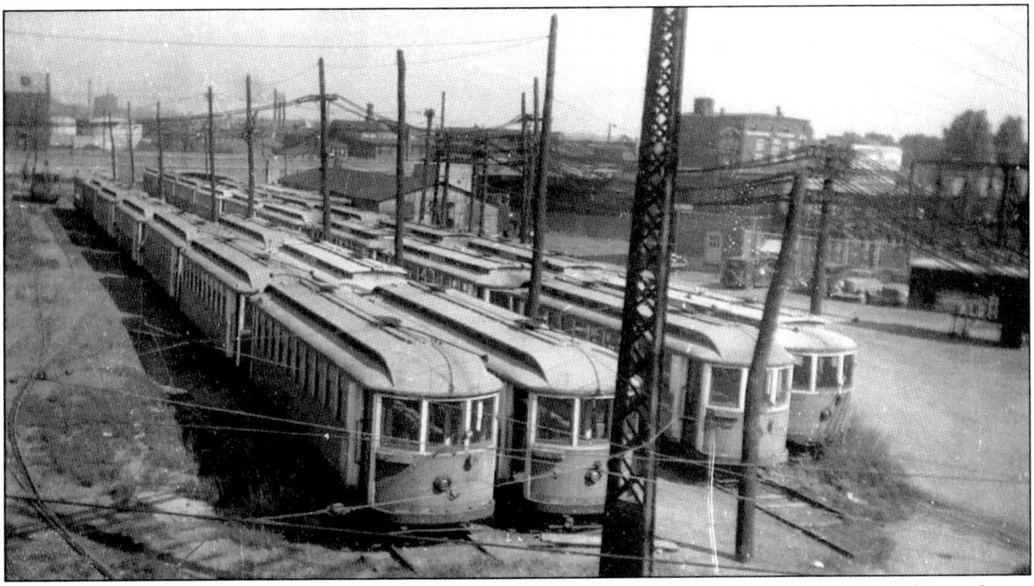

Cars lay over in the Bridgeport yard during the midday lull. Many older cars were only used two hours in the morning and two hours in the afternoon to cover the rush-hour runs from the large number of factories of the 1930s. During this era, Bridgeport was one of the major manufacturing cities in the country. (Courtesy Connecticut Motor Coach Museum Archives.)

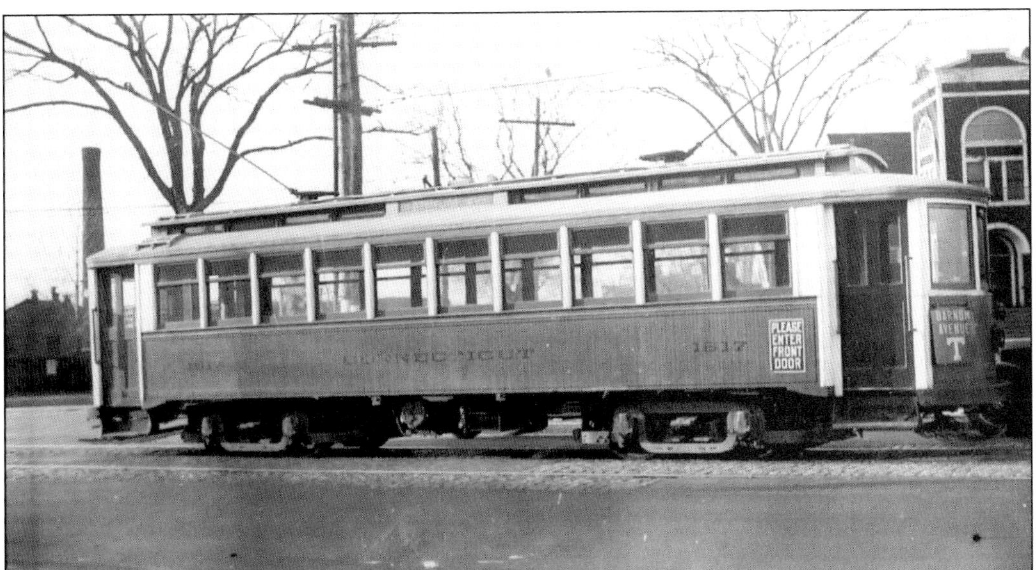

Car No. 1517 sits at the end of the Barnum Avenue line as it prepares to return to the railroad station. (Courtesy Connecticut Motor Coach Museum Archives.)

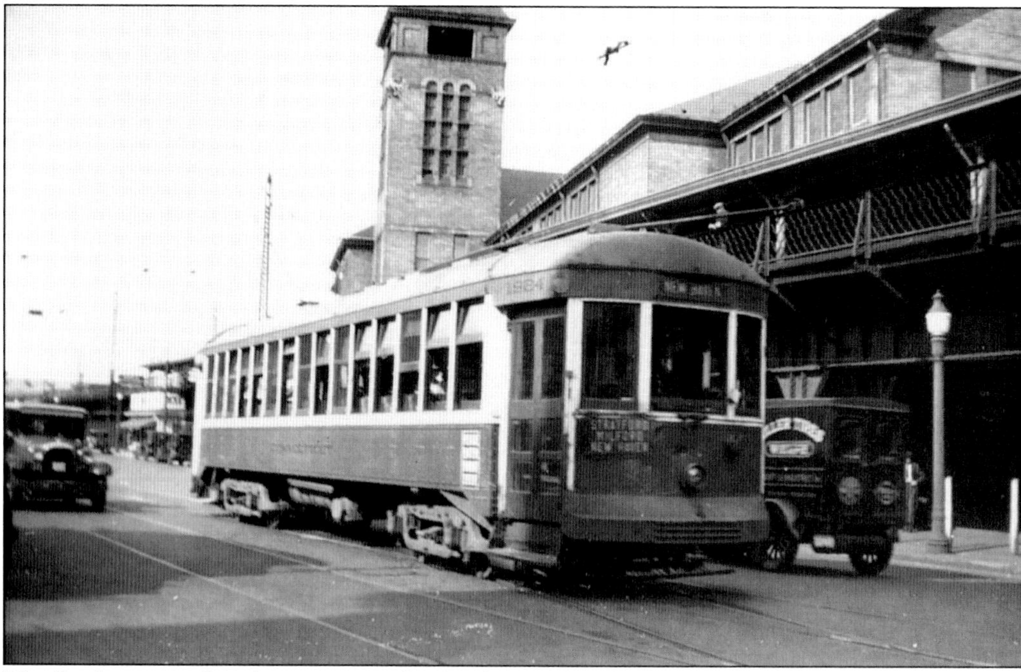

The Bridgeport railroad station was the focal point for all the lines in the city. Car No. 1924 is running on the New Haven to Bridgeport line, which was converted to a bus route on August 5, 1934. (Courtesy Connecticut Motor Coach Museum Archives.)

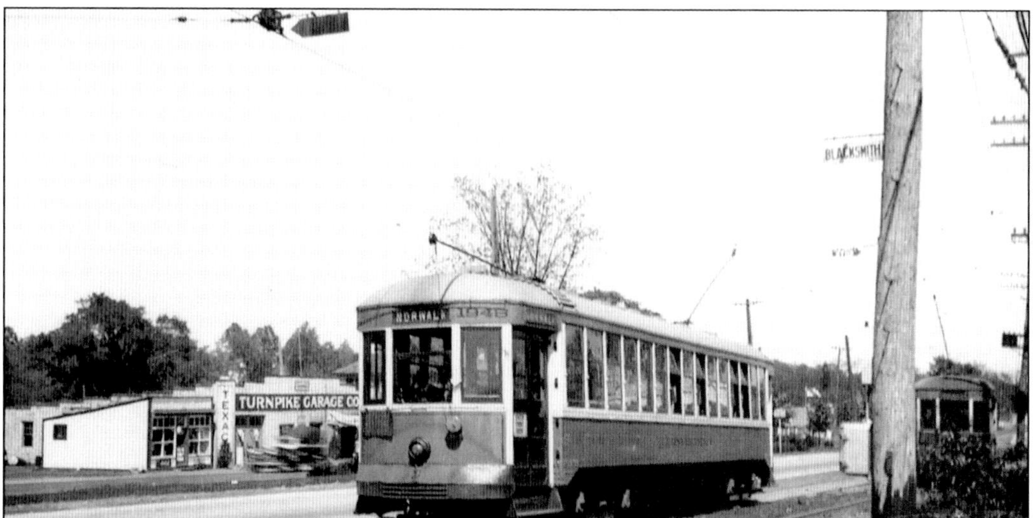

The Connecticut Company used the 1900-series cars for most long-distance routes like the Bridgeport to Norwalk run. Car No. 1945 was one of the cars turned over to the Connecticut Railway and Lighting Company when that company started to operate the Bridgeport Division in November 1936. The New Haven Railroad leased the Connecticut Railway and Lighting lines in 1906. When the railroad and the Connecticut Company went into receivership in 1935, the U.S. District Court voided the lease and returned the property to Connecticut Railway and Lighting. (Courtesy Connecticut Motor Coach Museum Archives.)

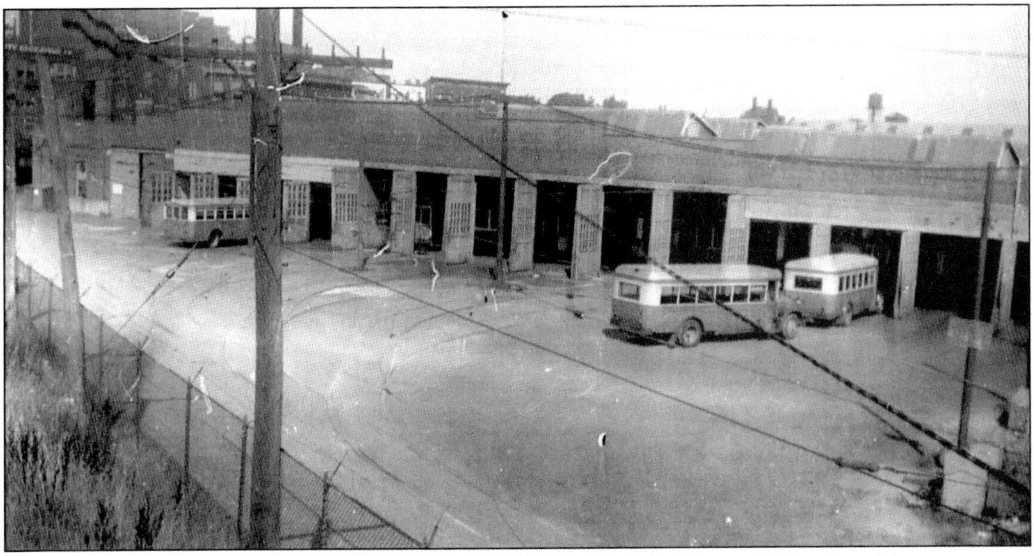

In the 1930s, buses began to appear in Bridgeport, and by June 1937, all public transit in Bridgeport had changed to bus. As late as 1920, streetcar companies across the nation operated only 75 motor coaches. In that era, motor coaches were basically motortruck chassis converted to a bus by mounting a bus body on the existing frame. This resulted in extremely poor riding quality. The Fageol Safety Coach Company in California produced the first vehicle specifically built to carry passengers in 1925. (Courtesy Connecticut Motor Coach Museum Archives.)

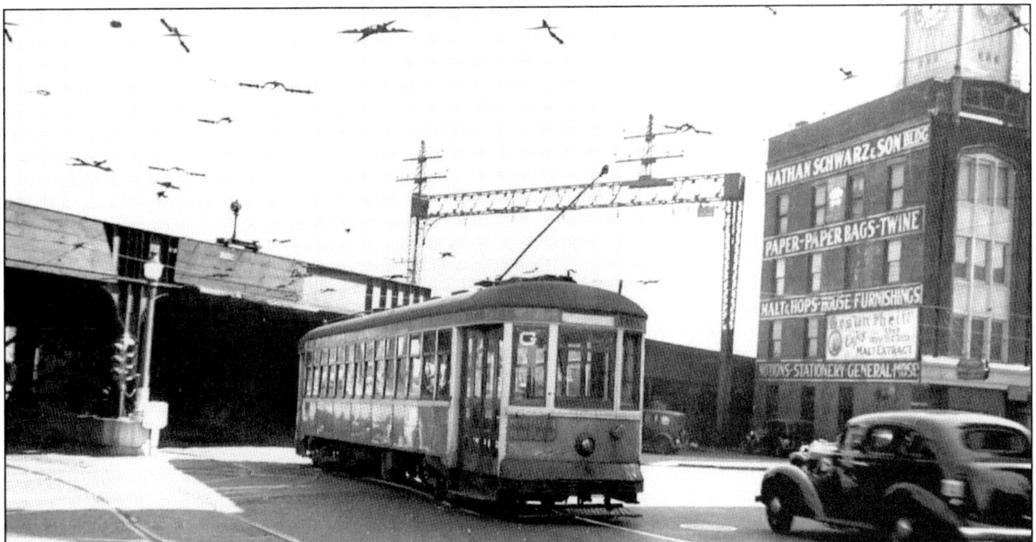

Connecticut Company car No. 1847 runs on the Fairfield Avenue line in Bridgeport in 1934. (Courtesy Connecticut Motor Coach Museum Archives.)

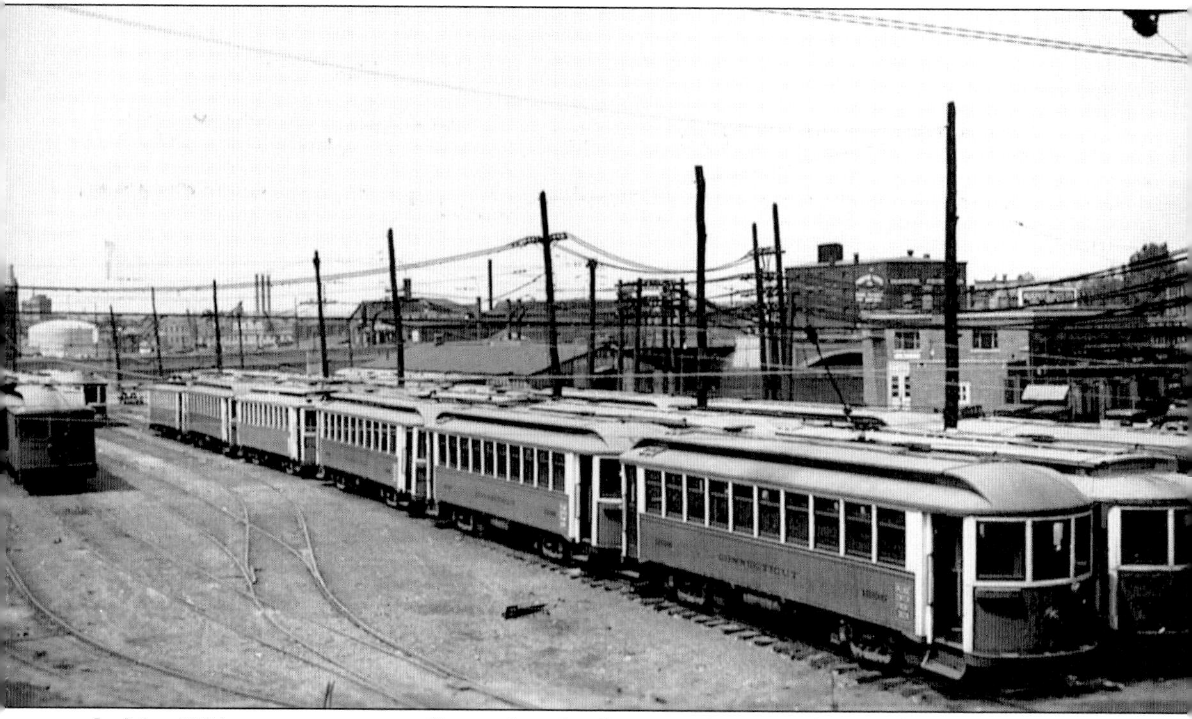

In May 1934, open cars were still stored in the Congress Street yard, as evidenced by the line of open cars sitting on the left side of this photograph. The Connecticut Company was one of the last major streetcar operators of open cars in this country. (Courtesy Connecticut Motor Coach Museum Archives.)

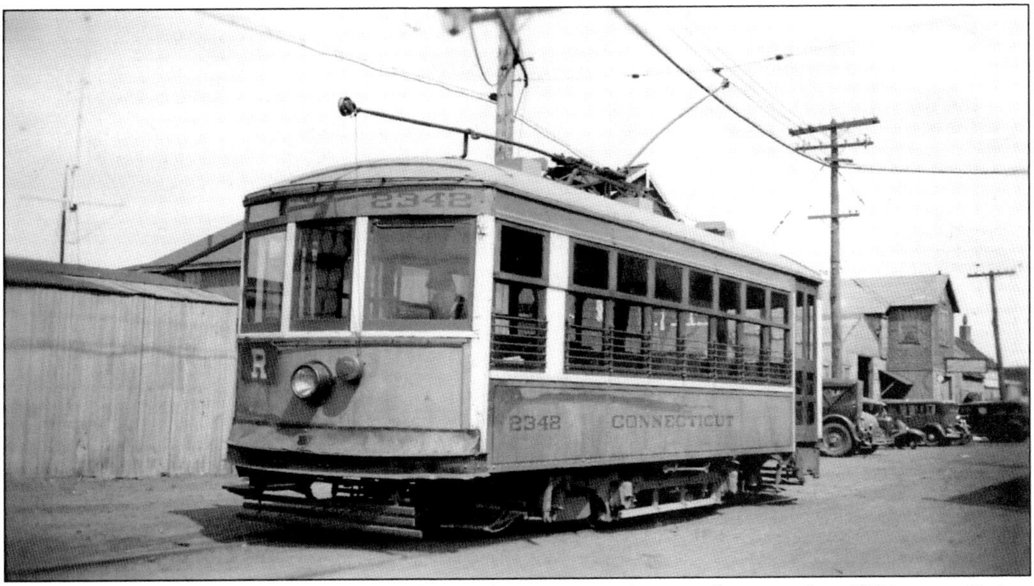

A single-truck Birney safety car travels on the Seaview Avenue line in this 1934 view. Being single-truck cars—cars with only one set of wheels, mounted in the middle—Birney cars were very unpopular with the public because they rode so rough. The companies, however, liked them because they were inexpensive to operate. In 1916, Charles Birney, an engineer with the firm of Stone and Webster, designed a single-truck car measuring 28 feet long and weighing seven to nine tons—about a third of the weight of a standard wood or steel car. These cars were designed to be run by one operator and were equipped with a "dead man control," which stopped the car in the event that the operator was disabled. The streetcar industry labeled them "safety cars." (Courtesy Fred Bennett collection.)

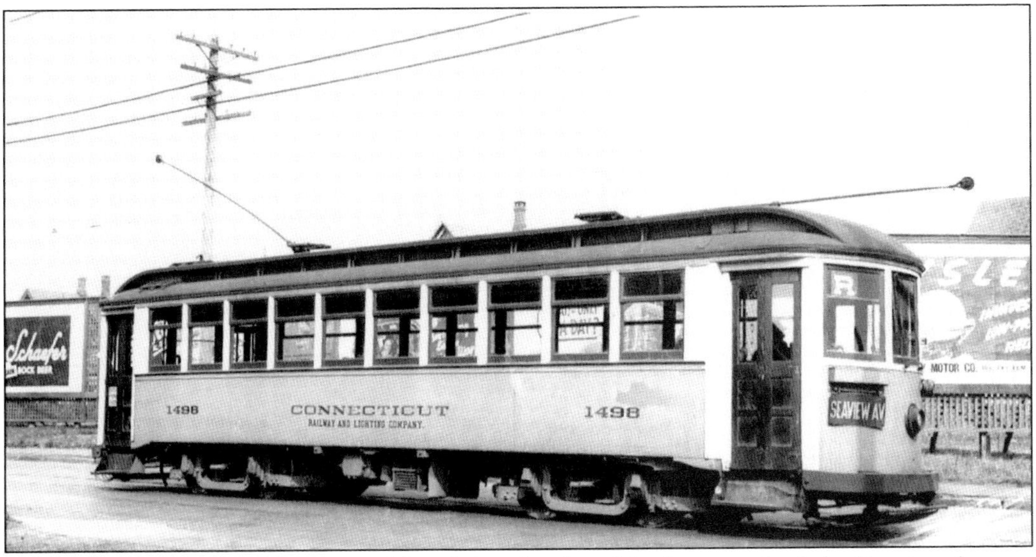

Streetcar service in Bridgeport would end shortly after this photograph of the Seaview Avenue line was taken in 1937. (Courtesy Connecticut Motor Coach Museum Archives.)

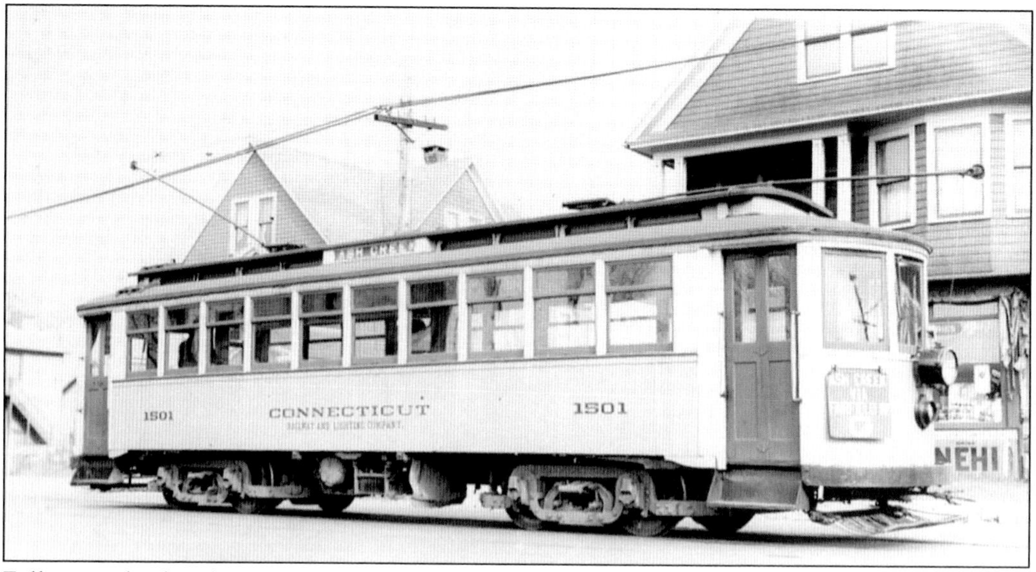

Following the dissolution of the Connecticut Company, the lines once operated by Connecticut Railway and Lighting in Bridgeport were returned to it. Car No. 1501 was re-lettered for Connecticut Railway and Lighting after November 1936. (Courtesy Connecticut Motor Coach Museum Archives.)

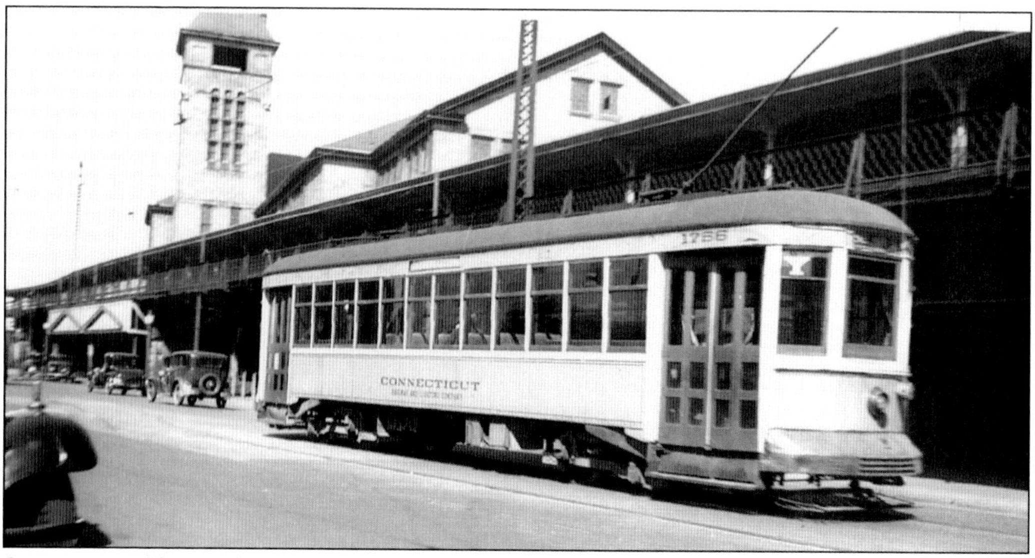

Semiconvertibles, such as car No. 1756 shown here at the Bridgeport railroad station in 1937, were designed to allow the windows to fold up into the body and to give passengers the feeling of riding in an open car. Because their windows could be closed, these cars, unlike the open cars, were used year-round. (Courtesy Connecticut Motor Coach Museum Archives.)

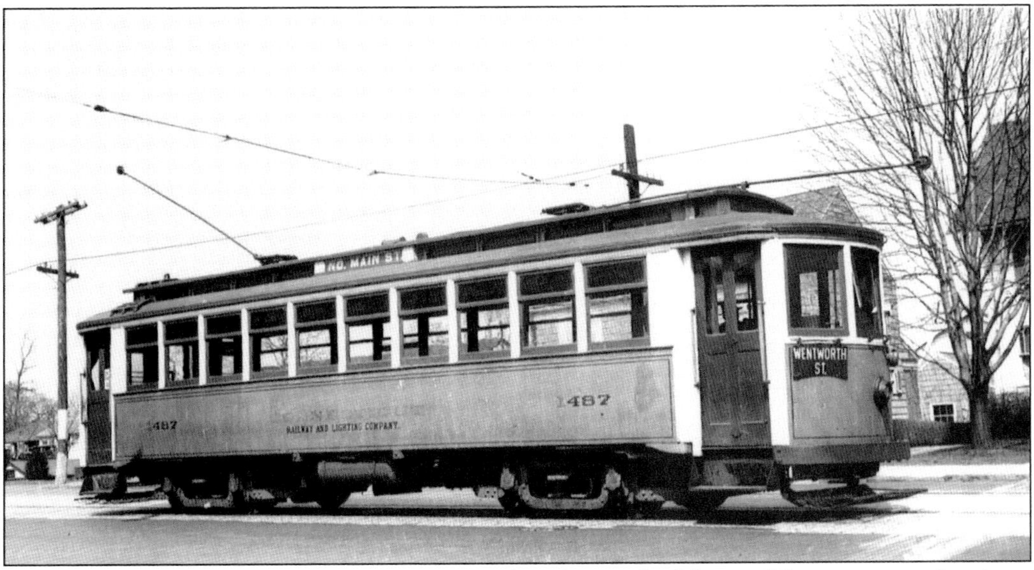

During peak hours, the trolley companies employed "turn back" cars. These were used only in high-volume areas and did not run the entire length of the route. Cars destined Wentworth Street, such as car No. 1487 shown at the end of the double track on North Main Street, were turn back cars on the S line in Bridgeport. (Courtesy Connecticut Motor Coach Museum Archives.)

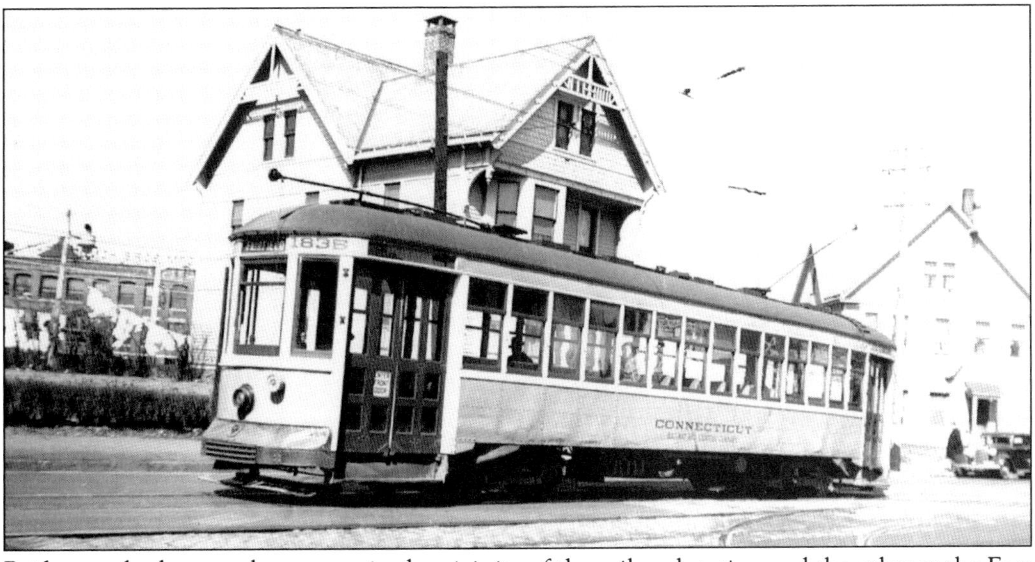

Bridgeport had two carbarns: one in the vicinity of the railroad station and the other at the East End Carbarn. Here car No. 1835 sits on Stratford Avenue just outside the East End Carbarn. (Courtesy Fred Bennett collection.)

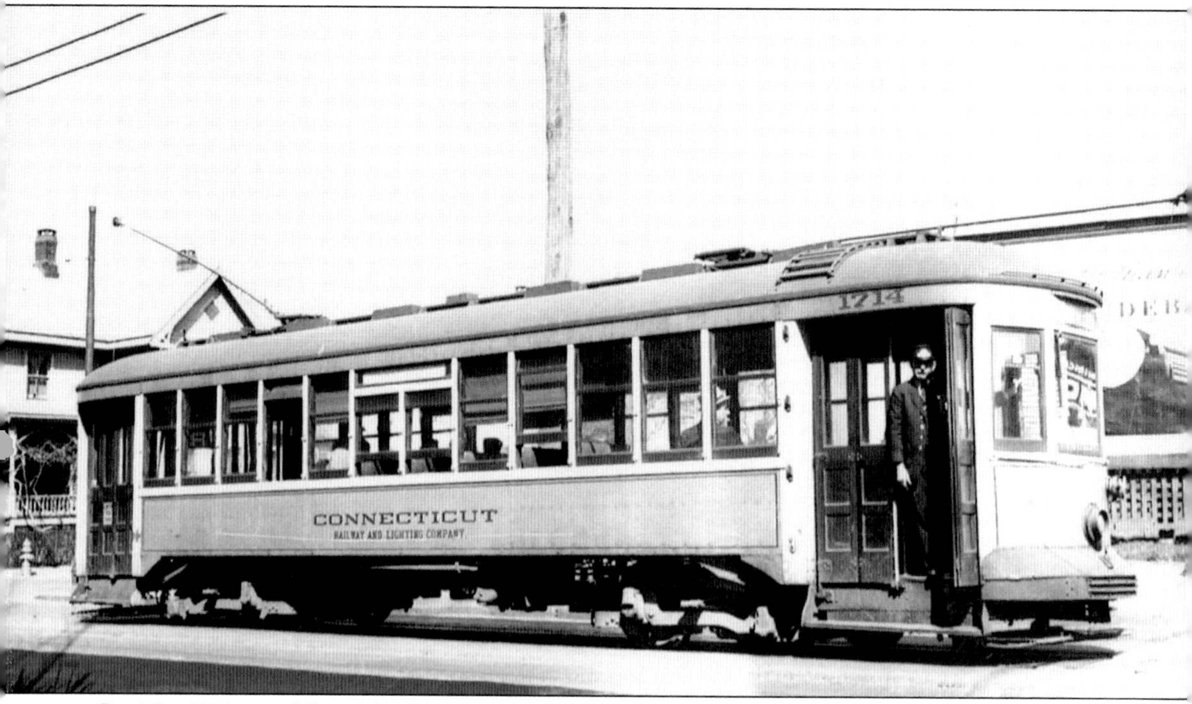

Car No. 1714 was delivered to the Connecticut Company in 1915 by the Wason Manufacturing Company of Springfield, Massachusetts. The car was designed to be operated by a two-man crew consisting of a conductor and motorman. By the early 1930s, all the cars in the Connecticut Company—except the open cars—were operated by one man who both ran the car and collected the fares. (Courtesy Fred Bennett collection.)

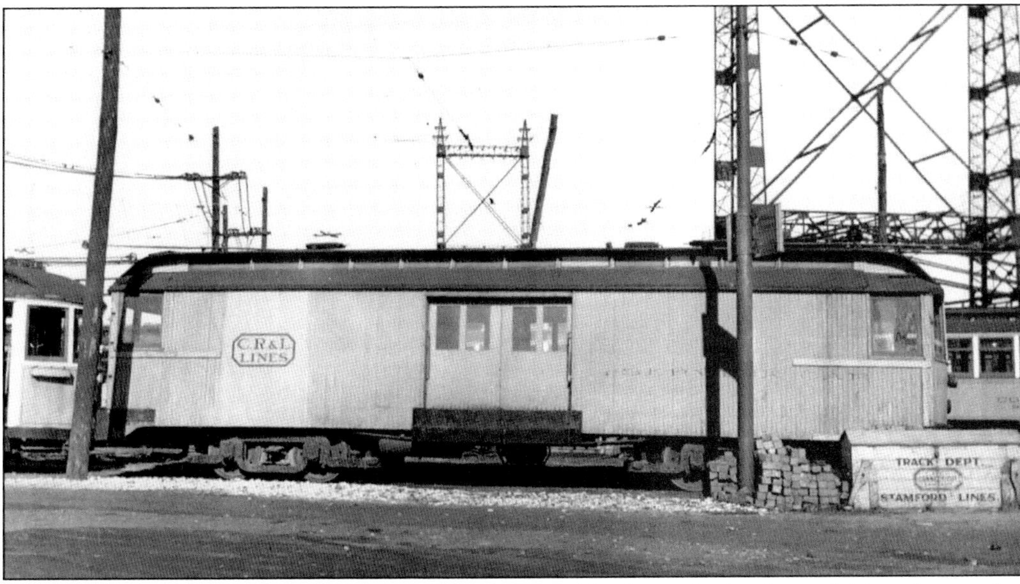

The Bridgeport Division of Connecticut Railway and Lighting had a fleet of 46 work cars that were used to maintain the overhead wire, maintain the track, and retrieve disabled cars out on the line. This service car most likely brought tools to job locations and responded to derailments like the one shown on page 11. (Courtesy Fred Bennett collection.)

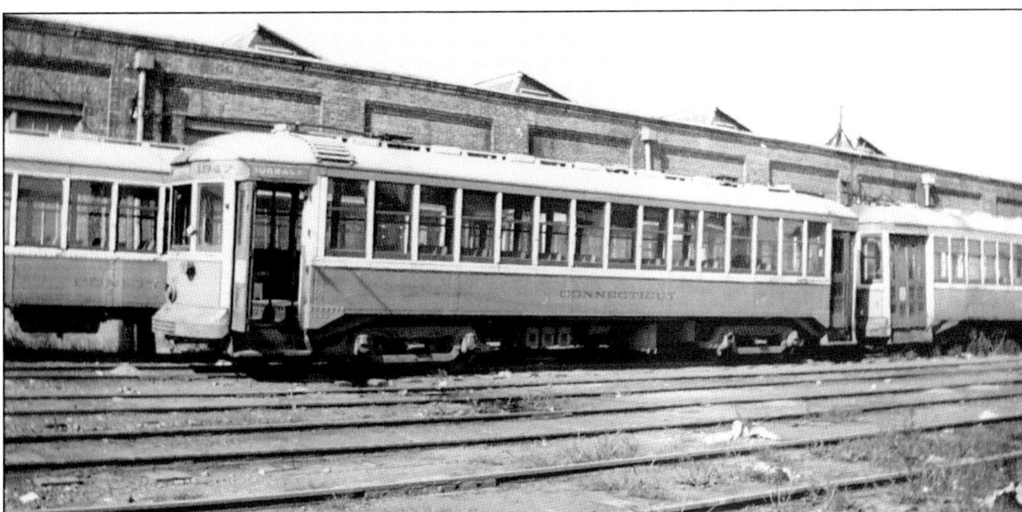

A group of 1900-series cars lays over at the Bridgeport barn, most likely on a Sunday. Fifty 1900-series cars were purchased in 1919 from the J. G. Brill Company of Philadelphia to handle long-distance runs between cities. Bridgeport used these cars on the Norwalk and New Haven runs. After all other lines closed, many ended up in New Haven and ran until that line also closed at the end of 1948. (Courtesy Connecticut Motor Coach Museum Archives.)

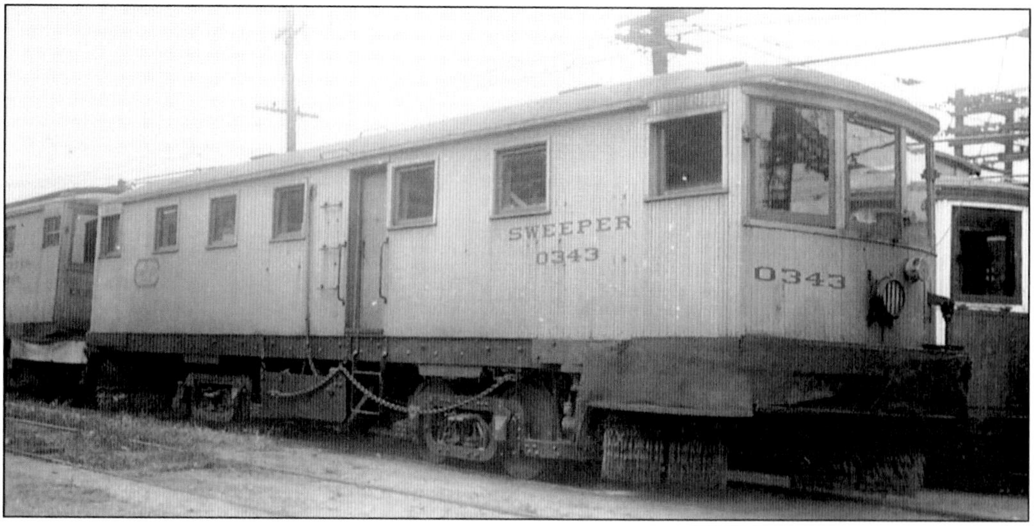

In order to keep running in the winter, trolley companies were forced to deal with the winter weather. In New England, that meant snow removal. Many street railway companies, like the Connecticut Company, built their own equipment using parts from obsolete cars that were being scrapped, as with snow sweeper No. 0343, which was built by the Bridgeport carshop in 1923. This car was scrapped in 1937 after the Bridgeport lines were converted to bus operation. (Courtesy Connecticut Motor Coach Museum Archives.)

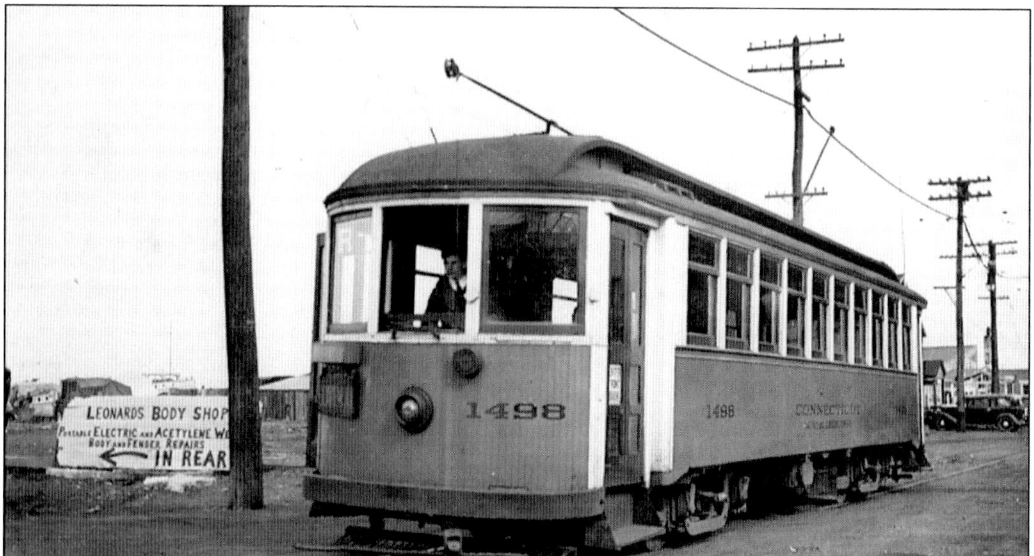

Car No. 1498 was built by the Osgood Bradley Car Company of Worcester, Massachusetts, in 1911 for the Bridgeport Division of the Connecticut Company. It spent its entire life in Bridgeport until being scrapped in 1937. During their lifetime, many cars moved around to various cities served by the Connecticut Company as service demands changed. (Courtesy Connecticut Motor Coach Museum Archives.)

Two

Danbury and Bethel Lines

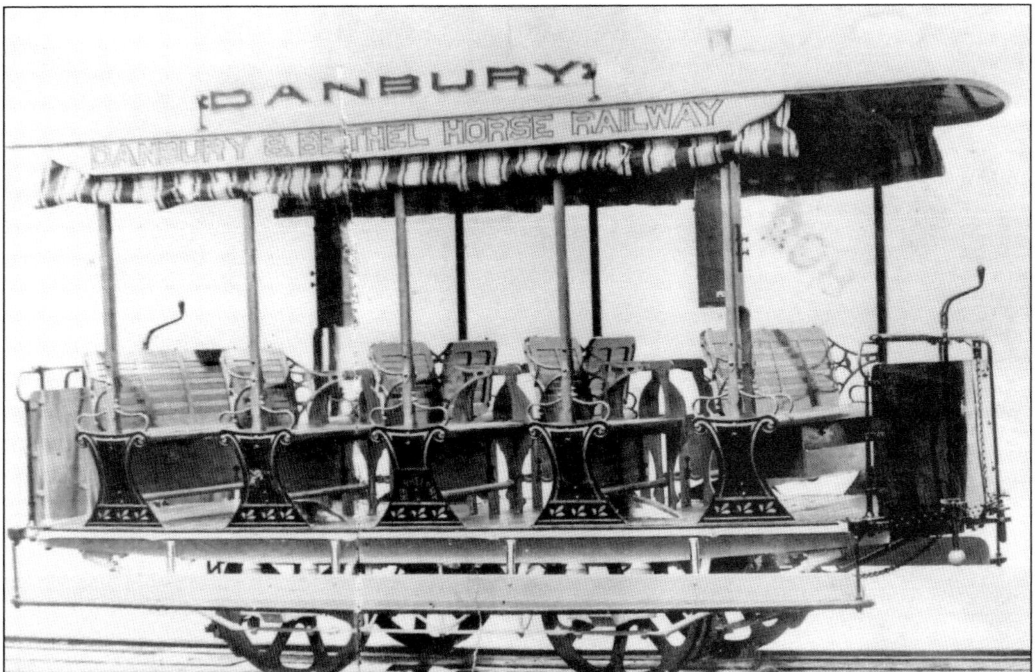

The Danbury and Bethel Horse Railroad was organized in 1884. In 1895, it was electrified at a cost of $355,000, which was raised from the sale of stocks and bonds to the public. At that time, the name was changed to the Danbury and Bethel Street Railway. By 1910, the line had expanded to a total of 16 miles. (Courtesy Fred Bennett collection.)

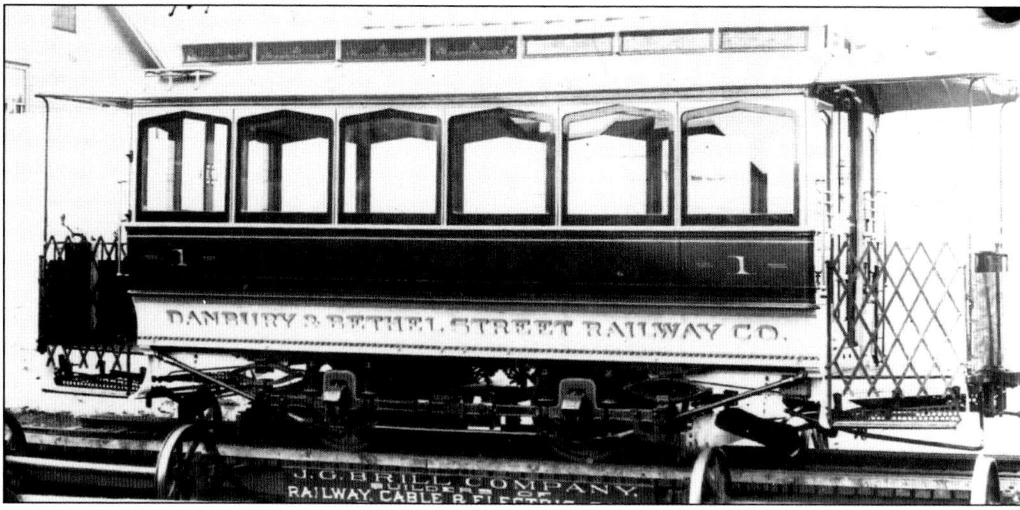

Often when cars were constructed, a builder's photograph was taken at the factory before delivery. Danbury and Bethel Street Railway car No. 1, shown at the J. G. Brill factory in Philadelphia, was one of the original cars purchased to electrify the line in 1895. (Courtesy Fred Bennett collection.)

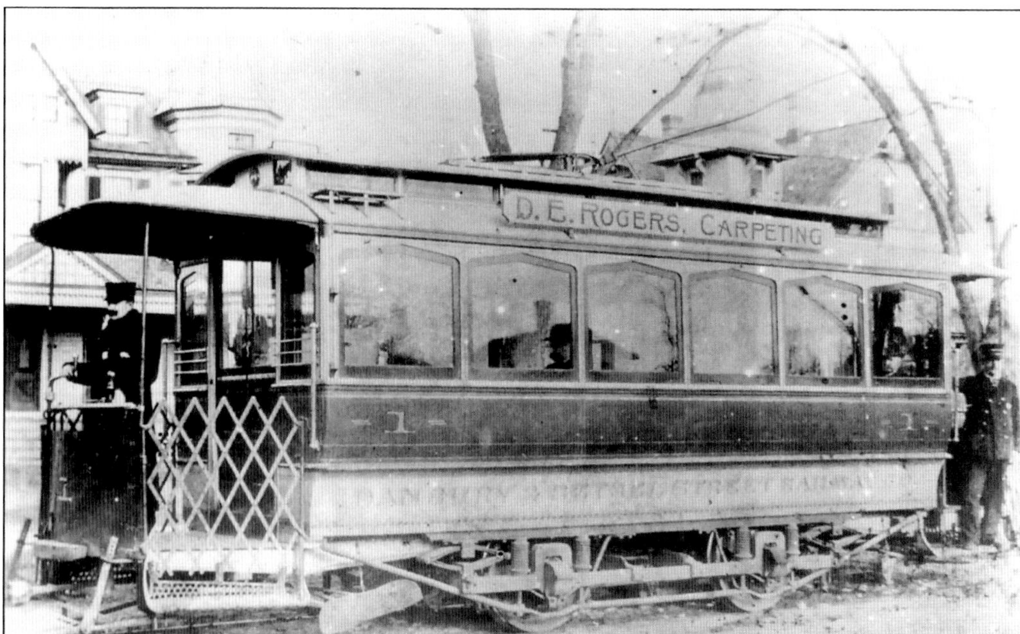

Commercial advertising on streetcars was very common in this era, as evidenced by Danbury and Bethel Street Railway car No. 1, in service in Danbury. Early streetcars had open platforms that gave the motormen plenty of fresh air. (Courtesy Connecticut Motor Coach Museum Archives.)

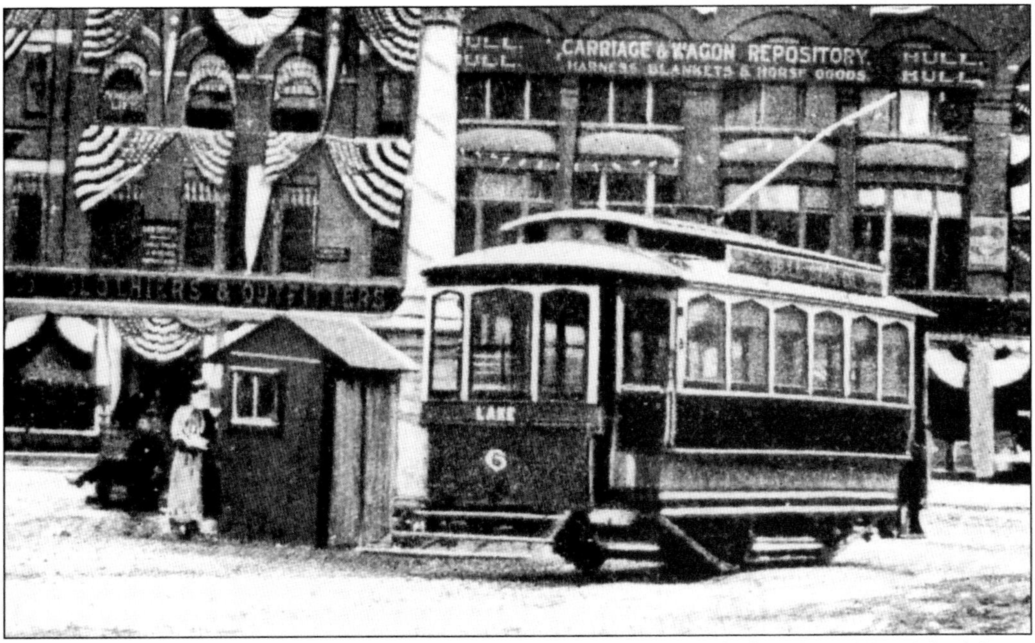

By the time this photograph was taken in 1900, the front vestibule of car No. 6 had been closed in to give the motorman some protection from the weather. This car was also one of the originals on the line. (Courtesy Fred Bennett collection.)

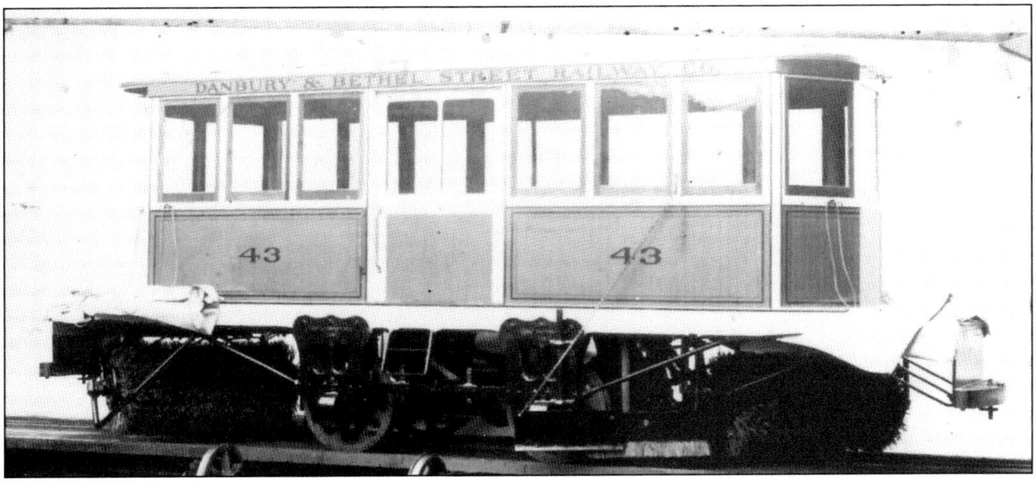

In some instances, new equipment was built for a specific purpose, like snow sweeper No. 43, pictured at the J. G. Brill factory in 1895. These cars proved vital in keeping the line open and the cars running in the harsh New England winter months. (Courtesy Fred Bennett collection.)

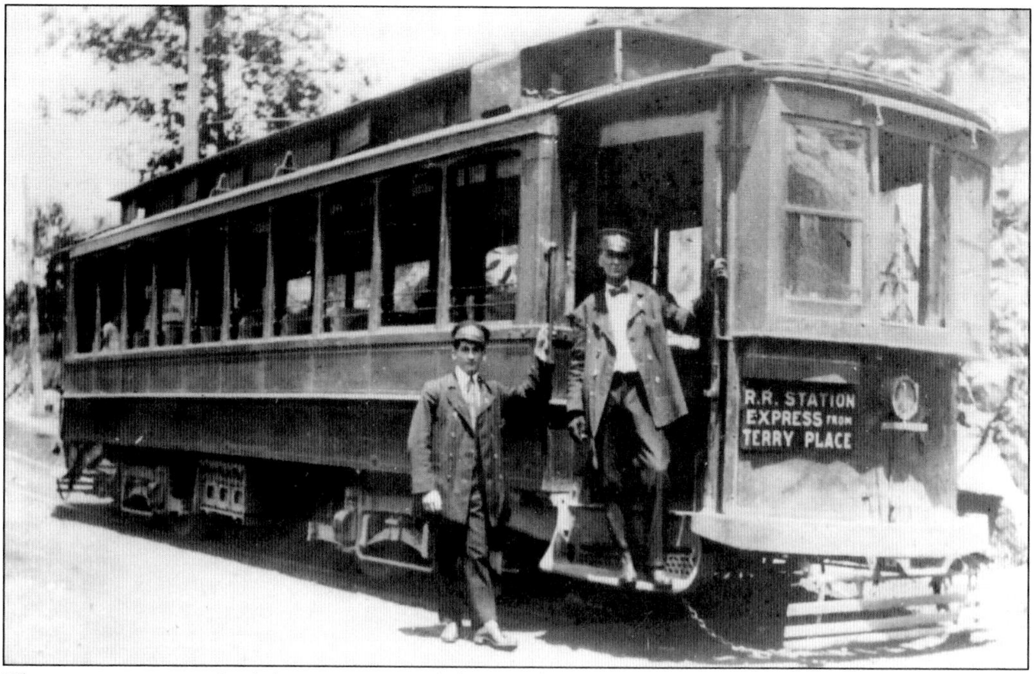

These two are proud of their car, one of the Danbury and Bethel Street Railway double-truck cars, in 1920. Windows have been added to the front, as this car originally came from the factory with an open vestibule. At this point in time, the company owned 26 closed cars, 7 open cars, and 3 snow sweepers and was $267,728 in debt. (Courtesy Fred Bennett collection.)

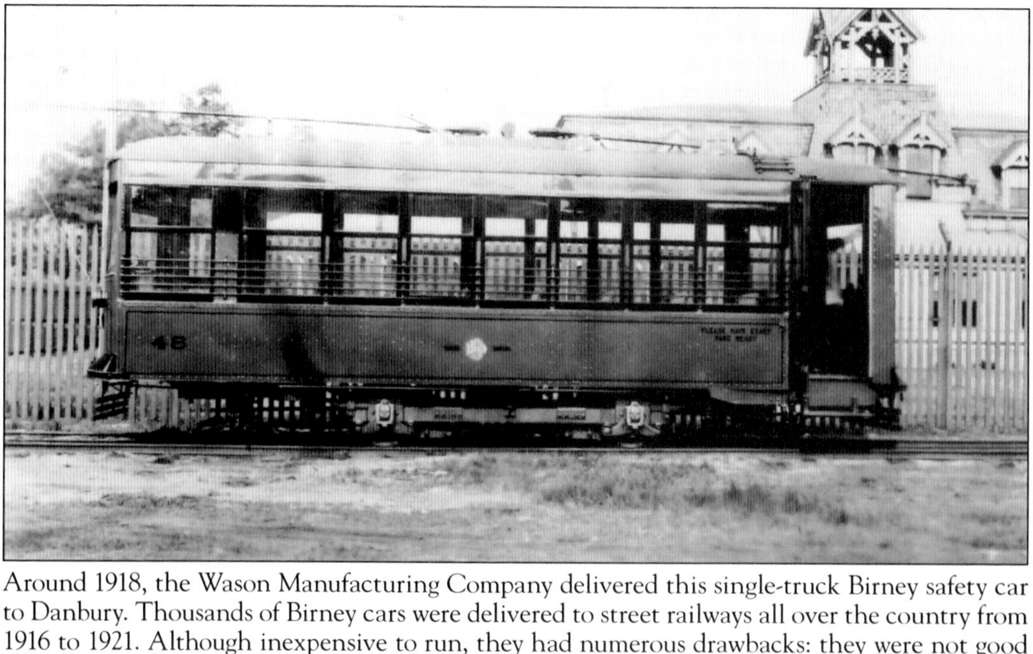

Around 1918, the Wason Manufacturing Company delivered this single-truck Birney safety car to Danbury. Thousands of Birney cars were delivered to street railways all over the country from 1916 to 1921. Although inexpensive to run, they had numerous drawbacks: they were not good in snow because of their light weight, they rode rough, and they had a reputation for derailing easily. (Courtesy Fred Bennett collection.)

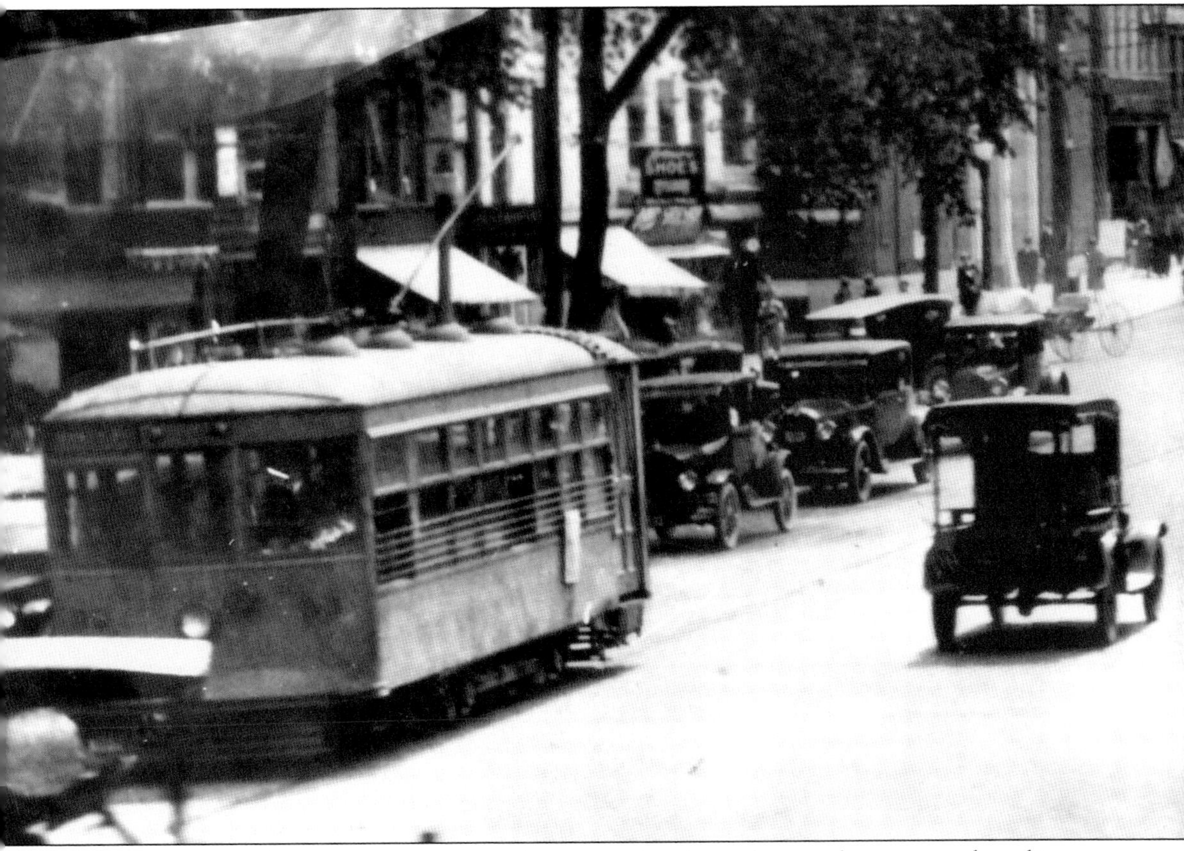

It was not unusual to see a Birney car in downtown Danbury sharing the street with its biggest competitor, the automobile. In 1914, the company expanded its power station to enable it to sell power to the cities of Danbury and Newtown. This actually helped support the money-losing streetcars. In 1917, the company went into receivership, not having paid dividends since 1908. The company was reorganized in 1925 as the Danbury and Bethel Traction Company, operating 13 miles of line. Finally on November 19, 1926, the company abandoned all service, the entire line was scrapped, and the equipment was sold for junk. (Courtesy Connecticut Motor Coach Museum Archives.)

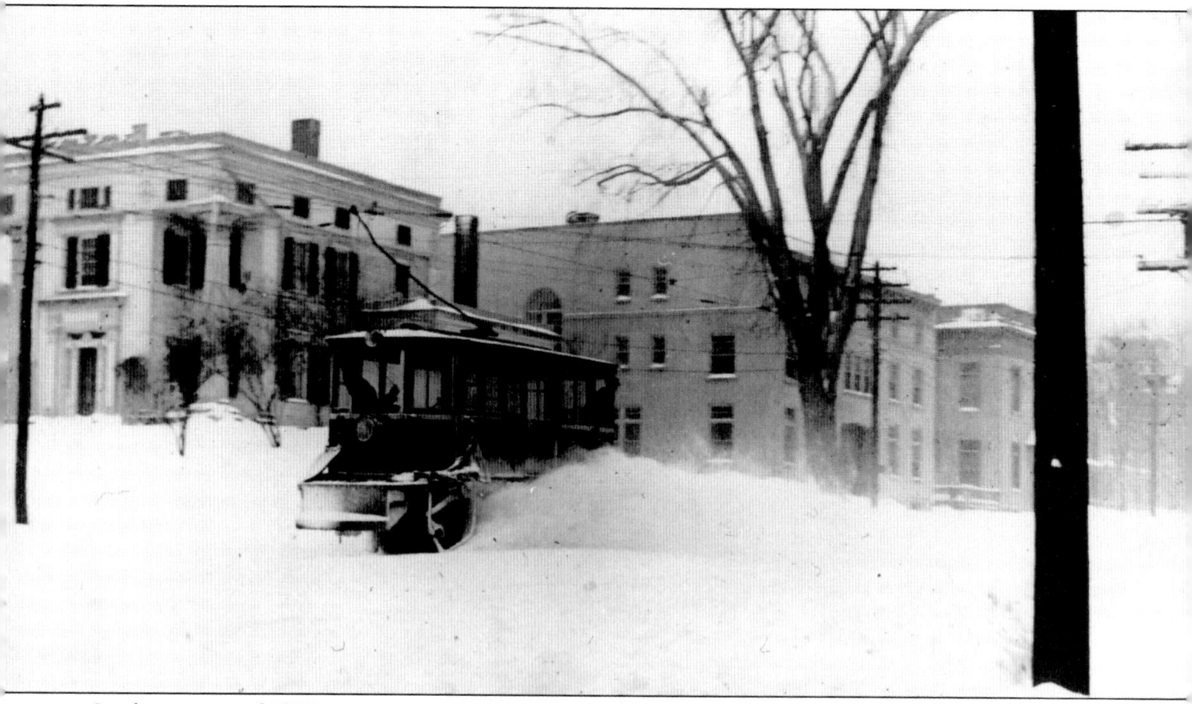

In the winter of 1920, a company snow sweeper clears the line in Danbury. Danbury was one of only two major cities in Connecticut (the other being Bristol) that did not have its streetcars operated by the Connecticut Company. (Courtesy Fred Bennett collection.)

Three

MERIDEN LINES

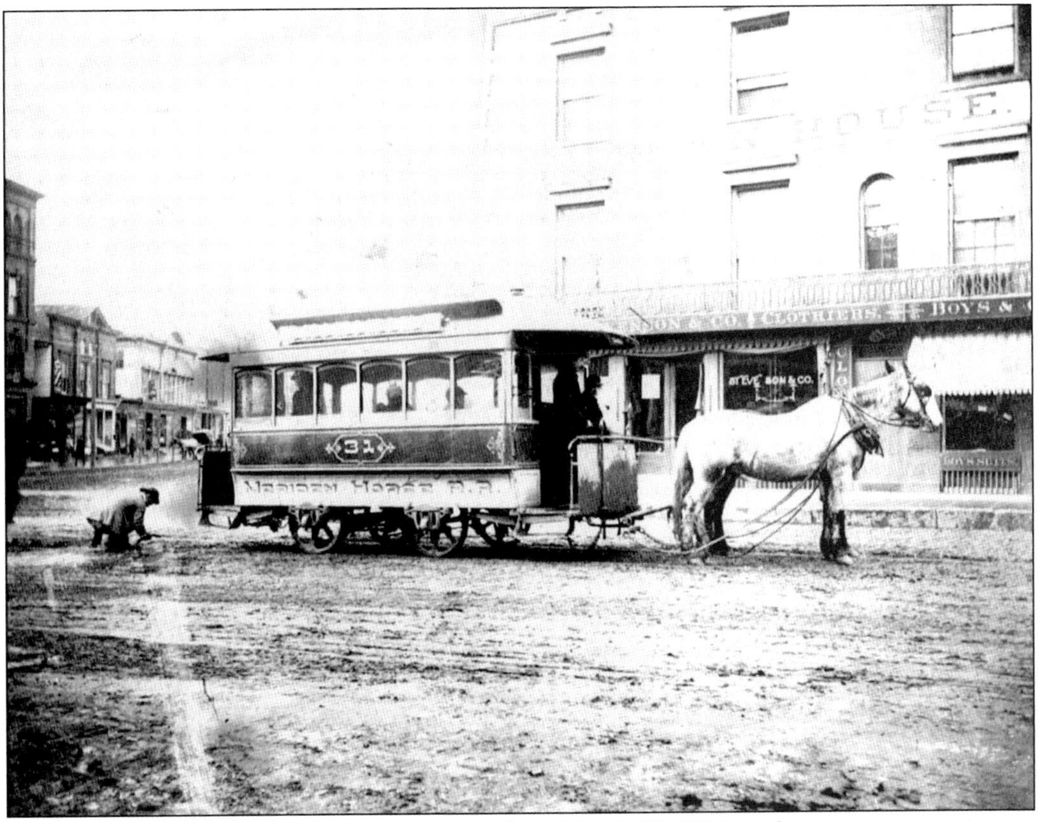

The Meriden Horse Railroad was incorporated on March 30, 1886, with operations starting on March 21, 1887. On January 10, 1888, the company stables were ravaged by a fire that destroyed 14 cars and killed 80 horses. The line was electrified in 1888 simply because electric cars were cheaper to run than horsecars and the company had to replace the equipment lost in the fire. (Courtesy Fred Bennett collection.)

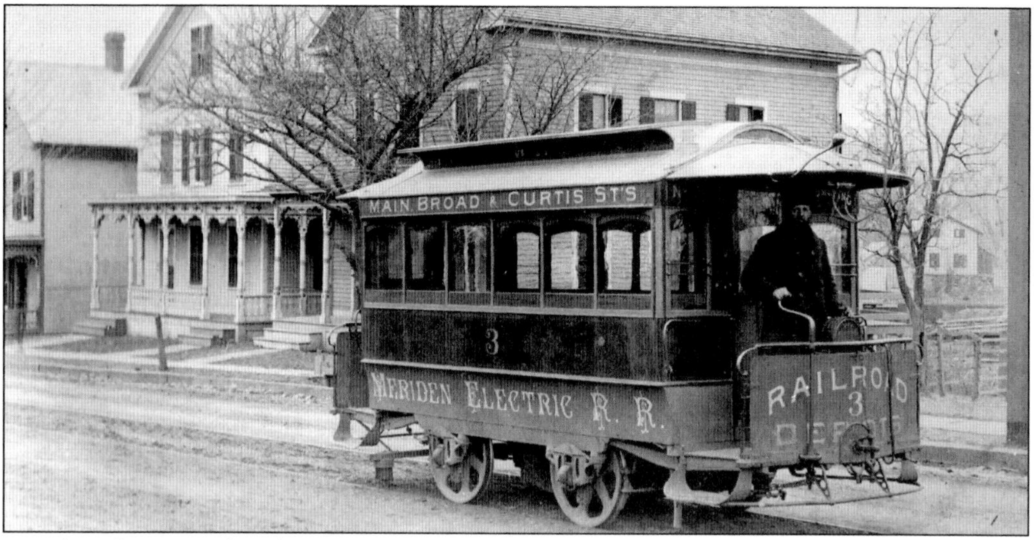

Meriden Electric Railroad car No. 3 was a converted horsecar. In 1888, the line was electrified using equipment supplied by Leo Daft, a pioneer in the streetcar industry. Daft's system used two overhead wires and a little four-wheeled carriage connected to the car by a flexible cable. The carriage was called a troller because of the way it was pulled along the wires. The biggest problem was the erratic behavior of the carriage; it would occasionally jump off the overhead wires and crash down on the roof of the car. Daft cars were finally banned in Meriden in 1892 when the mayor assigned a city official to investigate the problems. During an inspection trip, the investigator was struck on the head by one of the trollers. (Courtesy Fred Bennett collection.)

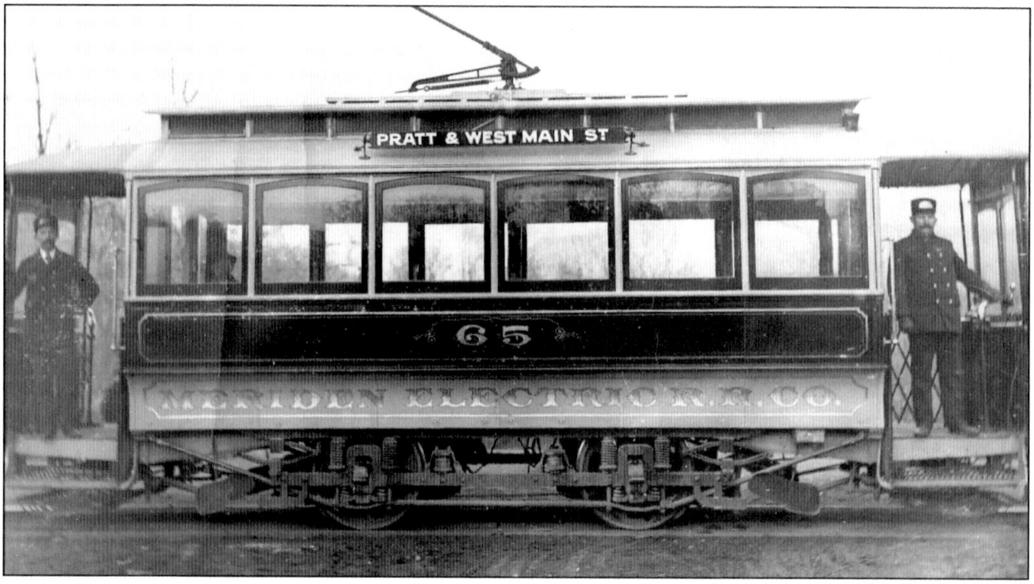

The Meriden Electric Railroad purchased car No. 65 from the J. G. Brill Company. This photograph was taken before 1903, when all cars with open vestibules had to be enclosed per order of the state. Meriden was the second city in Connecticut to electrify its horsecar lines, the first being Derby in May 1888. Hartford was the third city to electrify when the Hartford and Wethersfield Horse Railroad started running electric cars in September 1888. (Courtesy Connecticut Motor Coach Museum Archives.)

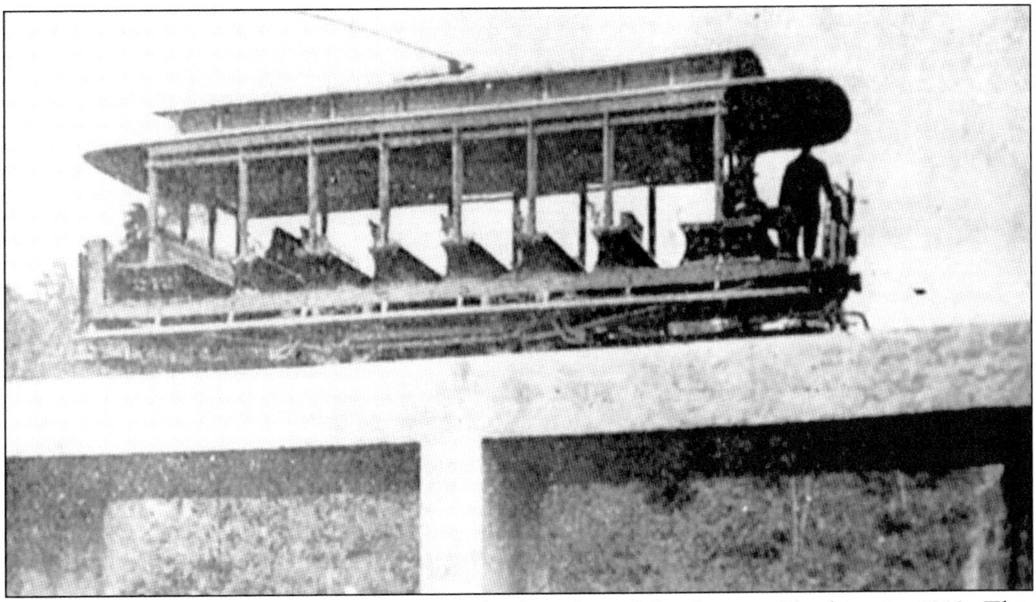

The 10-bench open car No. 242 ran on the line from Meriden to Cheshire in 1910. This line was originally built by the Meriden, Southington and Compounce Tramway Company in the late 1890s. It was acquired by the New Haven Railroad in 1907 and conveyed to the Connecticut Company on June 1 of that year. Thereafter, it was operated as part of the Meriden Division. Car No. 242 was built in 1894 and scrapped in 1916. (Courtesy Connecticut Motor Coach Museum Archives.)

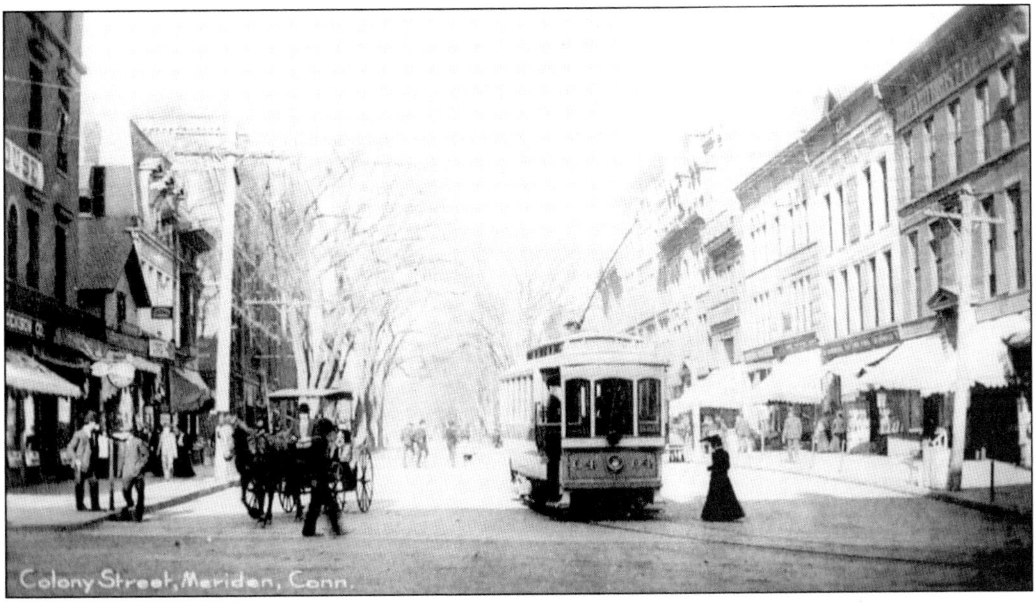

Meriden Electric Railway closed car No. 64 travels on Colony Street in 1905. Electric operation started on July 11, 1888; however, by October 1892, the line had been converted back to horse operation because of the numerous problems with the equipment designed by Leo Daft. In 1895, the line was electrified once again, using better equipment with more up-to-date technology. (Courtesy Fred Bennett collection.)

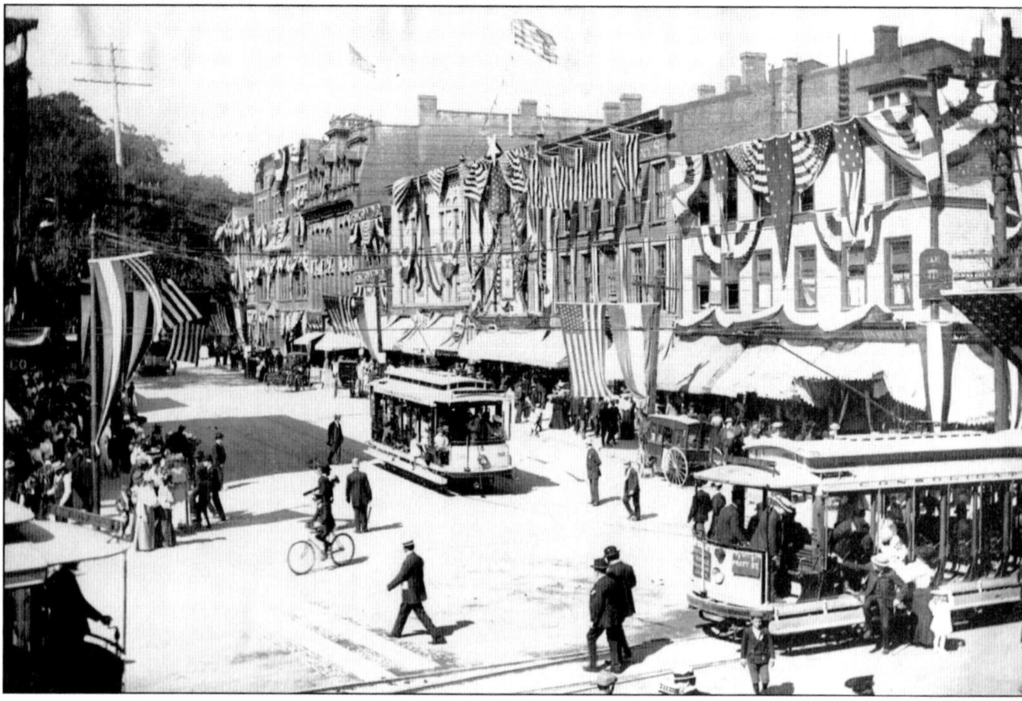

The festive atmosphere of the Fourth of July is apparent in Meriden's downtown in 1901. (Courtesy Fred Bennett collection.)

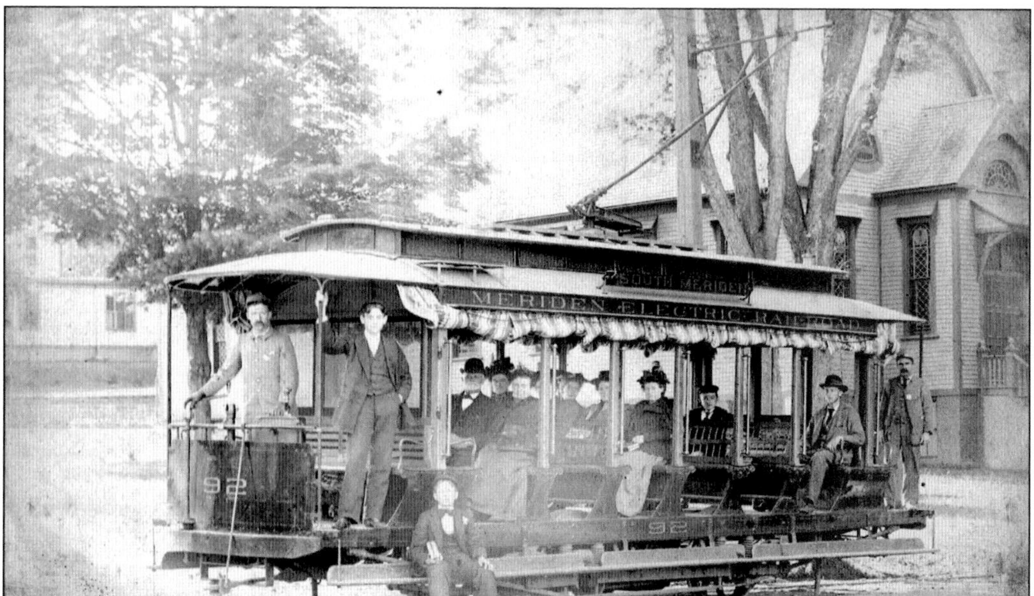

Meriden Electric Railroad open car No. 92 runs on the line to South Meriden. In 1925, Meriden's first motor coach line was established from the Meriden railroad station to Cambridge Street. The first streetcar line to be converted to motor coach was the Meriden to Wallingford line on September 22, 1929. The last line to operate was the Meriden to Plainville via Southington, which was converted to motor coach on September 28, 1931. (Courtesy Fred Bennett collection.)

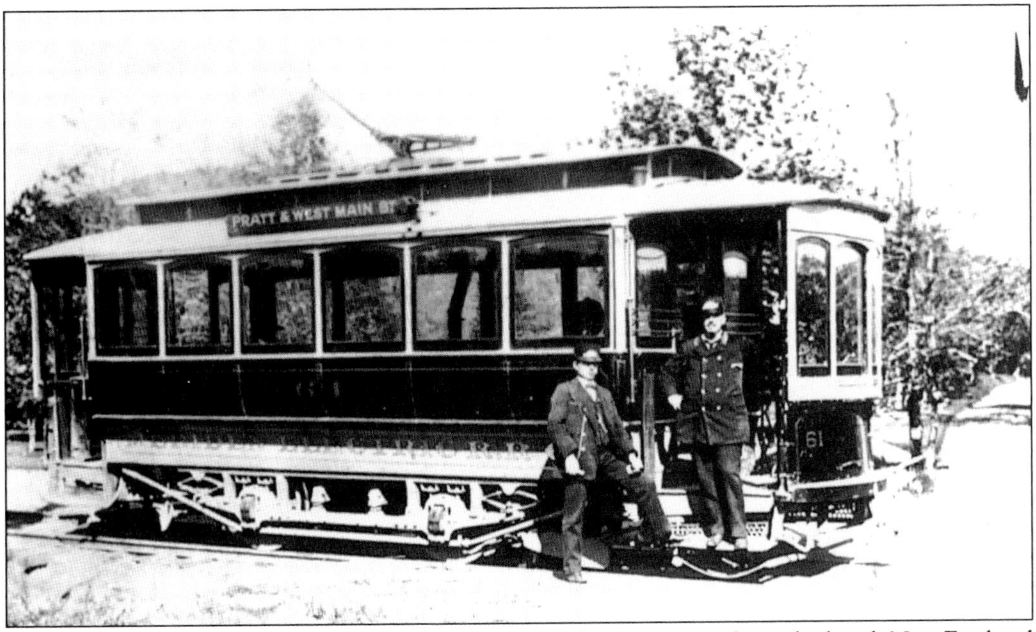

Car No. 61's vestibules have been closed in to protect the motorman from the harsh New England winters. Compare this image with that of car No. 65 on the bottom of page 36. (Courtesy Fred Bennett collection.)

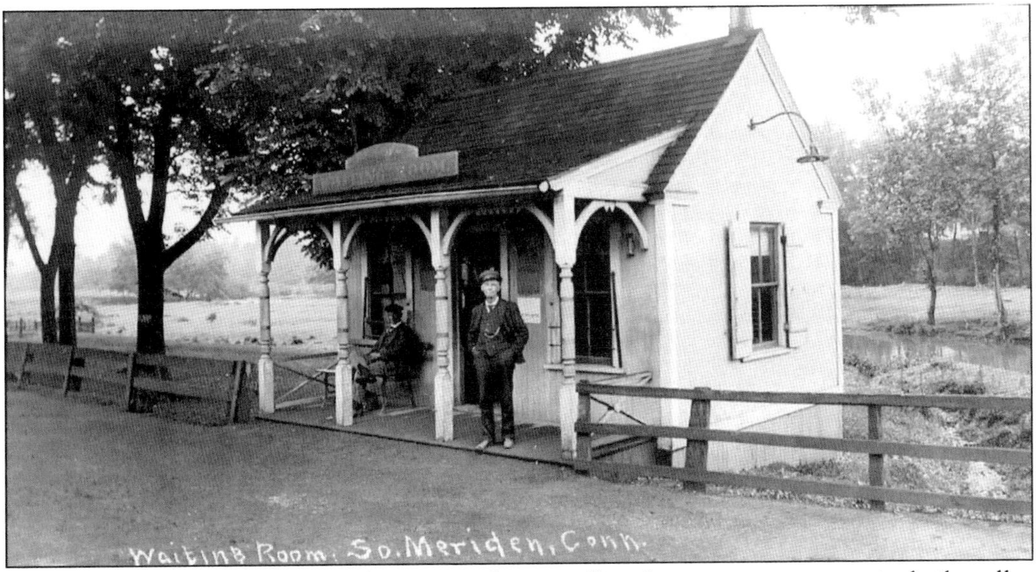

To protect their passengers from the wet weather as well as the sun, some companies built trolley waiting stations, such as this one in South Meriden. (Courtesy Fred Bennett collection.)

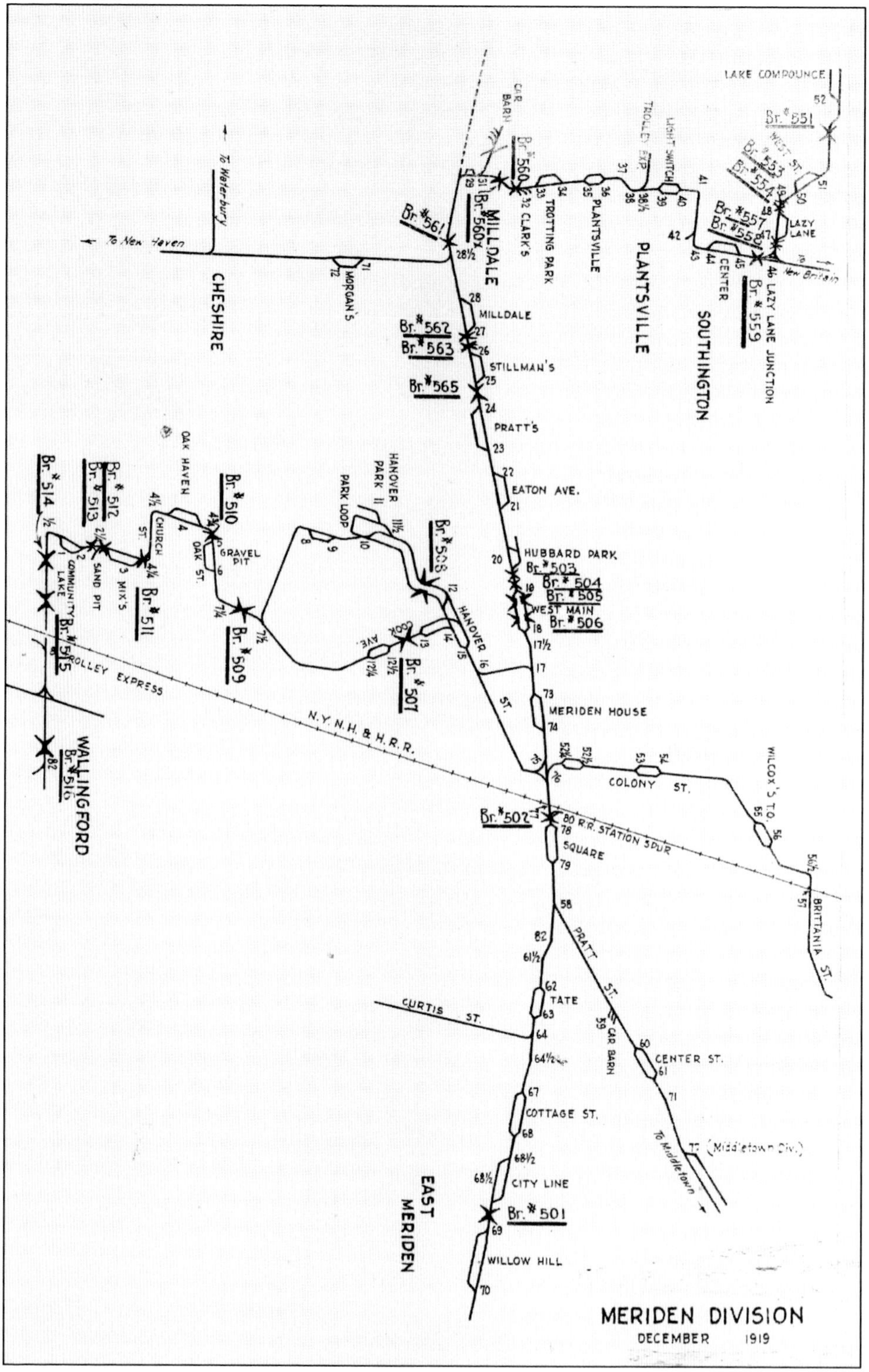

Shown here is a map of the streetcar system in Meriden. (Courtesy Connecticut Motor Coach Museum Archives.)

Four

Middletown Lines

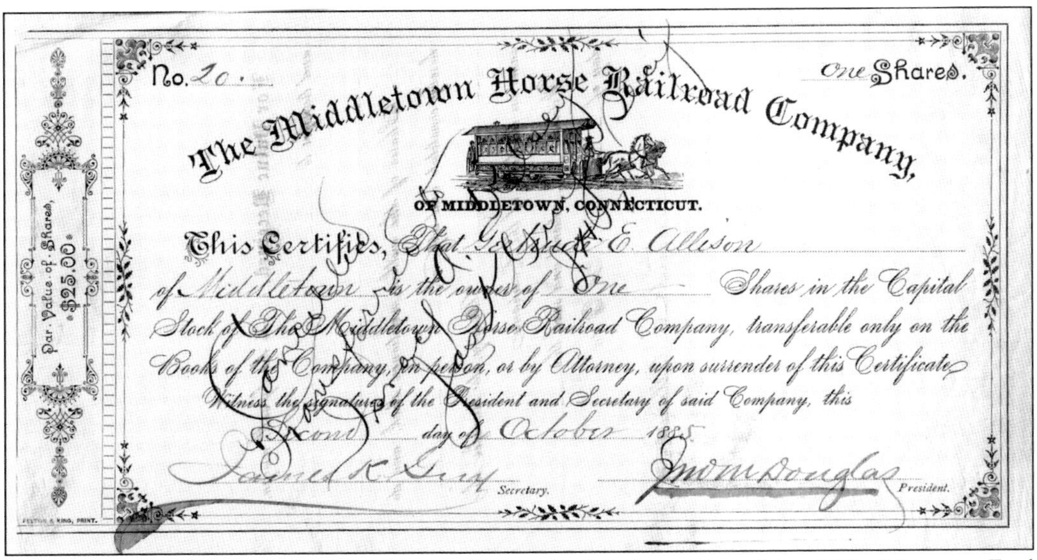

This stock certificate of the Middletown Horse Railroad was issued in 1885. (Courtesy Fred Bennett collection.)

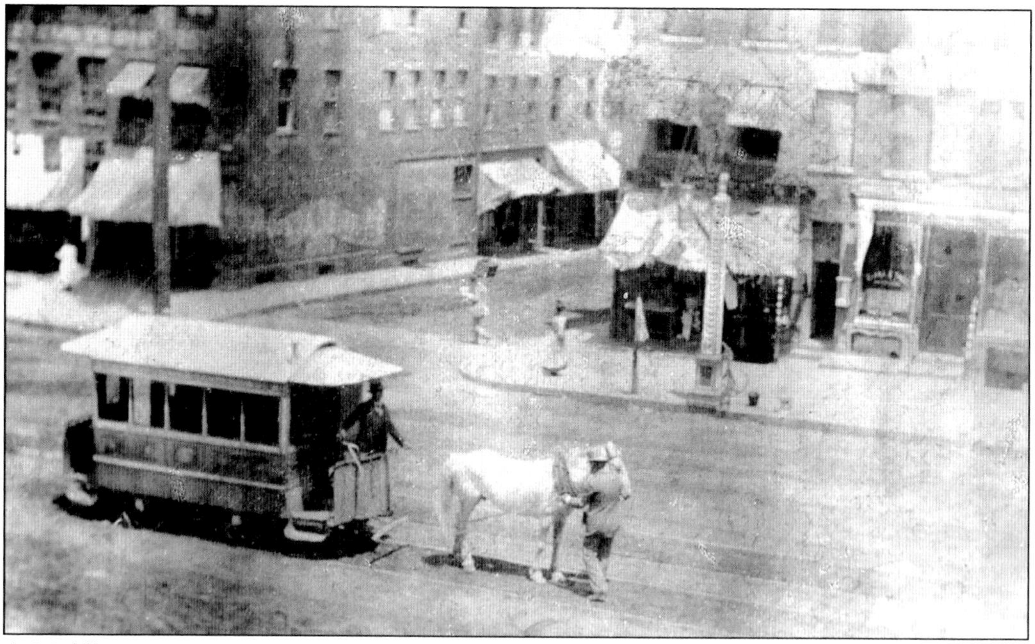

A Middletown Horse Railroad car runs on Main Street in 1886. Having their own horsecar line was a big advantage, for convenience and growth, to the citizens of a city like Middletown. In 1886, there were 525 horse railroads in 300 towns and cities in this country, powered by 100,000 horses and mules. (Courtesy Fred Bennett collection.)

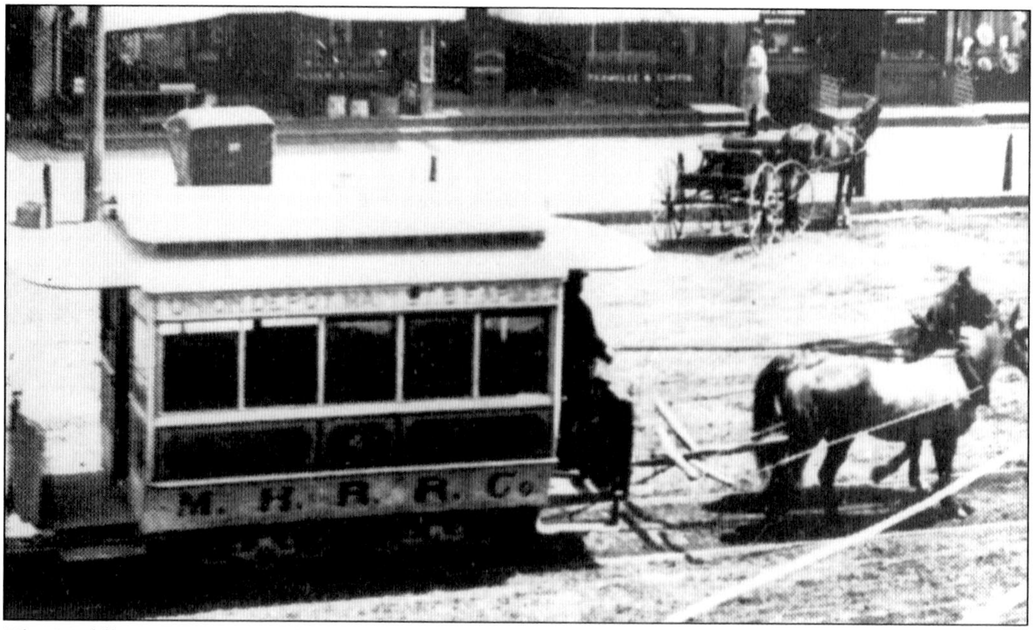

The Middletown Horse Railroad was incorporated in 1871, and in 1887, its charter was amended by the State of Connecticut to allow operation of electric cars. Horsecar passengers in the 1880s suffered the discomfort of hard seats, poor ventilation, and bitterly cold cars. However, these cars were far superior to the other available options like the rough-riding omnibus or stagecoach. (Courtesy Fred Bennett collection.)

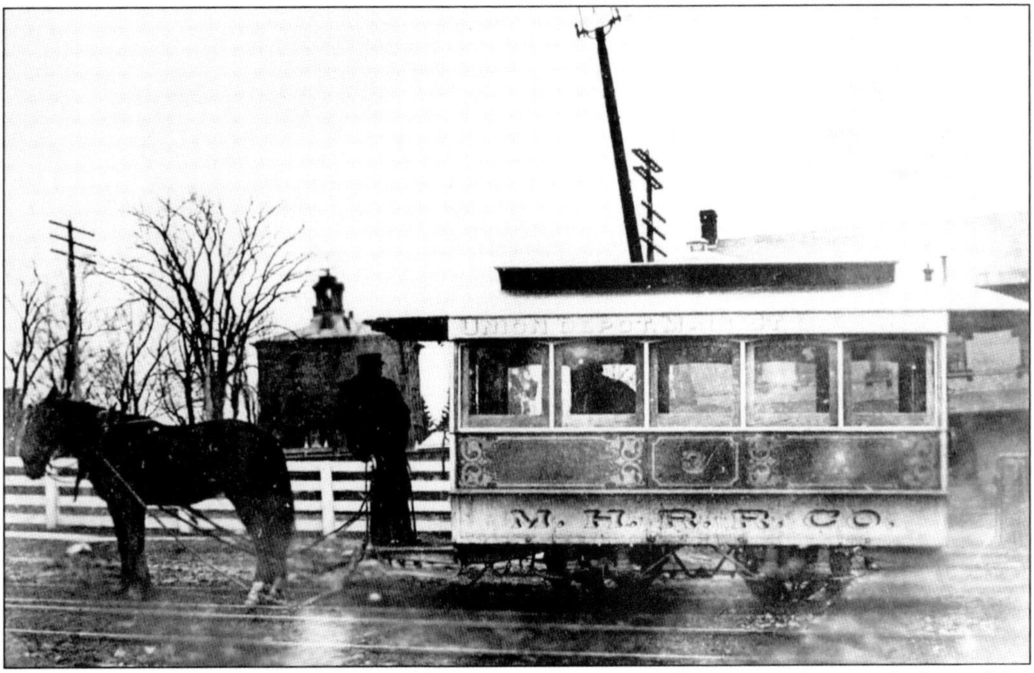

In the era when only men smoked in public, male passengers usually rode on the rear platform of the horsecar so the smoke would not offend the other passengers. (Courtesy Fred Bennett collection.)

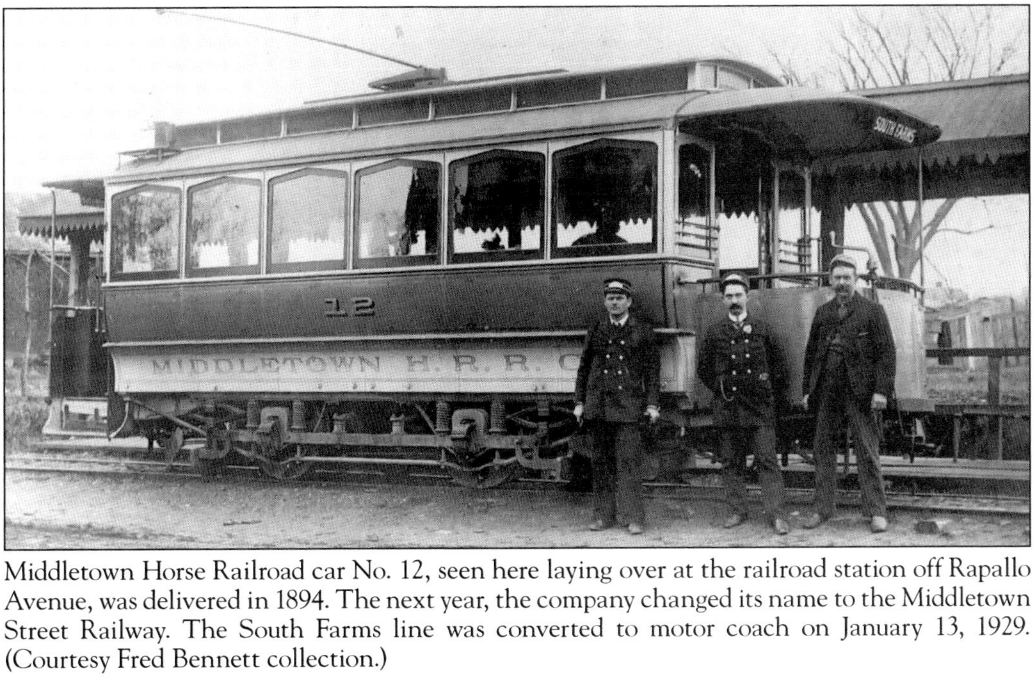

Middletown Horse Railroad car No. 12, seen here laying over at the railroad station off Rapallo Avenue, was delivered in 1894. The next year, the company changed its name to the Middletown Street Railway. The South Farms line was converted to motor coach on January 13, 1929. (Courtesy Fred Bennett collection.)

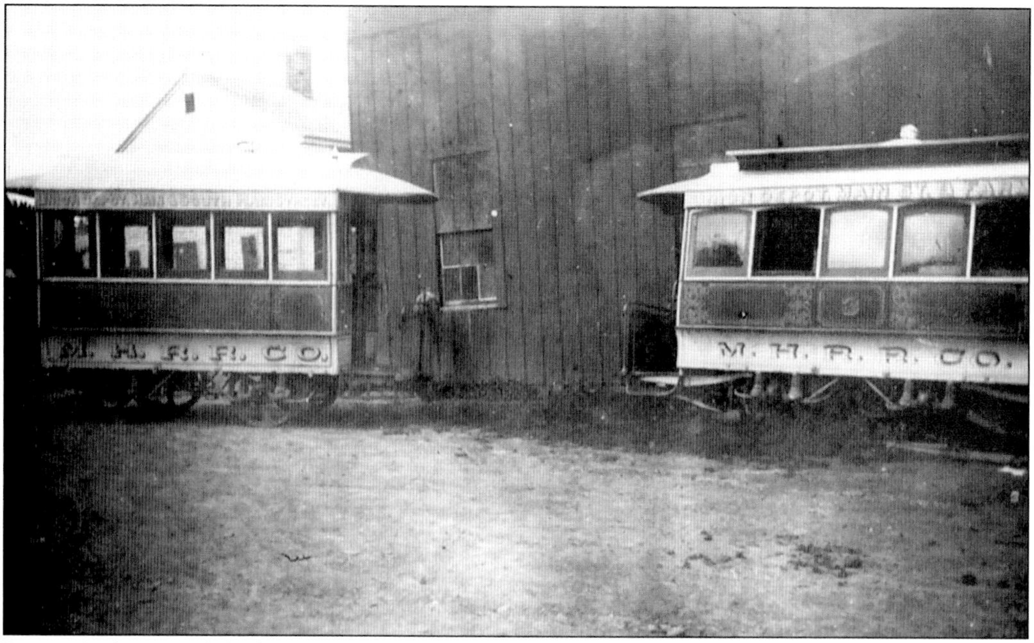

By 1895, the era of the horsecar was fading, having achieved its fullest growth in 1888. These two obsolete horsecars are ready to be scrapped in 1895 after being replaced by the new electric streetcars. This switch did not happen everywhere; horsecar lines in Mexico actually operated until the 1950s. (Courtesy Fred Bennett collection, Library of Congress photograph.)

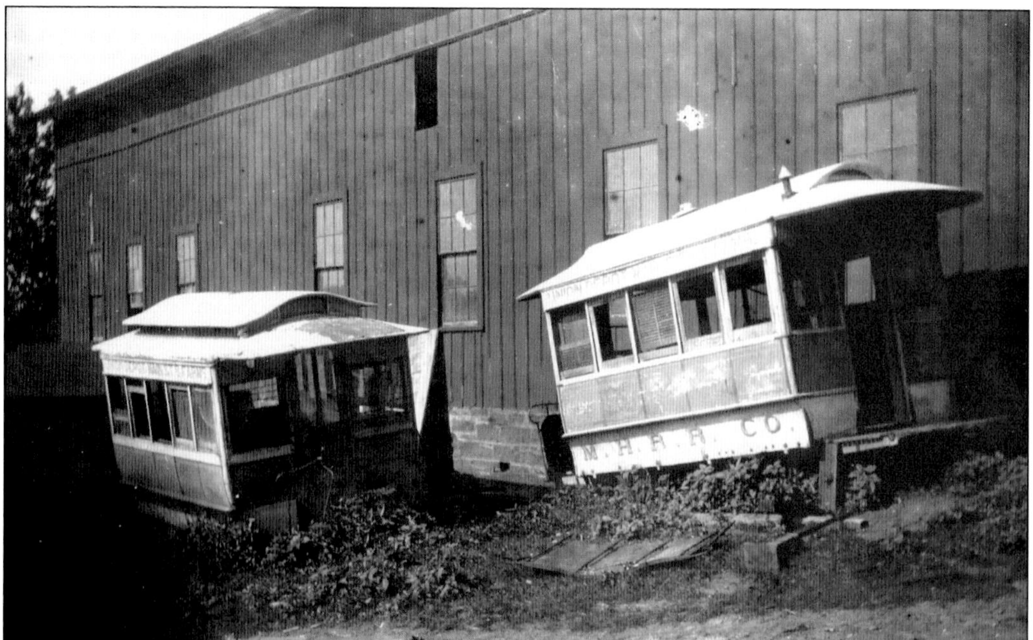

Some companies, like the Hartford and Wethersfield Horse Railroad, simply converted horsecars to electric rather than buy new cars. Other companies chose to purchase new electrified cars, leaving more forlorn horsecars waiting to be scrapped, such as these in 1895. (Courtesy Fred Bennett collection, Library of Congress photograph.)

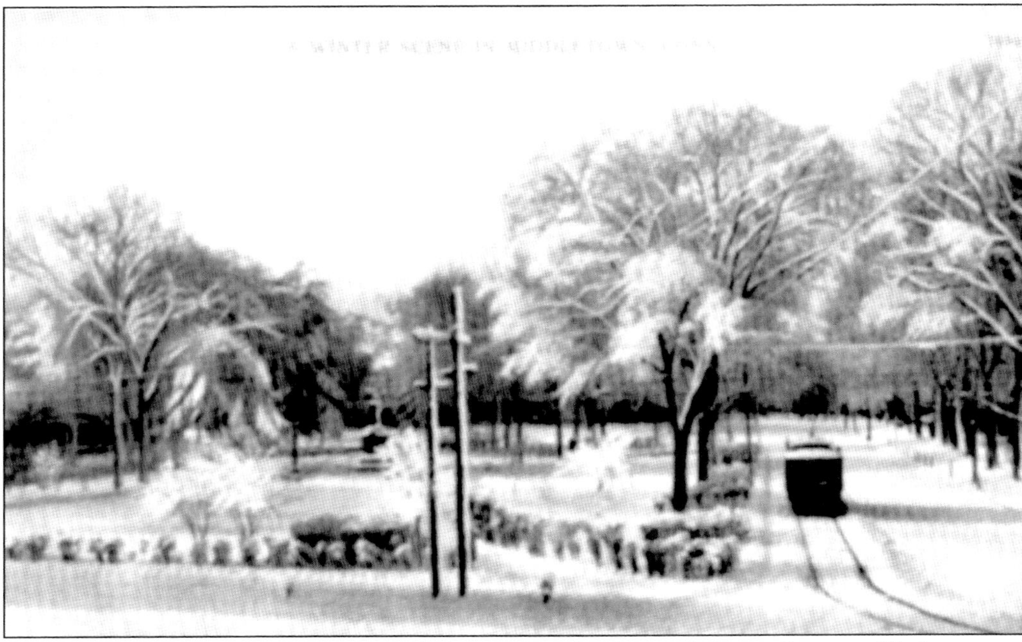

The romance of new fallen snow and the new technology of the trolley car fill this winter postcard scene of Middletown in 1900. (Courtesy Fred Bennett collection.)

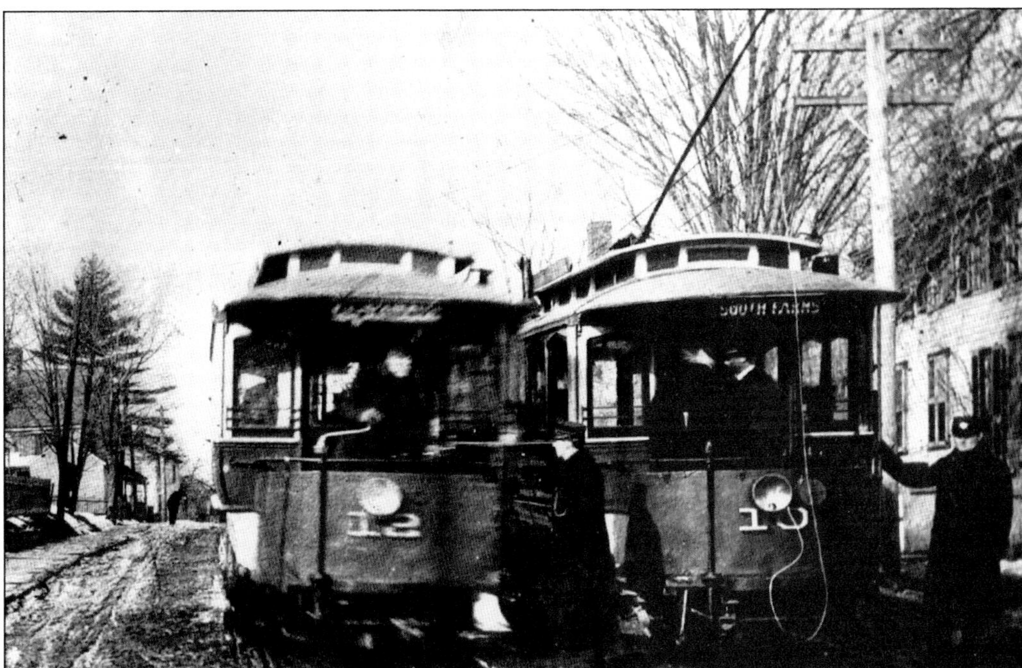

Two of the original cars purchased to electrify the Middletown Horse Railroad pass on Main Street in 1898. (Courtesy Fred Bennett collection.)

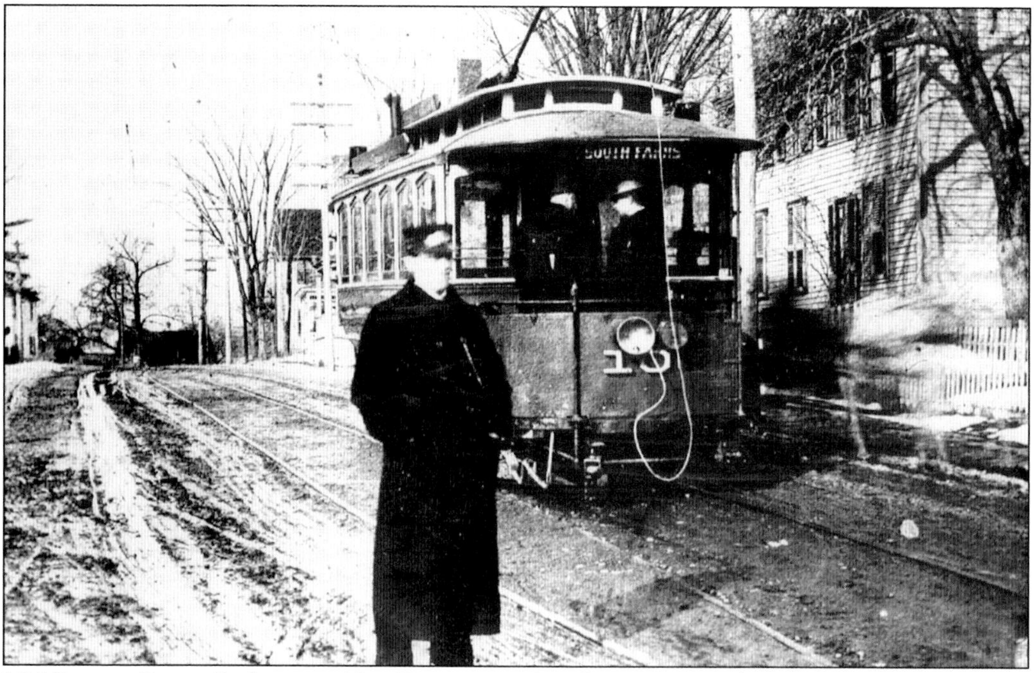

Middletown Street Railway car No. 10 is pictured with its crew in the winter of 1904. Built by the J. G. Brill Company in 1894, the car ran in Middletown until it was scrapped in July 1913. The early streetcars had little or no heat, so the crew often wore heavy fur coats during the winter. (Courtesy Fred Bennett collection.)

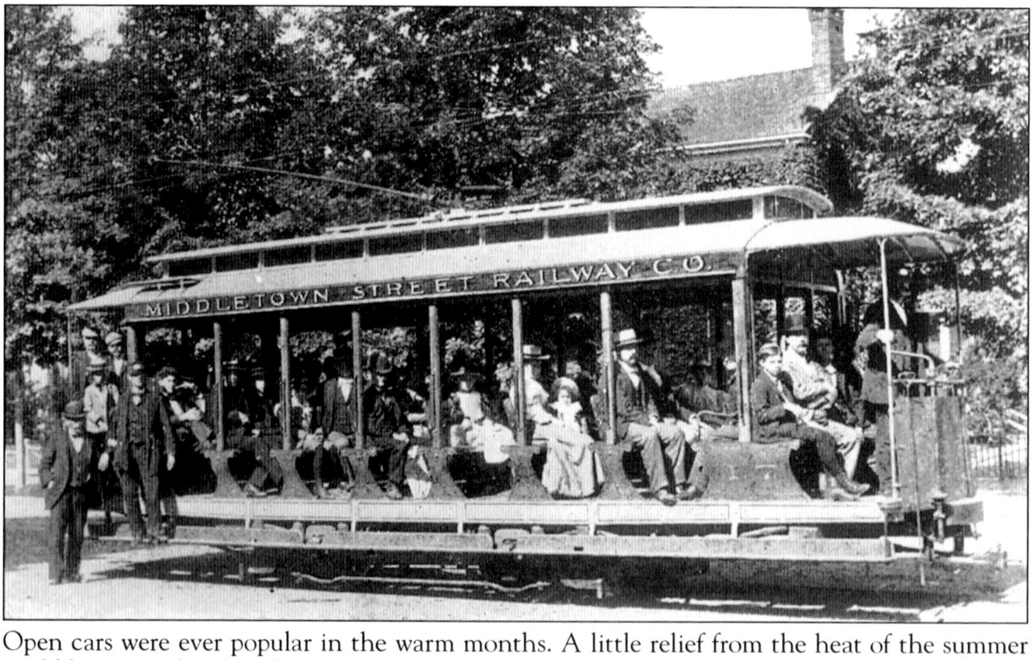

Open cars were ever popular in the warm months. A little relief from the heat of the summer could be enjoyed with a short ride on an open car. Middletown Street Railway car No. 17, seen here, later became Connecticut Company car No. 254 before being scrapped in Middletown in April 1923. (Courtesy Connecticut Motor Coach Museum Archives.)

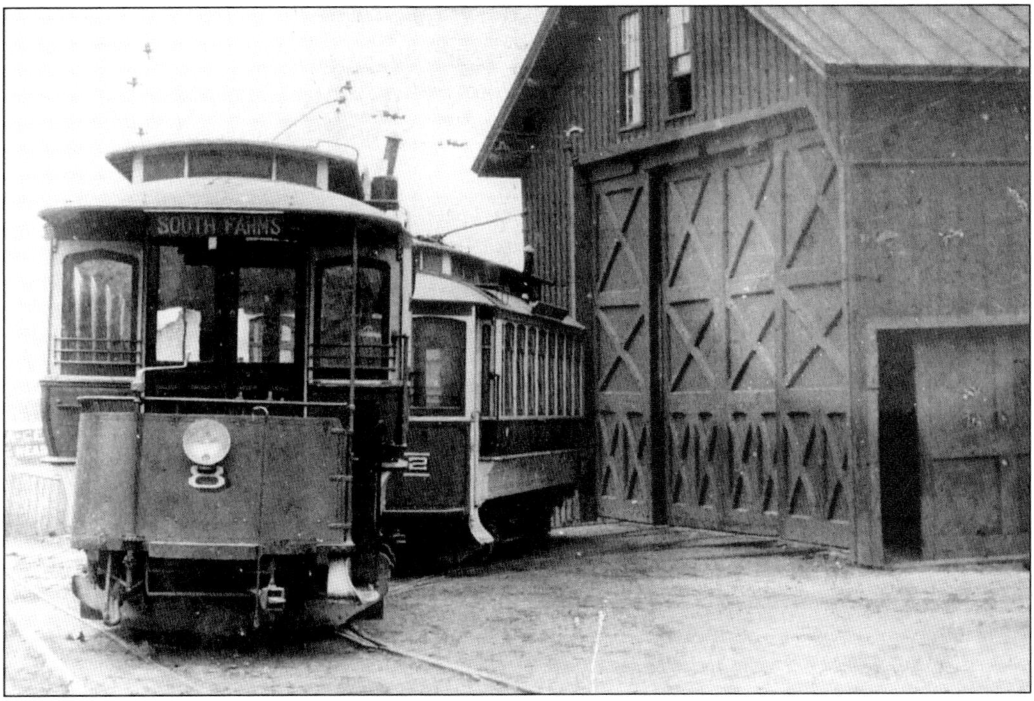

Two of the original electric cars on the Middletown Horse Railroad sit outside the carbarn in Middletown. (Courtesy Fred Bennett collection.)

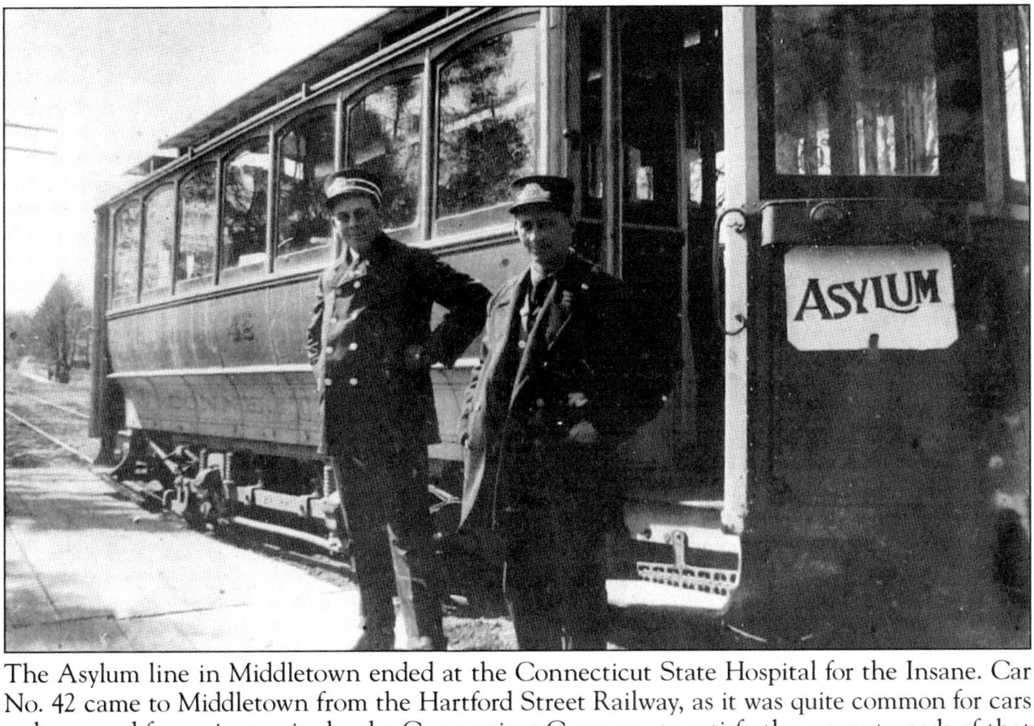

The Asylum line in Middletown ended at the Connecticut State Hospital for the Insane. Car No. 42 came to Middletown from the Hartford Street Railway, as it was quite common for cars to be moved from city to city by the Connecticut Company to satisfy the current needs of that community. (Courtesy Fred Bennett collection.)

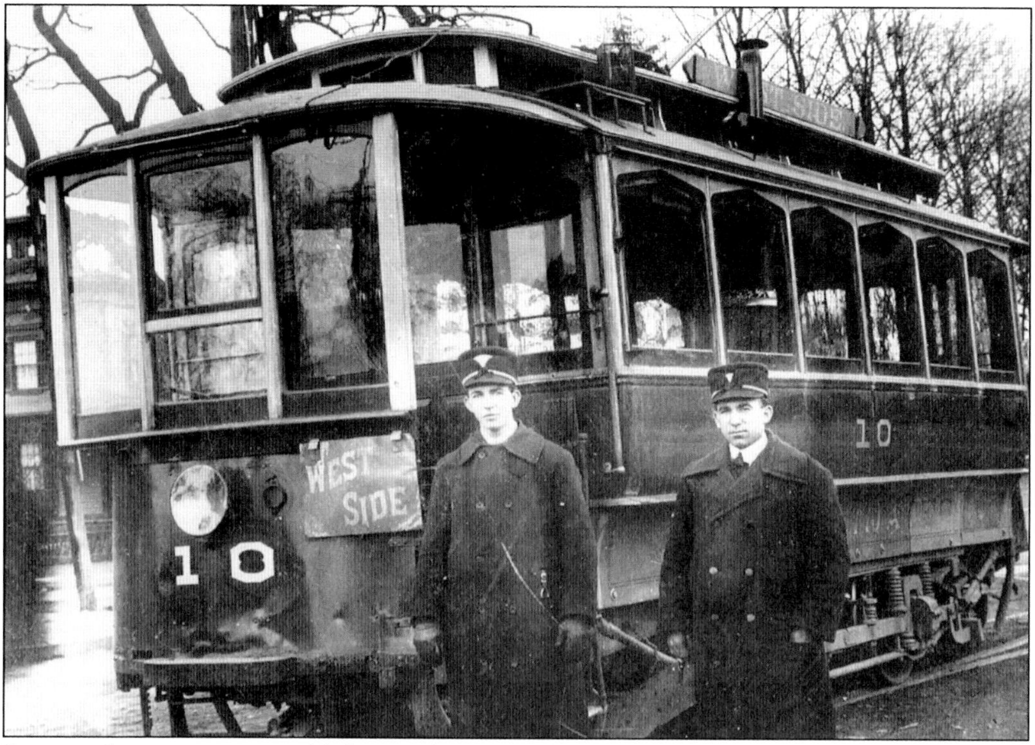

Street railway companies sold the conductors and motormen their uniforms for $10 each. In 1900, streetcar crews typically worked a six-and-a-half-day week for an average weekly wage of $12 to $15, depending on seniority. (Courtesy Fred Bennett collection.)

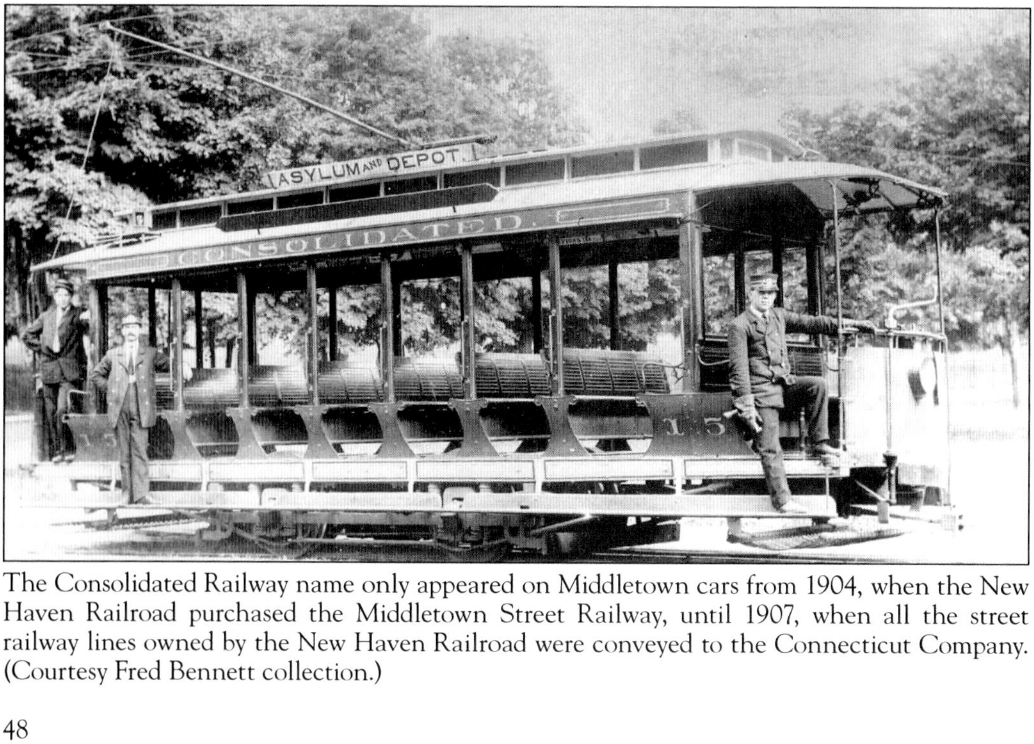

The Consolidated Railway name only appeared on Middletown cars from 1904, when the New Haven Railroad purchased the Middletown Street Railway, until 1907, when all the street railway lines owned by the New Haven Railroad were conveyed to the Connecticut Company. (Courtesy Fred Bennett collection.)

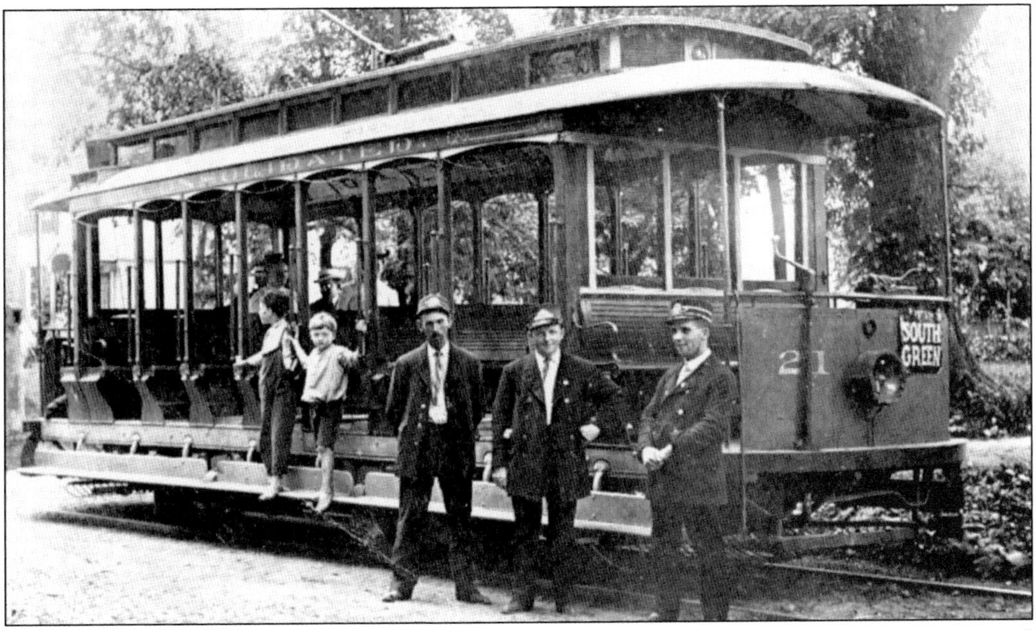

Consolidated Railway open car No. 21 became Connecticut Company car No. 472 in 1915 before being scrapped in 1920. Single-truck cars did not see many years of service after 1916, when over 400 were scrapped. Some were retained for use as work cars and ran until the 1940s. (Courtesy Connecticut Motor Coach Museum Archives.)

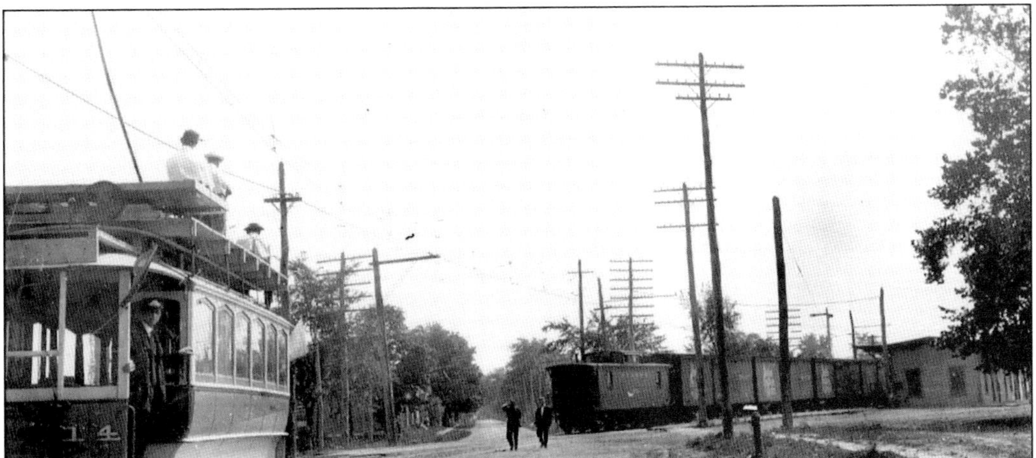

Trolley service between Hartford and Middletown began in 1909. The official first trip was held on May 24, 1909. From the Cromwell railroad station, the streetcars ran on the New Haven Railroad tracks to the Middletown railroad station. From there, they traveled up Rapallo Avenue to Main Street. On this line, streetcars shared the track with New Haven Railroad steam trains. Car No. 14, a former passenger car, was made into a line car in 1908 to install the overhead trolley wire on the railroad. (Courtesy Fred Bennett collection.)

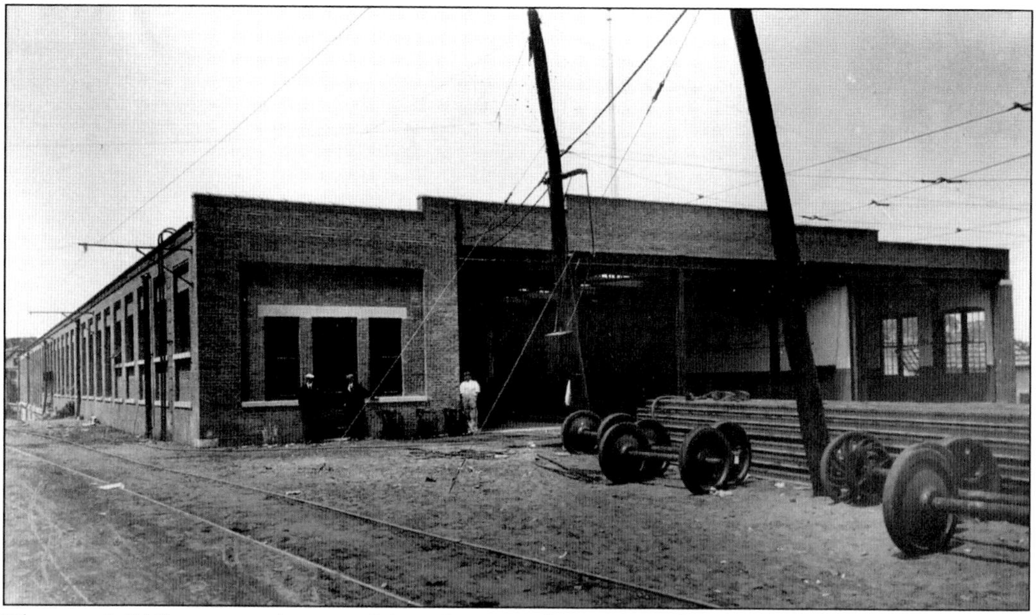

The new Middletown carbarn on Main Street is shown just after construction was completed, around 1910. This building was used as a bus garage after streetcar service ended on June 5, 1930. Today it is used as a warehouse. (Courtesy Fred Bennett collection.)

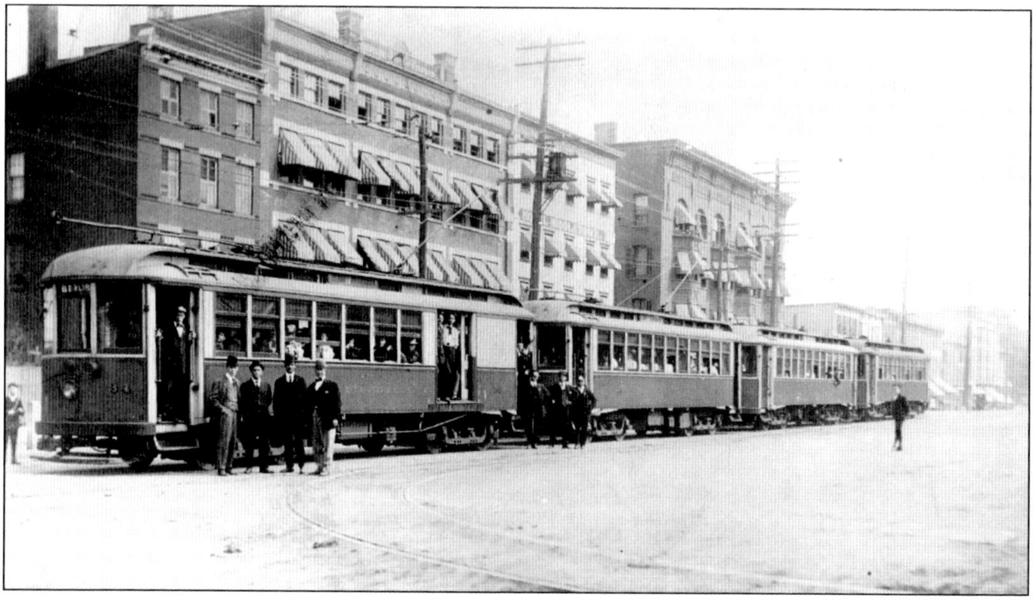

In 1920, a trip to the fair was a big event. Four Connecticut Company cars are lined up on Main Street in Middletown for a special excursion to the Berlin Fair, one of the largest in the area. The cars would run out to Westfield and then up the Berlin branch to the Berlin railroad station. The line from Westfield to Berlin was normally serviced by New Haven Railroad electric cars. (Courtesy Fred Bennett collection.)

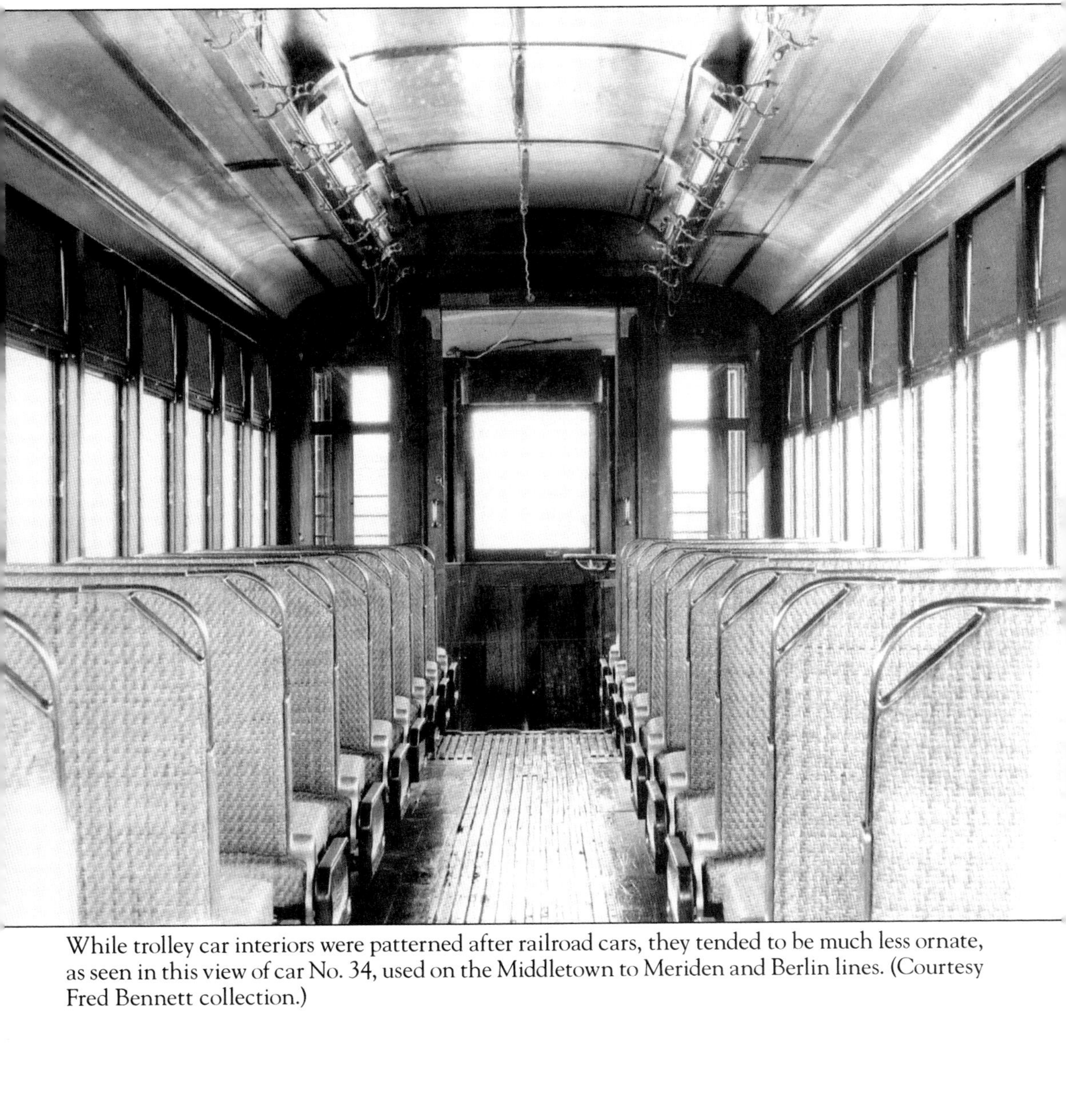

While trolley car interiors were patterned after railroad cars, they tended to be much less ornate, as seen in this view of car No. 34, used on the Middletown to Meriden and Berlin lines. (Courtesy Fred Bennett collection.)

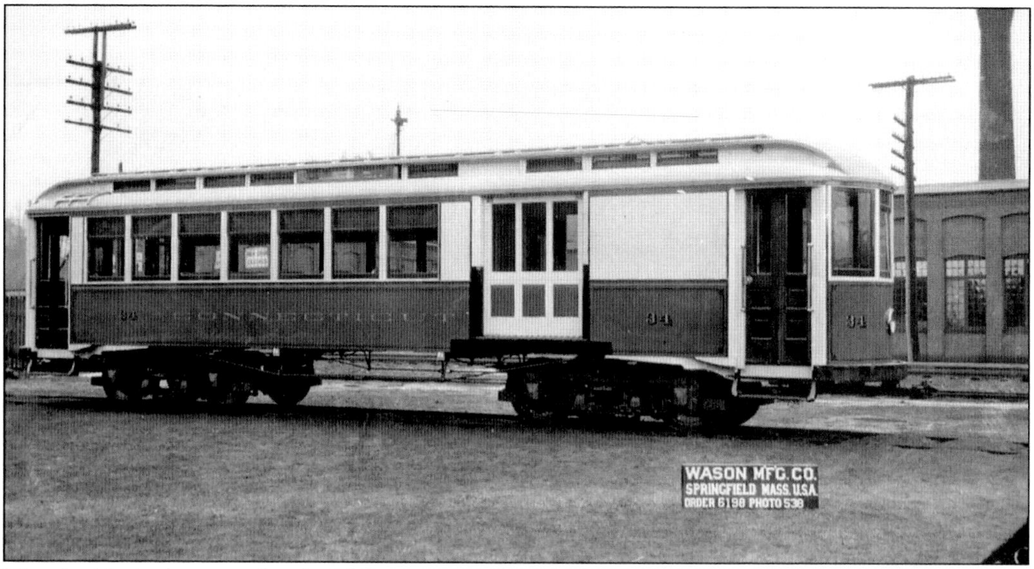

This builder's photograph of car No. 34 was taken at the Wason Manufacturing Company plant in 1907. The car was later transferred to the New Haven Railroad, where it became car No. 3711 for use on the line between Middletown and Berlin. On the New Haven, it was painted hunter green. (Courtesy Fred Bennett collection.)

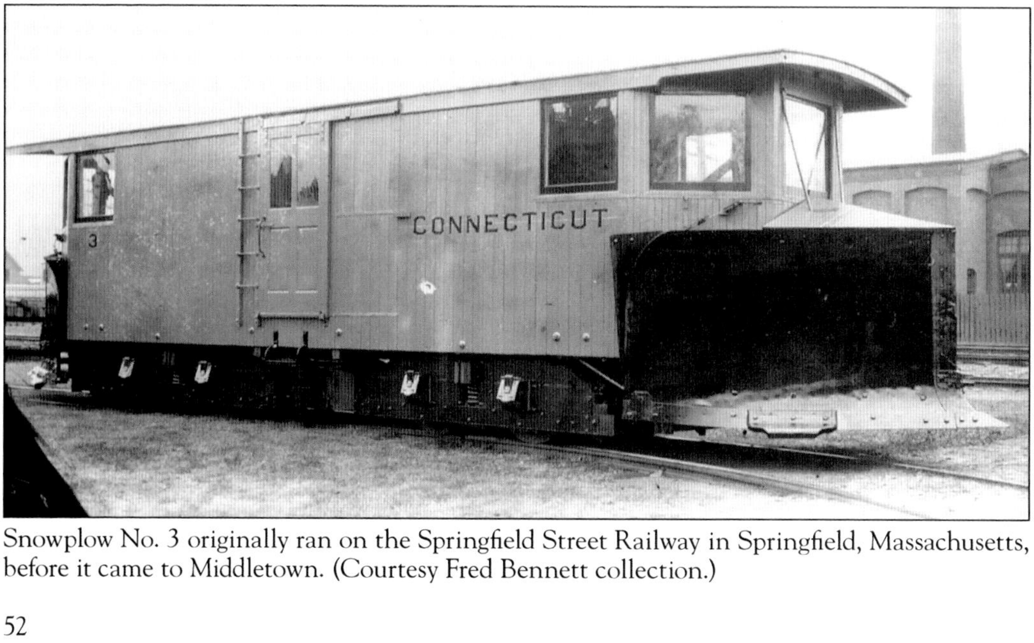

Snowplow No. 3 originally ran on the Springfield Street Railway in Springfield, Massachusetts, before it came to Middletown. (Courtesy Fred Bennett collection.)

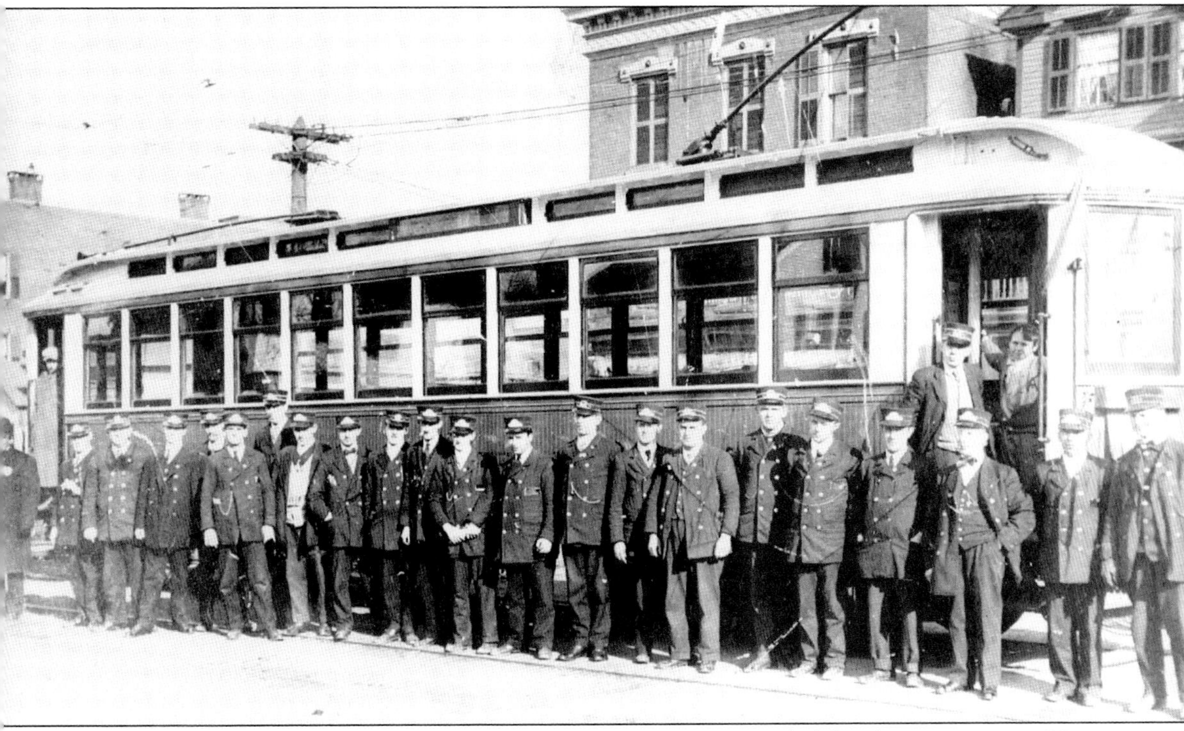

Crews were proud of the job they did and the service they provided for the community. Here conductors and motormen pose with a city policeman in front of the Middletown carbarn in 1911. (Courtesy Fred Bennett collection.)

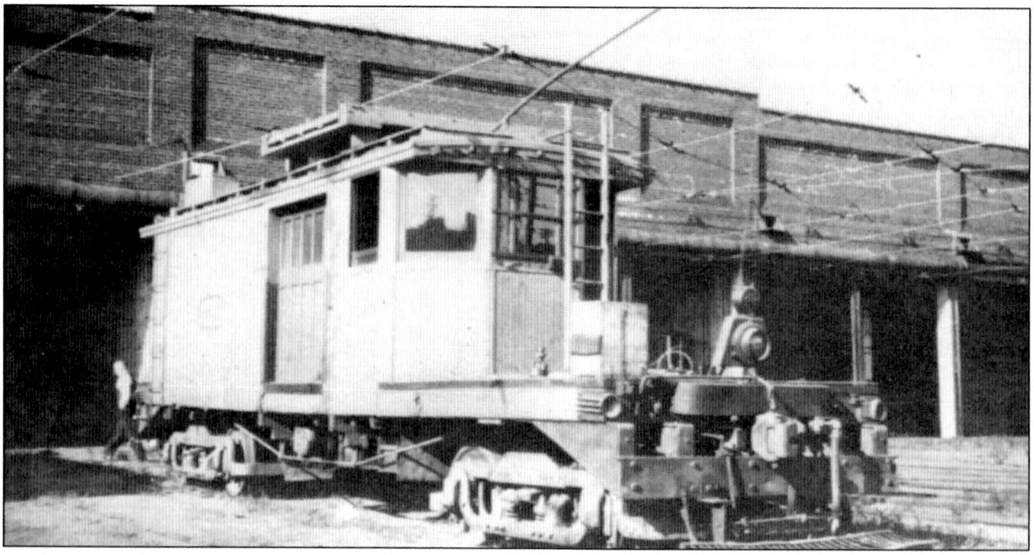

Middletown Division line car No. 14 is shown in this 1914 view in front of the carbarn on Main Street. It was equipped with a standard railroad coupler for retrieving New Haven Railroad cars that broke down on the Berlin to Middletown line, a service it performed in addition to its trolley line duties. This replaced the original car No. 14, pictured on page 49. (Courtesy Fred Bennett collection.)

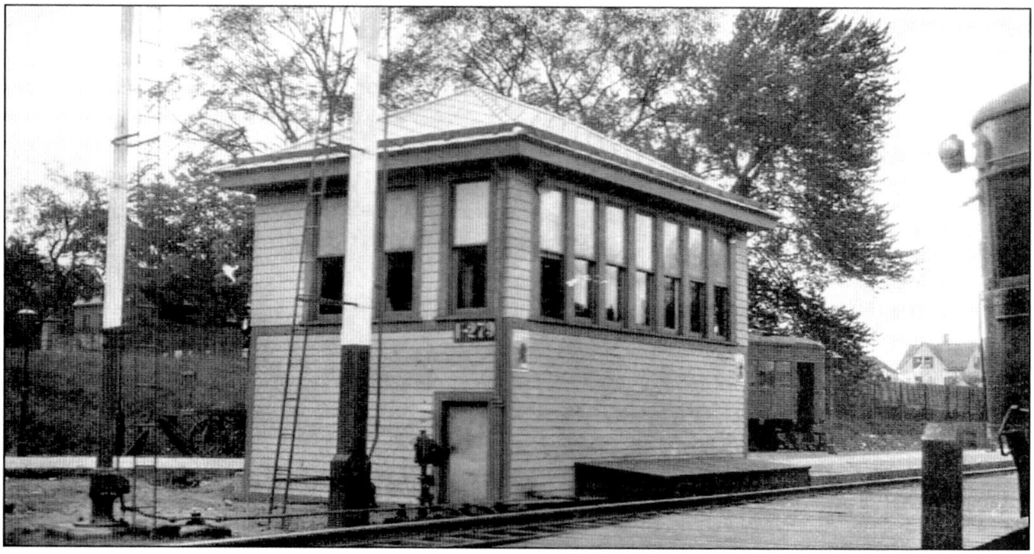

Signal Station F-279 protected the junction of the Hartford to Old Saybrook line and the New Haven to Willimantic line where they crossed in Middletown. Hartford to Middletown streetcars ran on the Hartford line between Cromwell station and Middletown. (Courtesy Connecticut Motor Coach Museum Archives.)

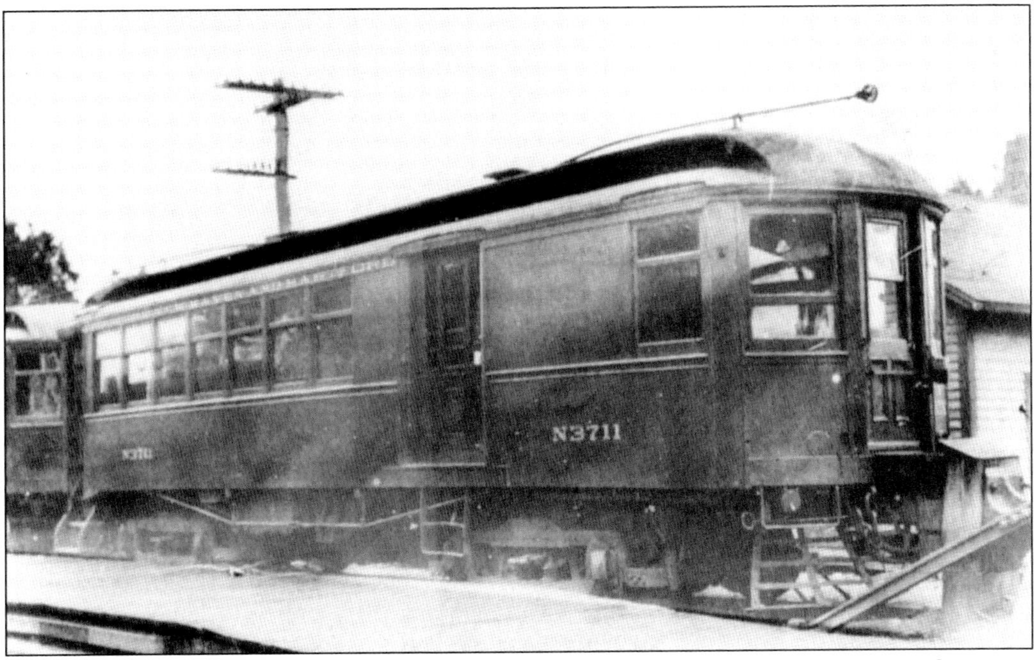

Some trolley cars found new lives after the trolley era ended. Former Connecticut Company car No. 34 is pictured here after it was sold to the New Haven Railroad. (Courtesy Connecticut Motor Coach Museum Archives.)

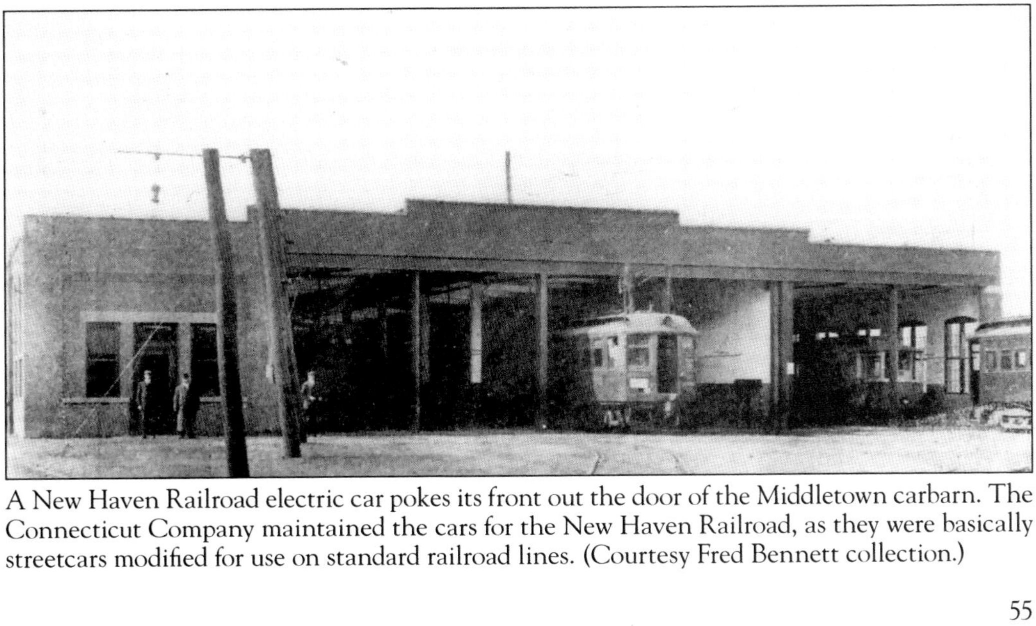

A New Haven Railroad electric car pokes its front out the door of the Middletown carbarn. The Connecticut Company maintained the cars for the New Haven Railroad, as they were basically streetcars modified for use on standard railroad lines. (Courtesy Fred Bennett collection.)

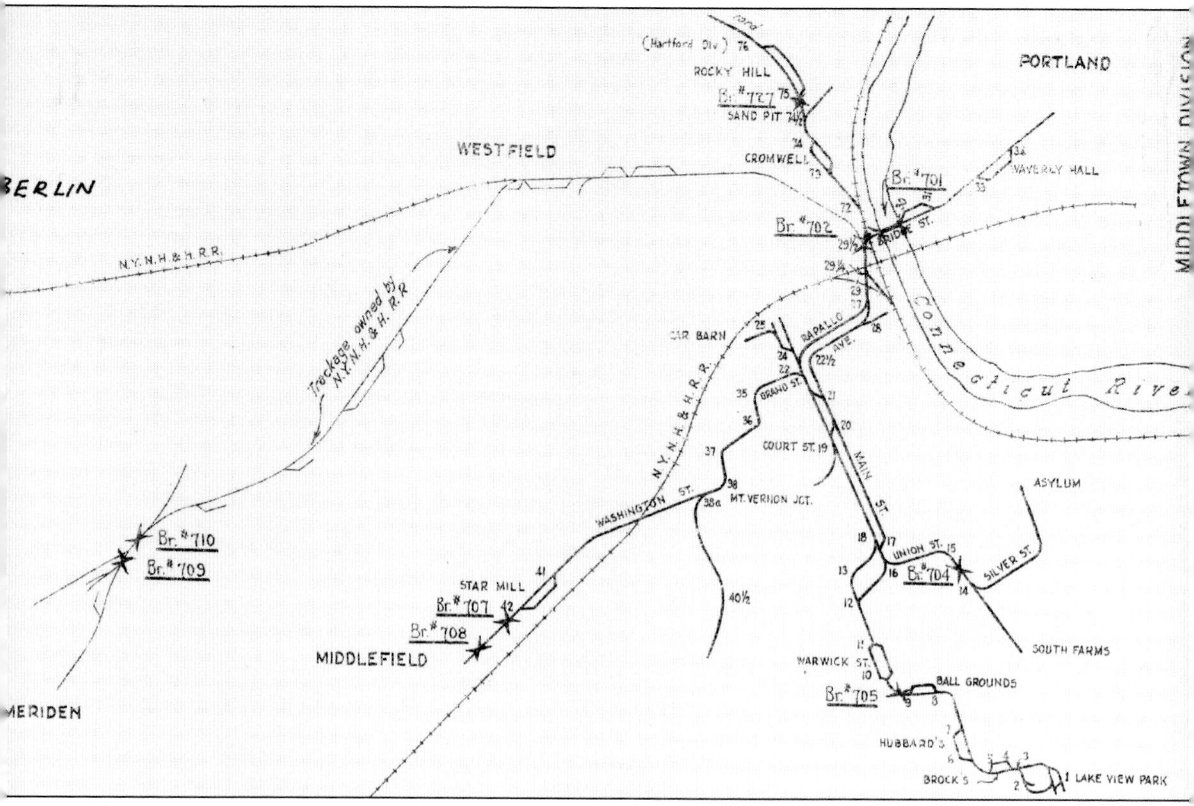

This map details the street railway system in Middletown. (Courtesy Connecticut Motor Coach Museum Archives.)

Five

New Haven

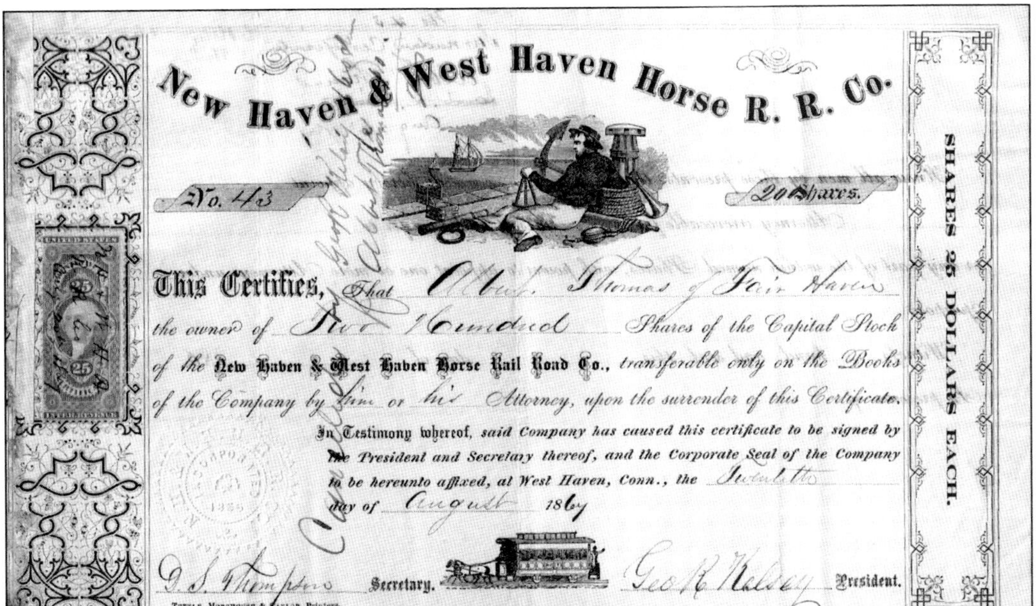

Shown here is a stock certificate of the New Haven and West Haven Horse Railroad. The company was incorporated on July 20, 1865, under special laws of Connecticut authorizing a horse railroad over certain streets in West Haven. In October 1892, the Winchester Avenue Railroad purchased the company and merged operations. (Courtesy Fred Bennett collection.)

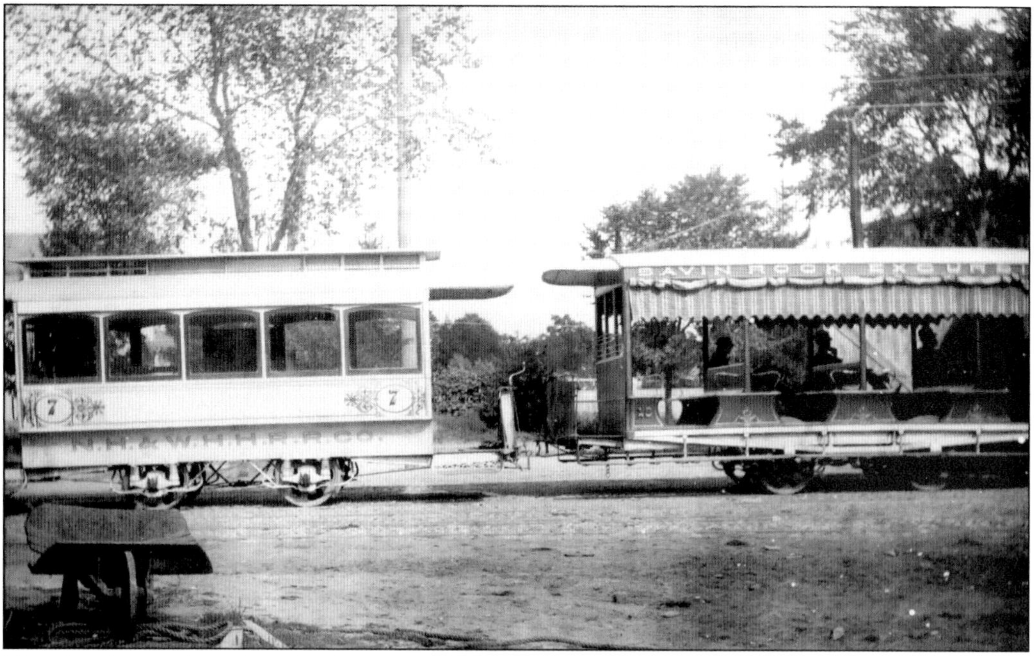

The New Haven lines bought three cars from the Union Railroad of Providence to replace those that had been lost when a carbarn burned down in 1892. Two of these cars are pictured in 1895 in service for the New Haven and West Haven Horse Railroad. (Courtesy Fred Bennett collection.)

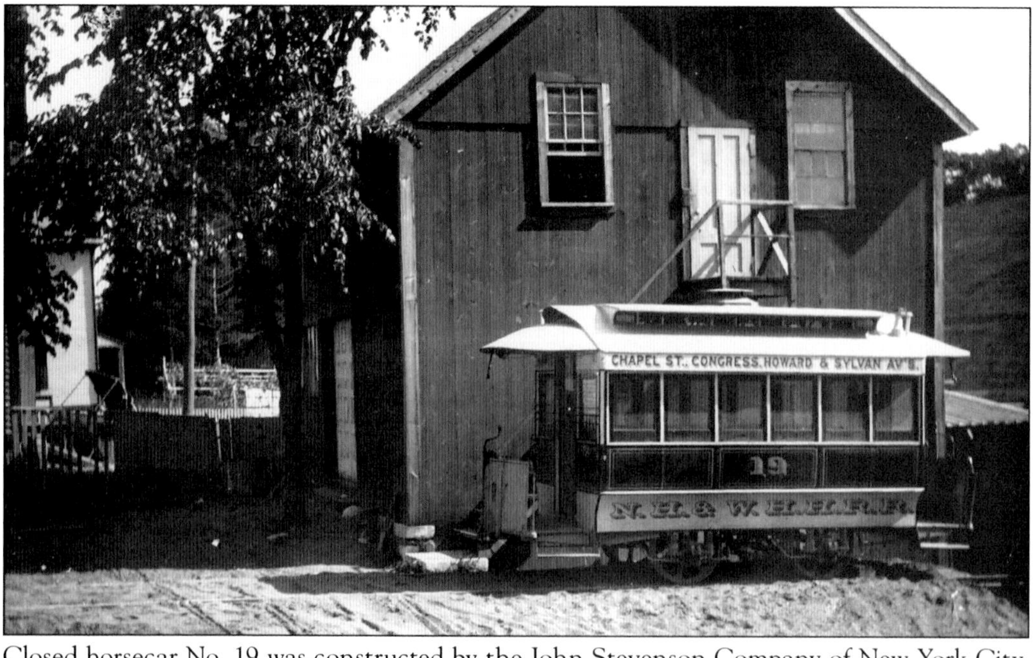

Closed horsecar No. 19 was constructed by the John Stevenson Company of New York City. The early horsecar builder delivered its first car in 1831 to the New York and Harlem Railroad. The 1880s were the peak years for the industry; there were more than 100,000 horses, 18,000 cars, and 3,000 miles of track in the country. (Courtesy Fred Bennett collection, Library of Congress photograph.)

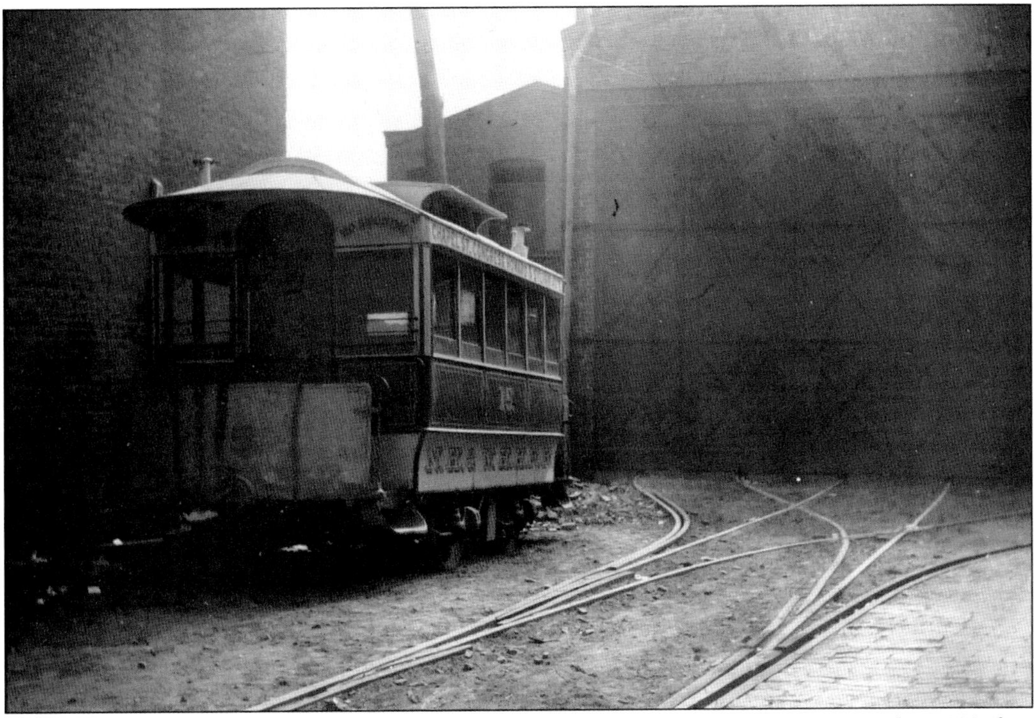

In this view, closed car No. 15 is pictured at the West Haven stables prior to the 1892 fire. (Courtesy Fred Bennett collection, Library of Congress photograph.)

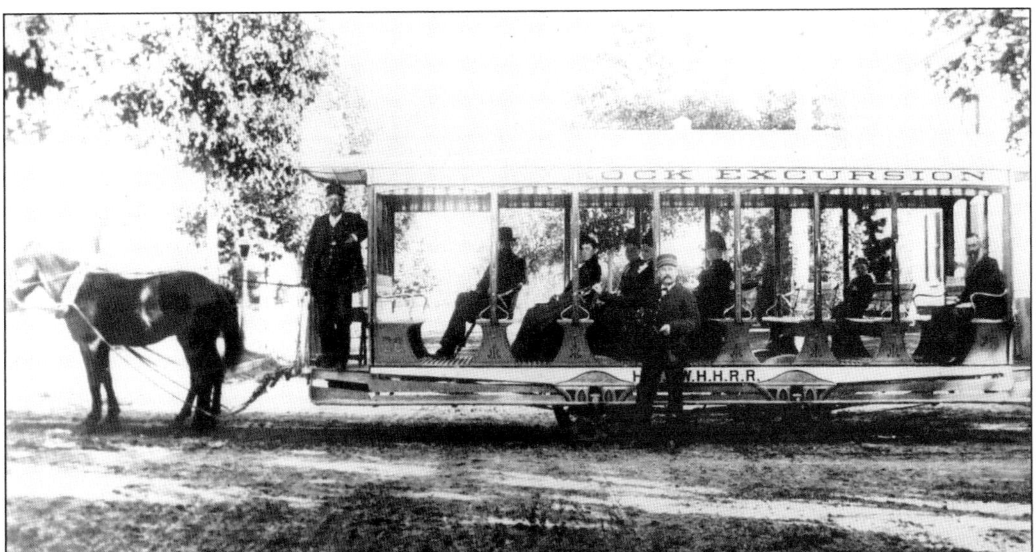

During the summer, a visit to the shore or an amusement park was a long-anticipated outing. The passengers on open car No. 28, shown at Savin Rock Park in 1888, are undoubtedly enjoying the ride. The car is lettered "H.H.&W.H.H.R.R." This is rather a mystery as there are no records surviving today that show a corporation name matching these letters. These cars operated on the New Haven and West Haven Horse Railroad, so it most likely was a subsidiary formed for accounting reasons. (Courtesy Fred Bennett collection.)

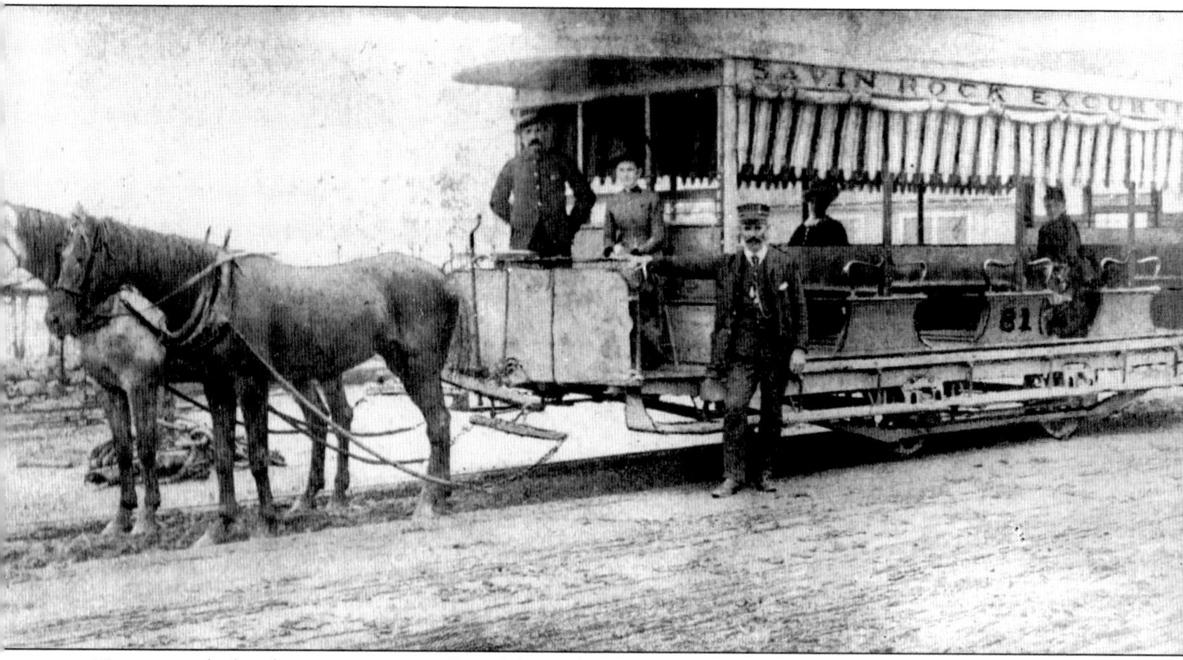

Horsecars helped cities to expand and brought suburbs closer with a new and better means of transportation. By the 1890s, however, a steady decline had begun for the industry, and by 1900, horsecars had all but disappeared from American cities. (Courtesy Fred Bennett collection.)

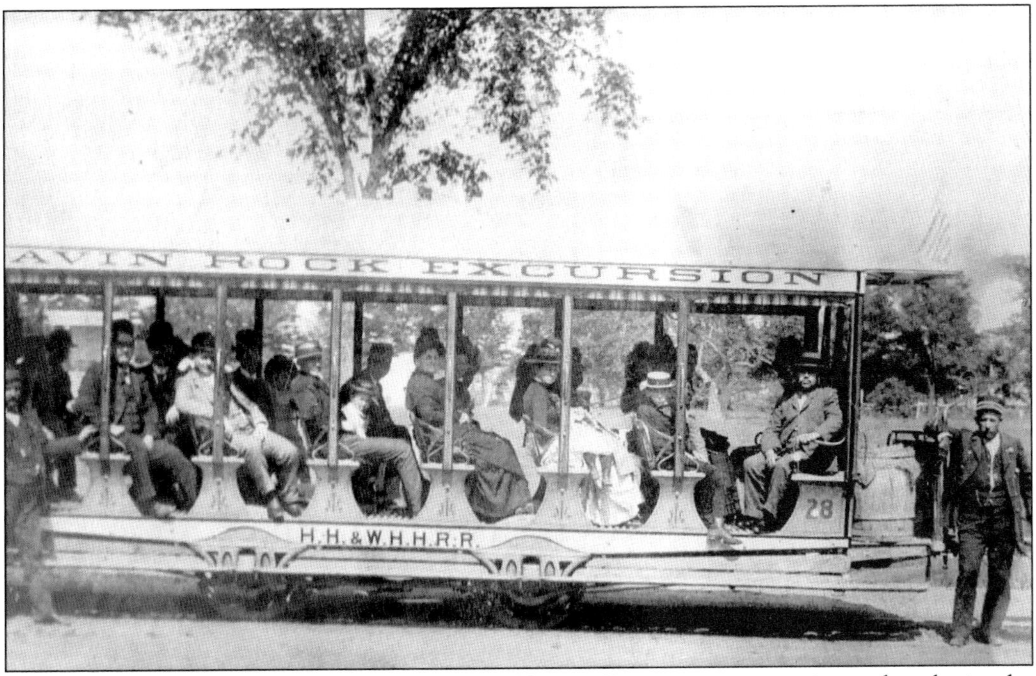

One line ended at Savin Rock Park in West Haven. Service to cemeteries and parks in the 1890s was a potential gold mine for a streetcar company. Weekends, when people could engage in leisure activities, proved a good time to take the trolley for an outing to these areas. (Courtesy Fred Bennett collection.)

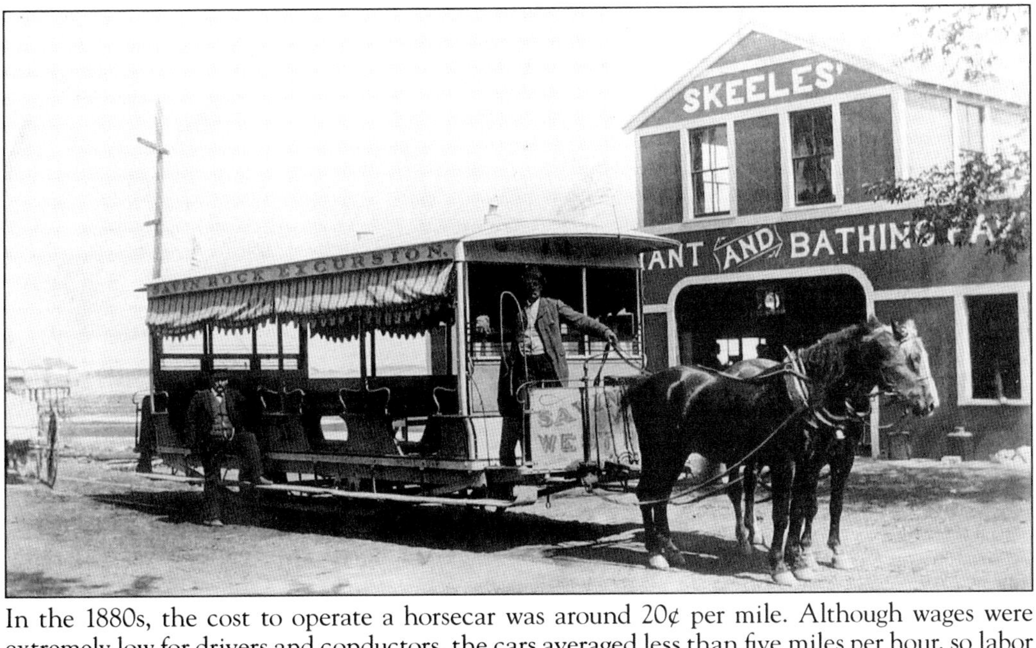

In the 1880s, the cost to operate a horsecar was around 20¢ per mile. Although wages were extremely low for drivers and conductors, the cars averaged less than five miles per hour, so labor per mile was quite high at the time. (Courtesy Fred Bennett collection.)

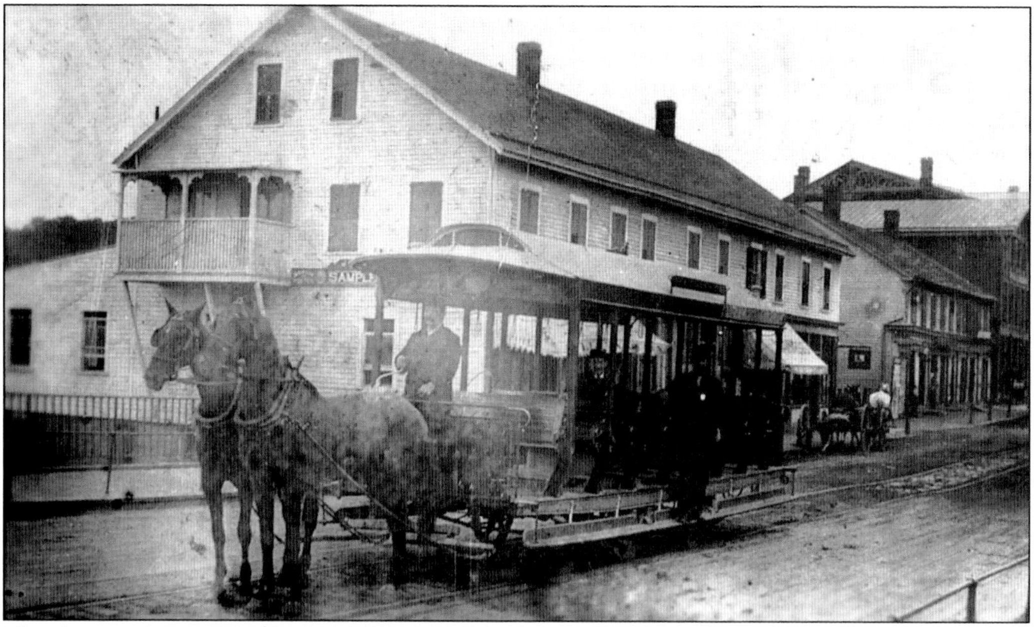

The largest horsecar operator in New Haven was the Fairhaven and Westville Railroad. Incorporated in 1860, the line ran its first car on May 6, 1861. Over the years, the company absorbed all the street railway operators in the city until May 20, 1904, when it was purchased by the New Haven Railroad. In 1907, the Connecticut Company became the operator of all the streetcars in New Haven. (Courtesy Fred Bennett collection.)

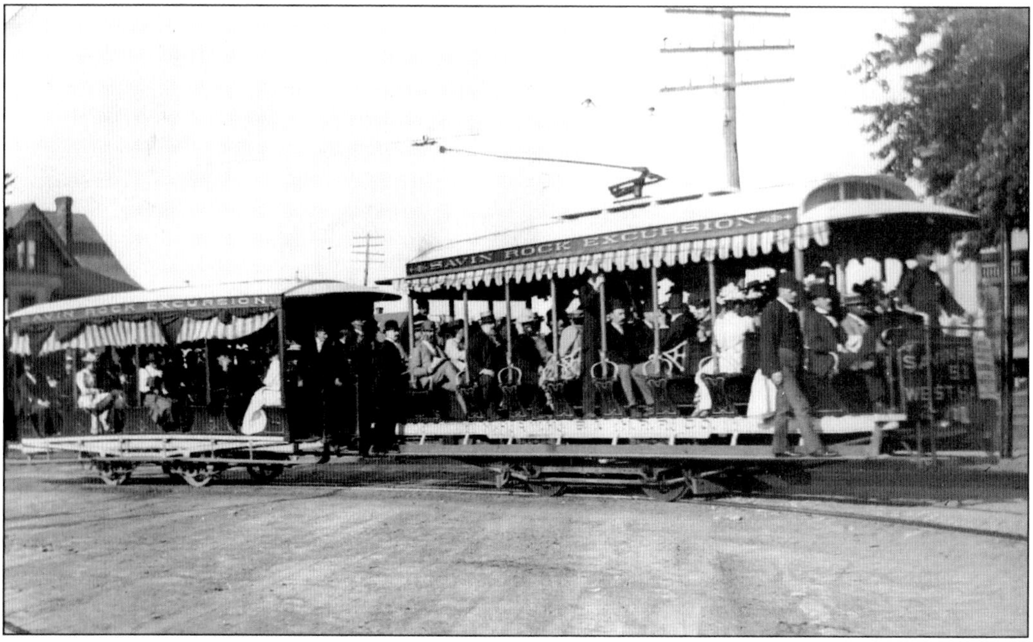

The New Haven and West Haven Horse Railroad operated two-car trains using a streetcar to pull a non-powered trailer car. While this required a three-man crew, it was economically beneficial on lines with heavy riding. The use of trailer cars never caught on in Connecticut, although they were used on some lines in Boston. (Courtesy Fred Bennett collection.)

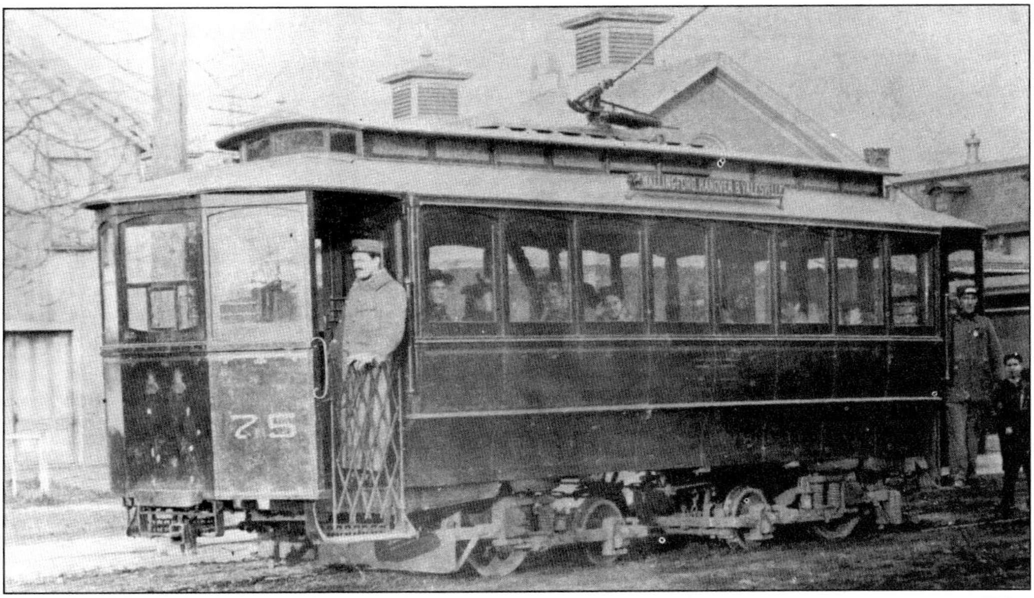

The streetcar lines in Wallingford were operated as part of the New Haven system. The Wallingford Tramway Company, incorporated in 1903, was authorized to operate a street railway from Wallingford to North Haven to connect with the Fairhaven and Westville Railroad in the village of Montowese, a total of seven miles of track. In 1904, the company was acquired by the Worcester and Connecticut Eastern Railway, a subsidiary of the New Haven Railroad. (Courtesy Connecticut Motor Coach Museum Archives.)

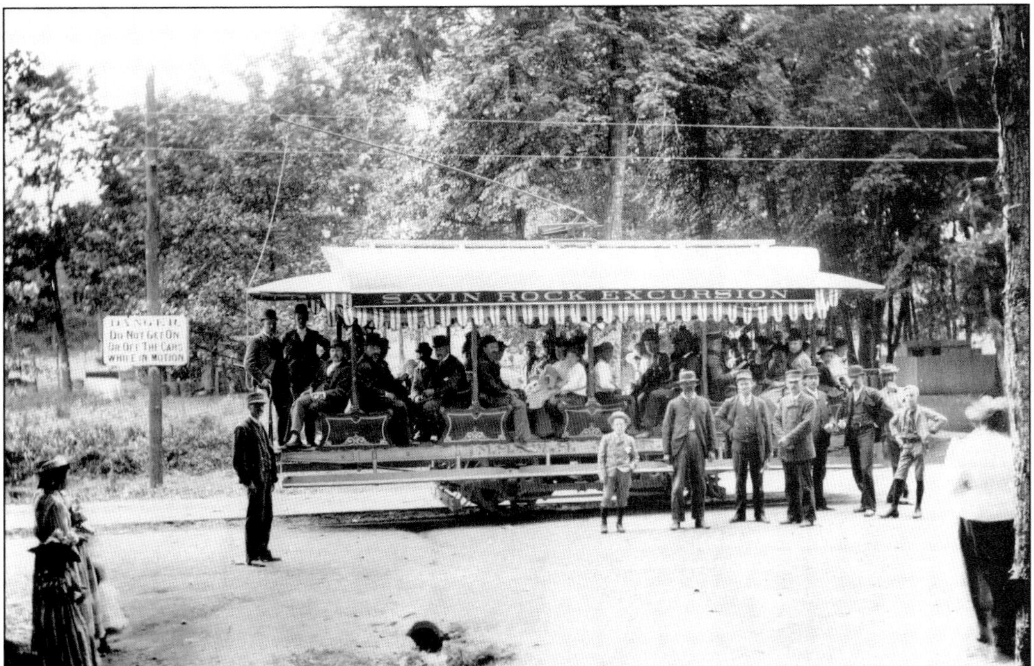

Keeping up with improvements in technology, the New Haven and West Haven Railroad ran its first electric car in July 1892. (Courtesy Fred Bennett collection.)

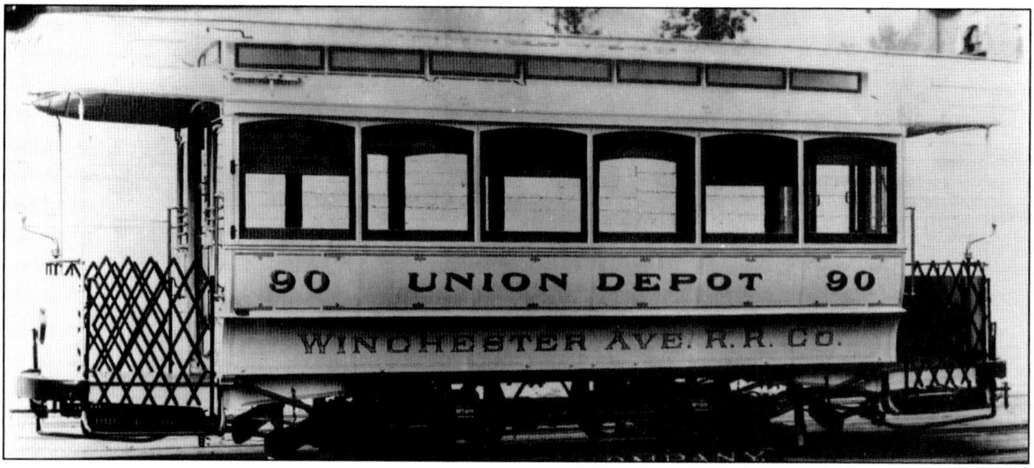

The Winchester Avenue Railroad was chartered in June 1889 but did not start operations until 1891. Car No. 90, built in Philadelphia by the J. G. Brill Company, was delivered to the Winchester Avenue line in 1896. It ran in New Haven until being scrapped in 1916. (Courtesy Branford Electric Railway Association Archives.)

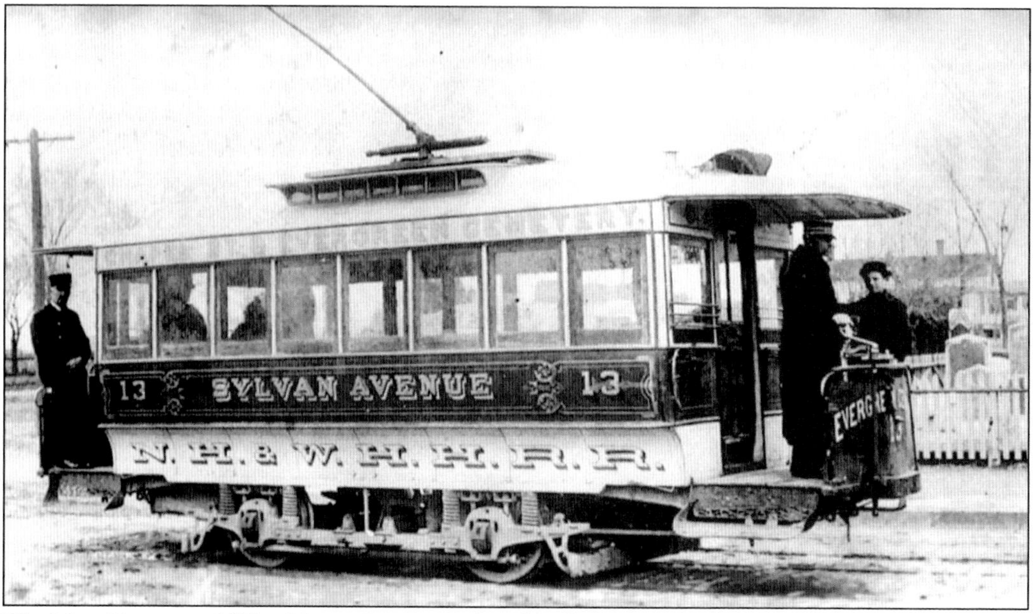

The New Haven and West Haven Horse Railroad had a short branch that ran up Sylvan Avenue to Evergreen Cemetery. In June 1931, it became the first streetcar line in New Haven to be converted to motor coach. Car No. 13 was originally built as a motorized horsecar in 1870 but was converted to electric operation around 1895. (Courtesy Branford Electric Railway Association Archives.)

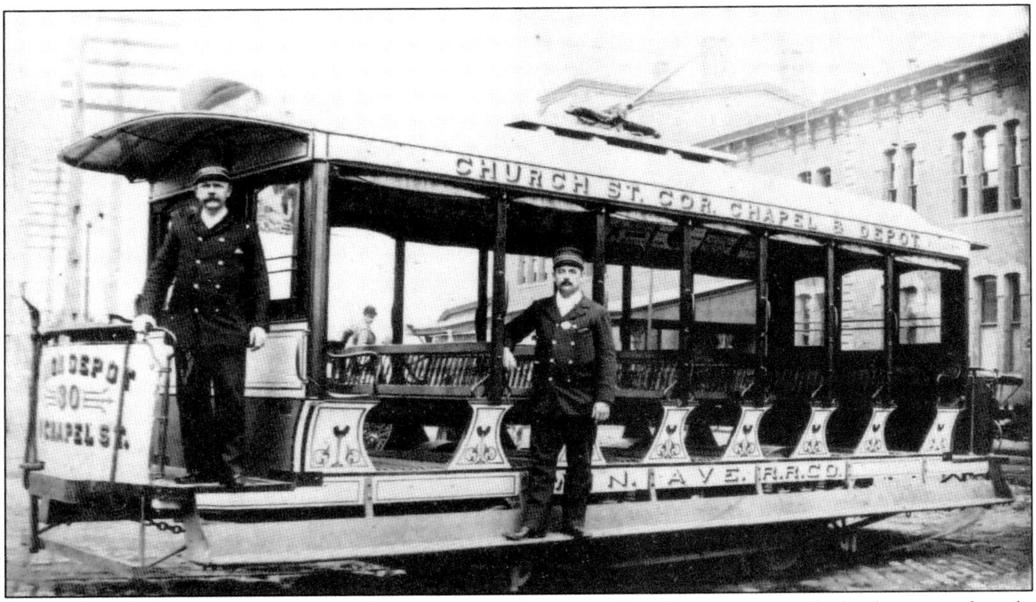

The Winchester Avenue Railroad operated six lines in New Haven, one of which was a shuttle car between the New Haven Railroad station and the green. Car No. 30, pictured with motorman C. S. Allen and conductor O. T. Woodford, rests at the station between runs. (Courtesy Branford Electric Railway Association Archives.)

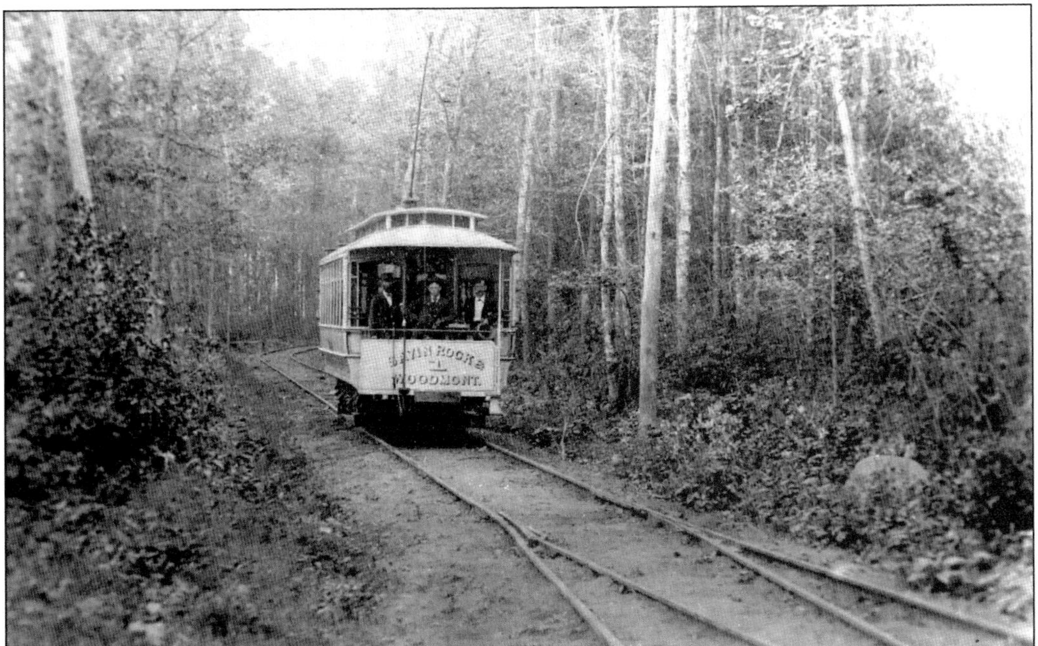

Cozy Nook, located in the Woodmont section of West Haven, is shown in this 1899 view. This line was built by the West Shore Railroad, which was organized in 1893. In December 1895, the line was leased to the Winchester Avenue Railroad for 99 years. Interestingly the West Shore Railroad remained a business entity reporting to the Public Utilities Commission until the late 1940s. (Courtesy Fred Bennett collection.)

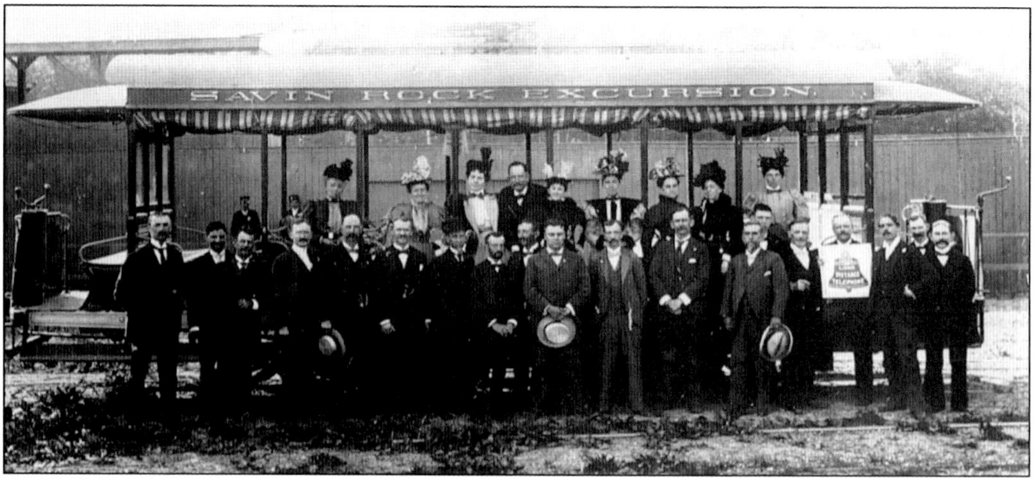

In the summer of 1899, the Southern New England Telephone and Telegraph Company sponsored a field trip to Savin Rock Park, and chartering a streetcar was the most convenient way for a big group to visit such an attraction. The company had opened the first commercial telephone exchange in the world in New Haven in 1878. (Courtesy Fred Bennett collection.)

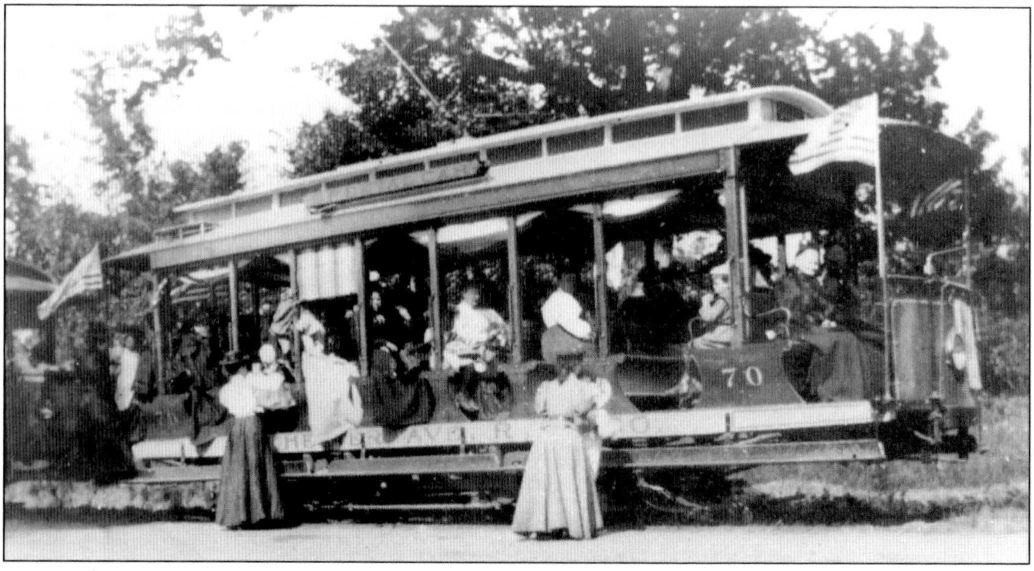

A Winchester Avenue Railroad open car is dressed for a celebration, with flags flying, at Savin Rock Park. This excursion from the city was most likely a Fourth of July event. (Courtesy Fred Bennett collection.)

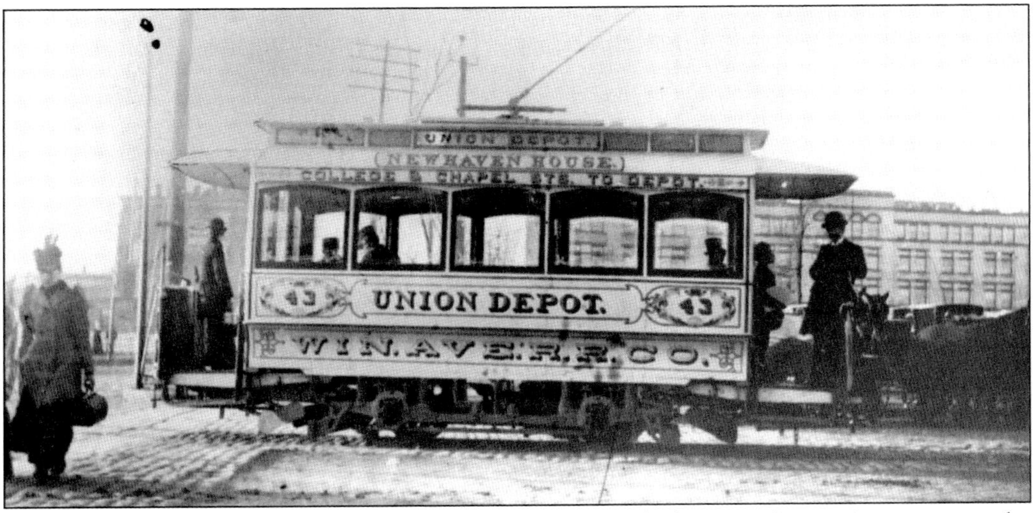

Most streetcars were fairly plain in the early 1900s, although this Winchester Avenue car is the exception. No doubt the cost of all this lettering made the cost prohibitive. (Courtesy Branford Electric Railway Association Archives.)

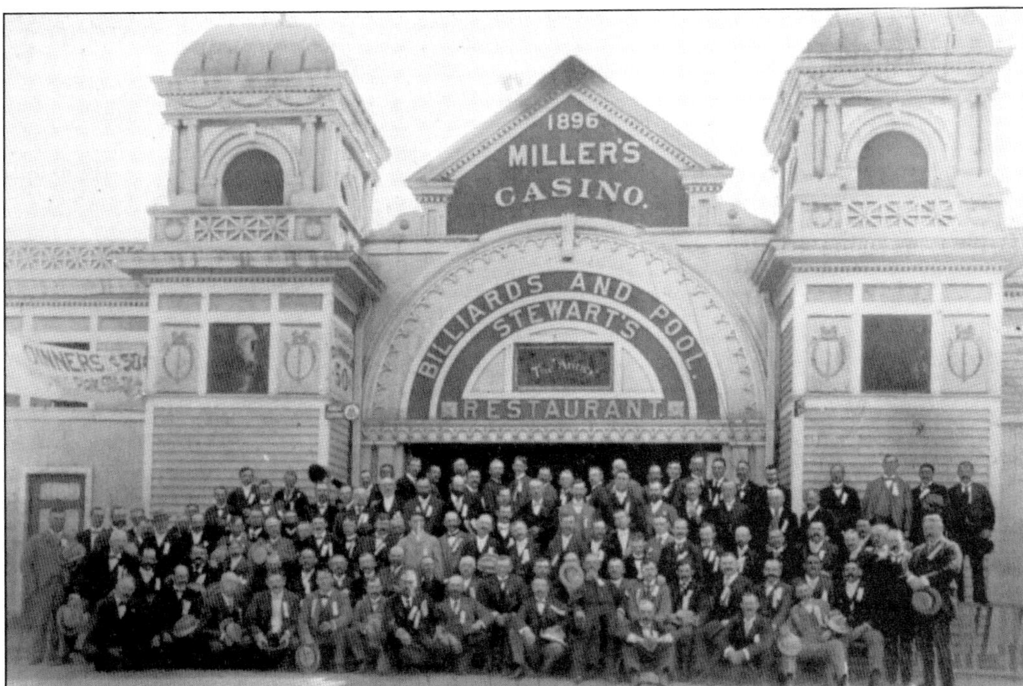

Miller's Casino, situated at Savin Rock Park, was served by the Winchester Avenue Railroad. In this 1900 view, a delegation of Connecticut legislators enjoys an outing. They probably traveled to and from the casino by streetcar from the railroad station in New Haven. Miller's Casino included a restaurant, billiard parlor, and dance pavilion all under one roof. (Courtesy Fred Bennett collection.)

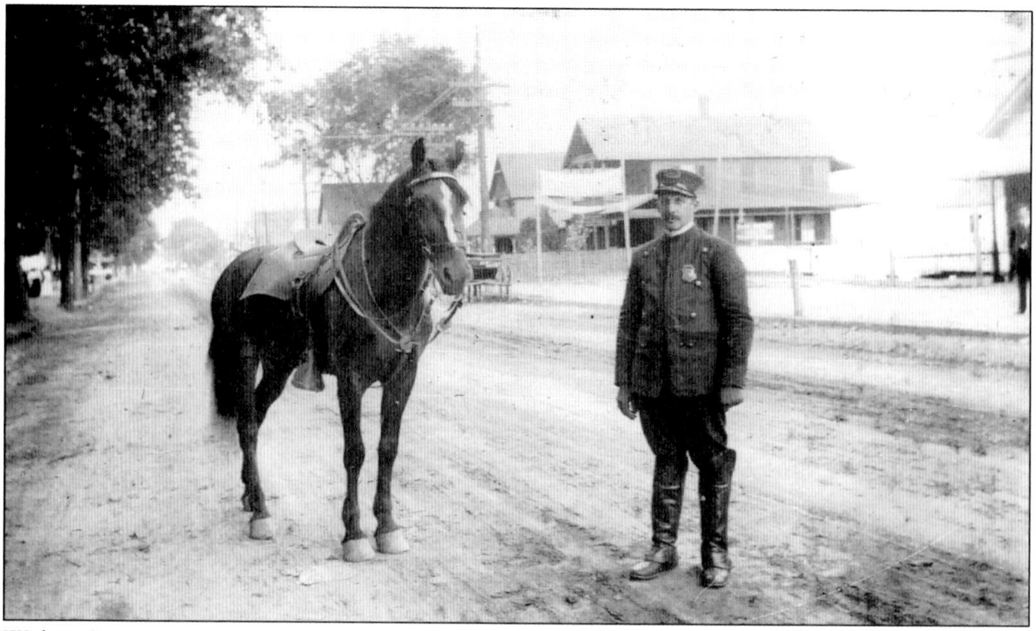

Walter Straton served as the regular police officer at Savin Rock Park in West Haven during the early 1900s. Responsible for handling any rowdy customers, he was actually paid by the Winchester Avenue Railroad, the owner of the park, and only worked six months out of the year. Straton was the grandfather of Fred Bennett, one of the authors of this book. (Courtesy Fred Bennett collection.)

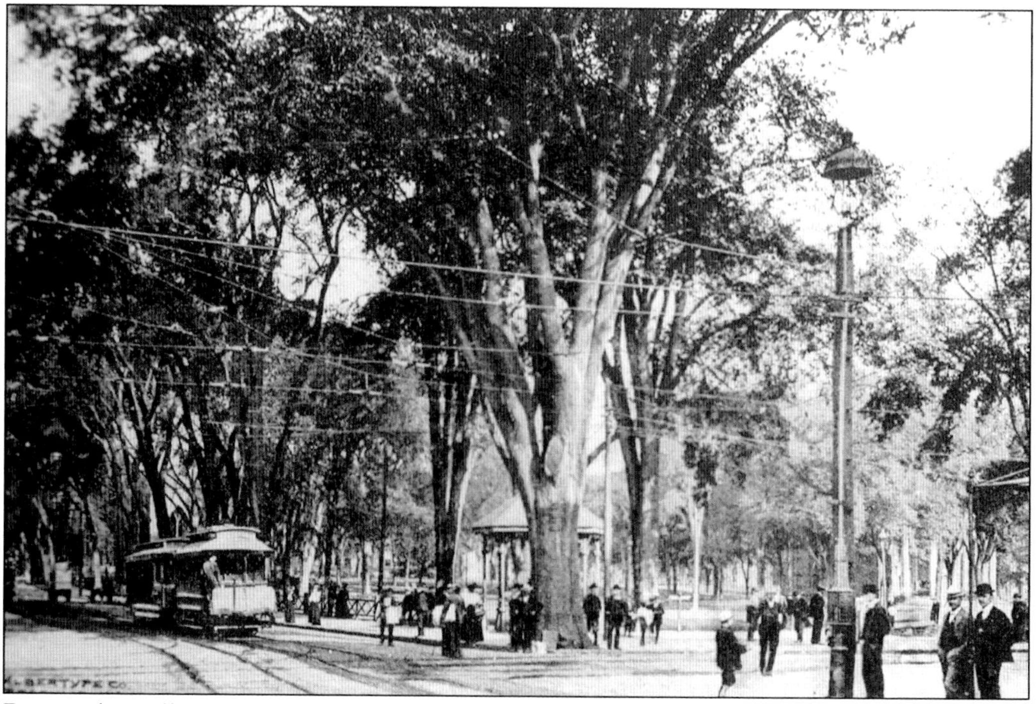

During the trolley era, the New Haven Green was bustling with people. Here two Winchester Avenue Railroad open cars await passengers in 1900. (Courtesy Fred Bennett collection.)

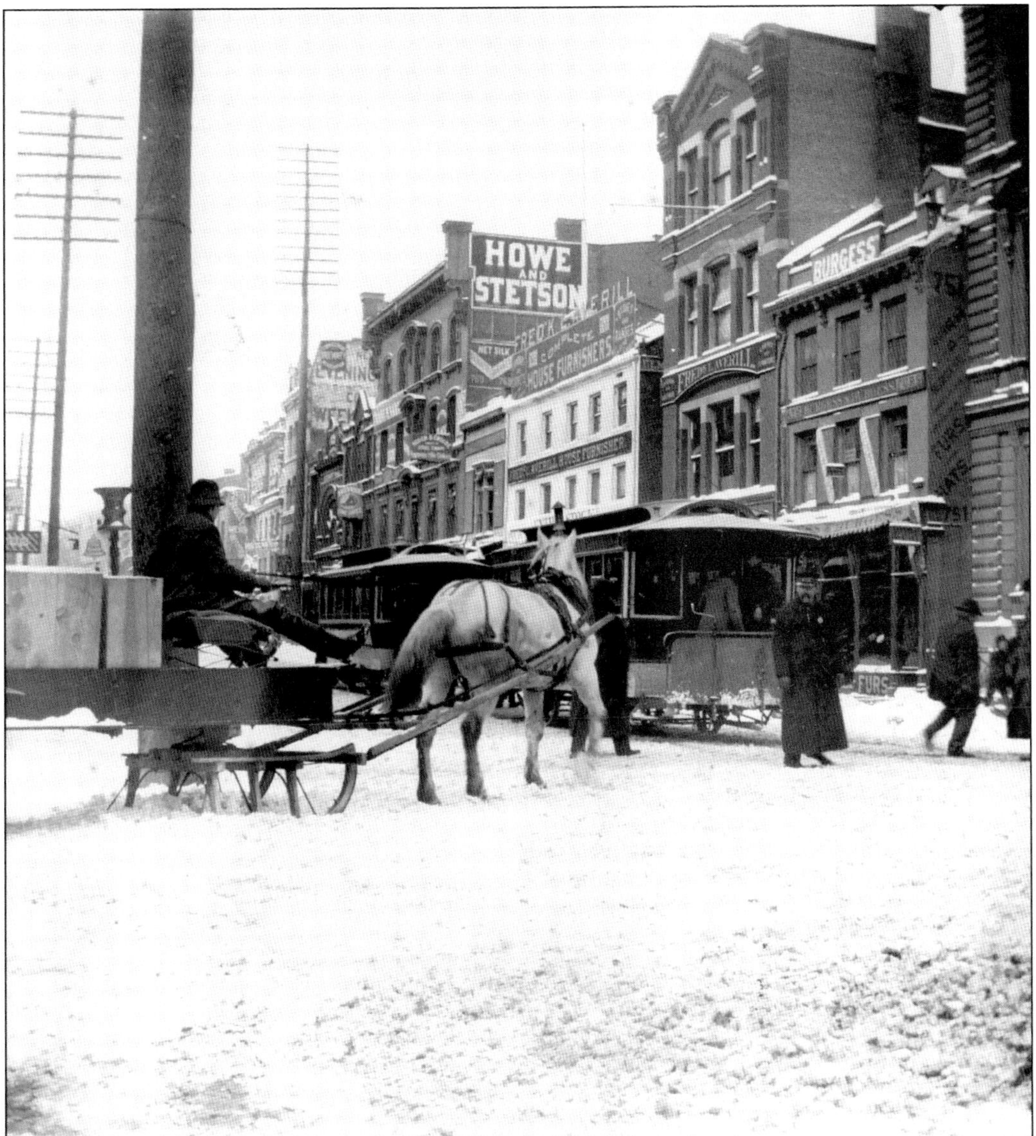

Horsecars and sleighs share the streets during the winter of 1890. Electric streetcars did not run here until June 1892, when the New Haven and West Haven Horse Railroad operated the first electric cars in the New Haven area. (Courtesy Fred Bennett collection.)

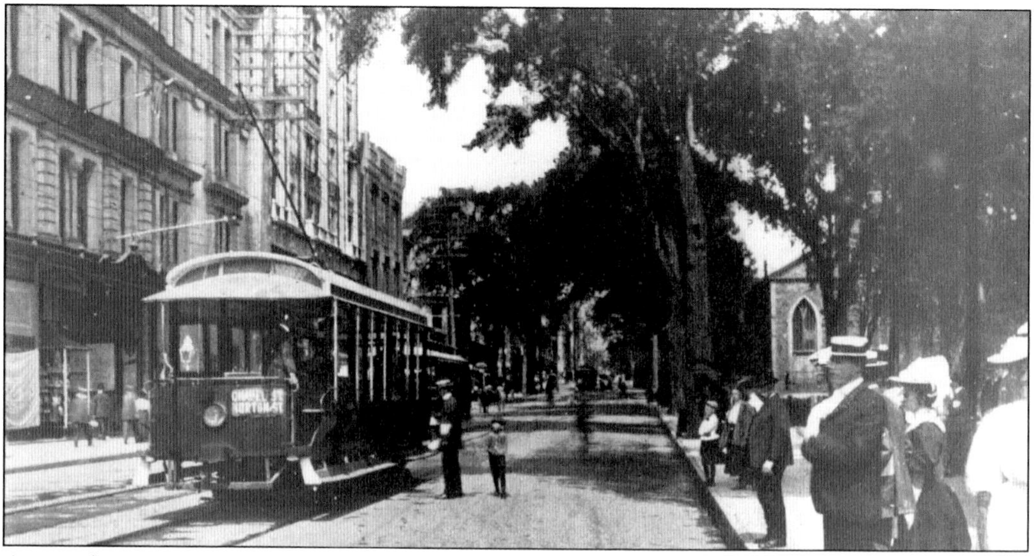

A Winchester Avenue Railroad open car is pictured by the New Haven Green at Chapel Street in 1900. The first successful streetcar line in the country began operating in Richmond, Virginia, in 1888. The Richmond Union Passenger Railway contracted with the Sprague Electric Railway and Motor Company, founded by Connecticut native Frank Julian Sprague, to build a complete electrical railway system for the city. (Courtesy Fred Bennett collection.)

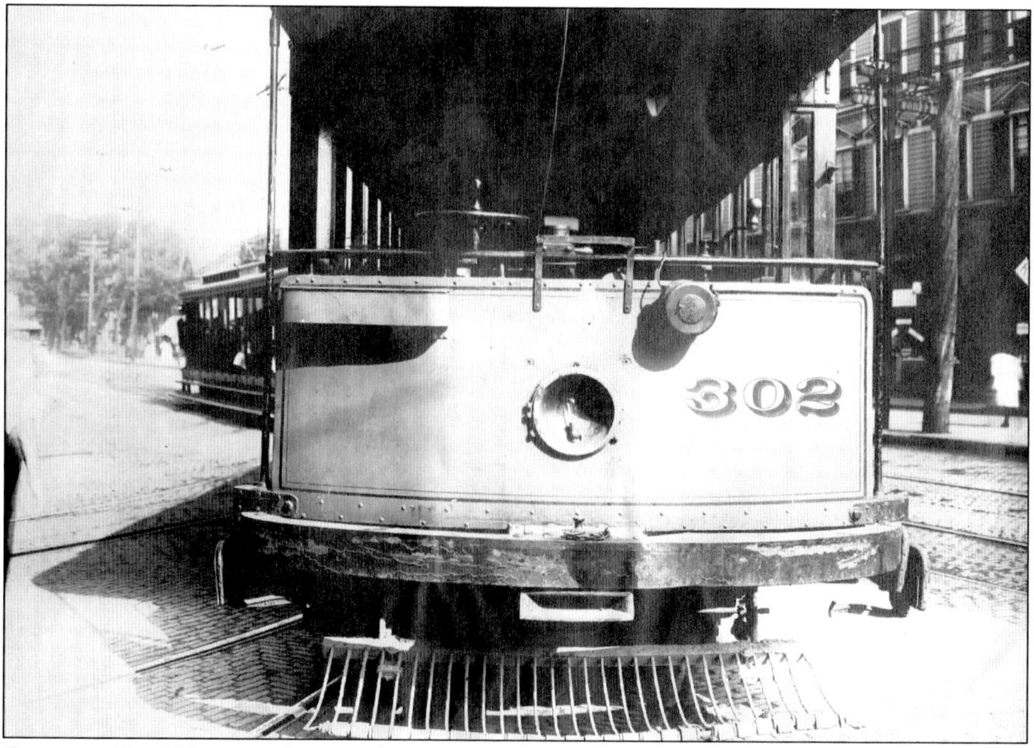

Open car No. 302 is seen here at the railroad station in New Haven. The safety fender would keep pedestrians from being run over by the wheels if they were to fall in front of the car. (Courtesy Fred Bennett collection.)

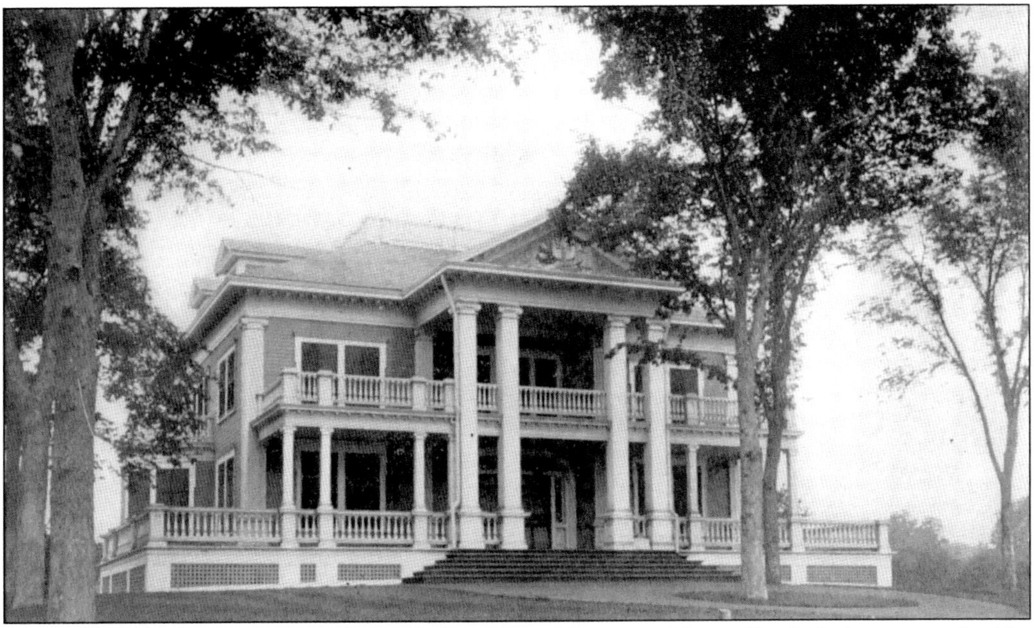

Colonial Park, a summer resort located about one mile west of Savin Rock Park, was reached by streetcar on the Woodmont line. The Connecticut Building, shown in this 1900 photograph, was originally erected at the 1893 Colombian Exposition in Chicago. After the fair closed, the structure was dismantled, brought to Connecticut, and reassembled at Colonial Park as a tourist attraction. It burned in 1918. (Courtesy Fred Bennett collection.)

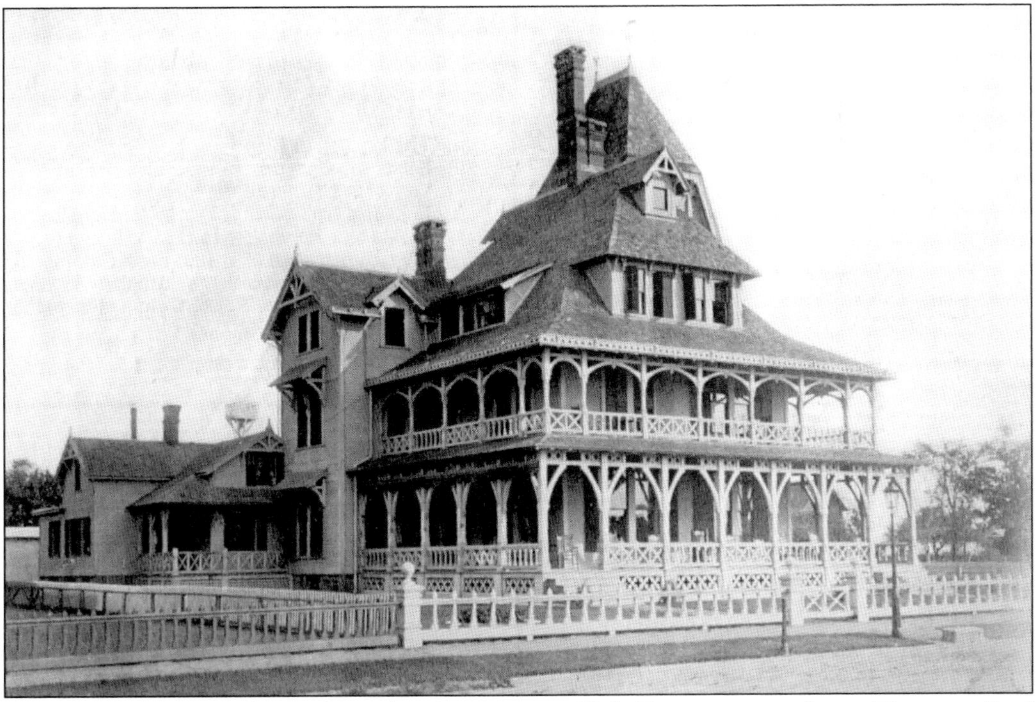

Situated on the Woodmont line, the Ansantawae Club House appears here. (Courtesy Fred Bennett collection.)

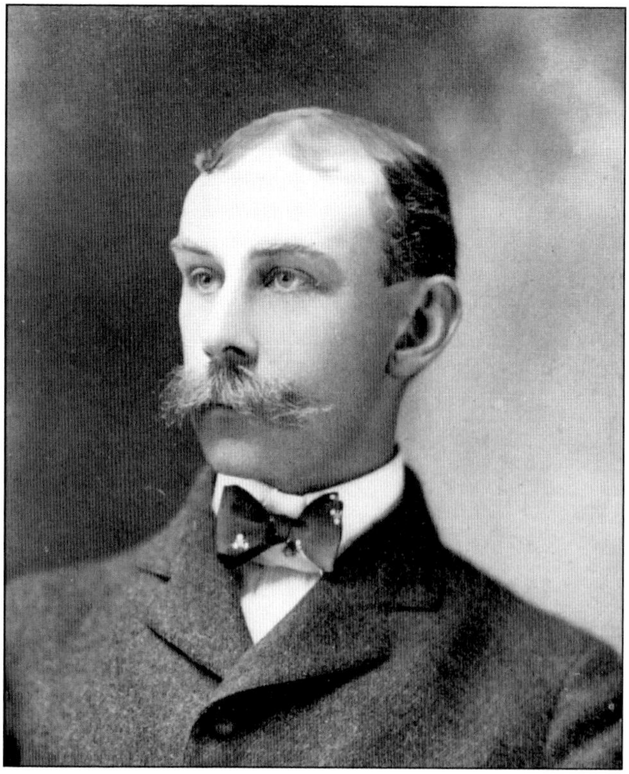

Albert E. Pond served as treasurer and general manager of the Winchester Avenue Railroad. (Courtesy Fred Bennett collection.)

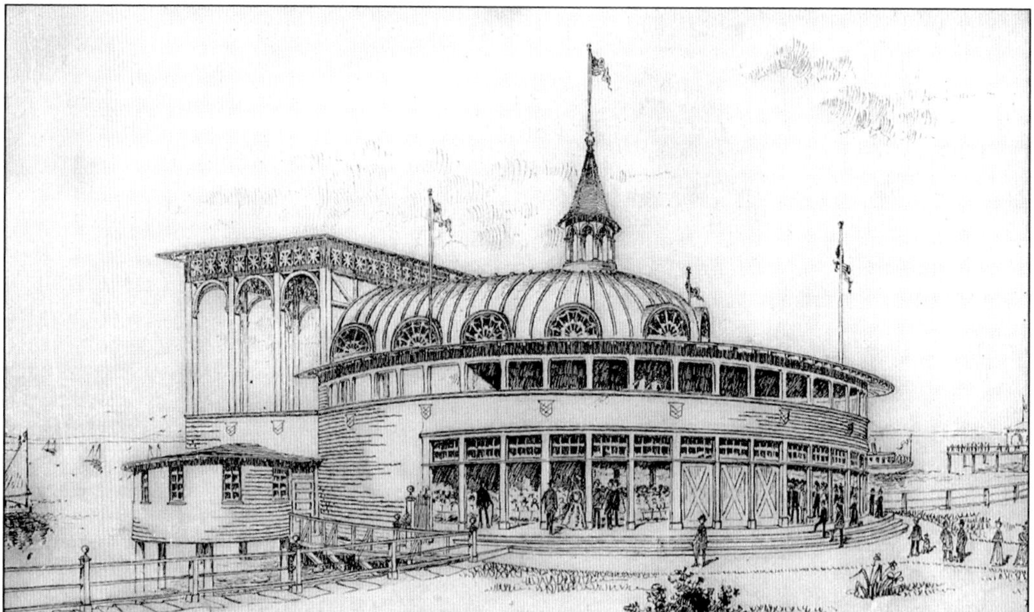

The new theater at Savin Rock Park is depicted in this 1900 architectural drawing. (Courtesy Fred Bennett collection.)

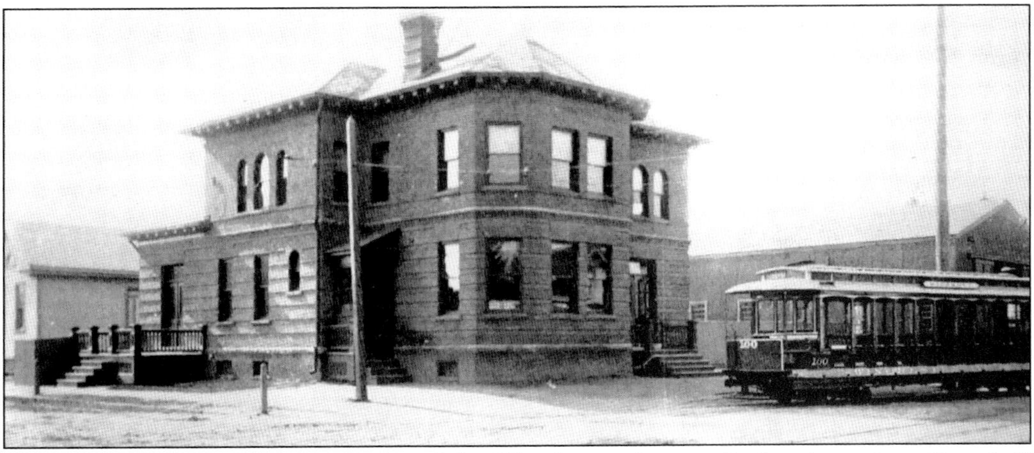

In 1900, the office and waiting room of the Winchester Avenue Railroad stood on Campbell Avenue in West Haven. (Courtesy Fred Bennett collection.)

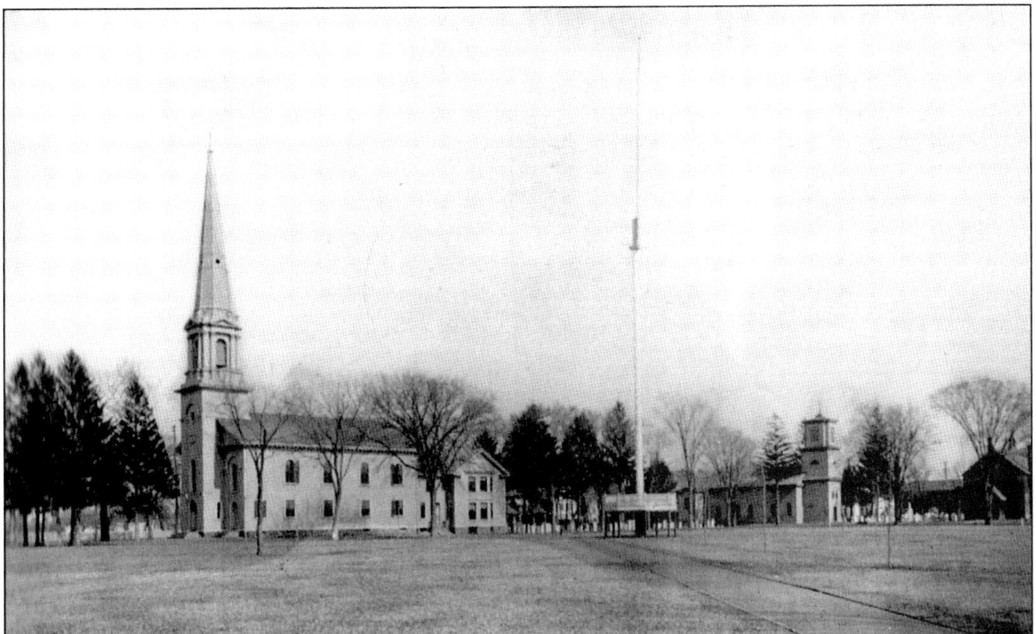

Every New England town had a green. Winchester Avenue Railroad cars passed the West Haven Green on their way to Savin Rock Park and Woodmont. (Courtesy Fred Bennett collection.)

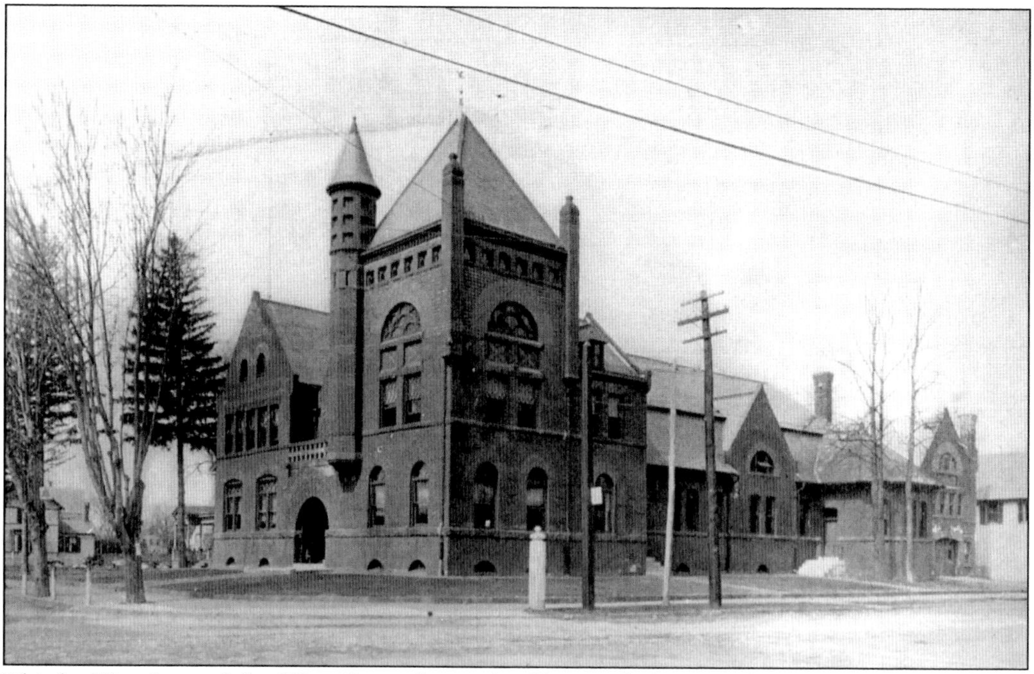

This building housed the West Haven borough offices and also served as the central fire station in 1900. The streetcar line passed in front of the building en route to Savin Rock Park. The borough of West Haven was a part of Colonial New Haven and then the town of Orange. It did not become a separate town until 1921 and was the last town incorporated in Connecticut. (Courtesy Fred Bennett collection.)

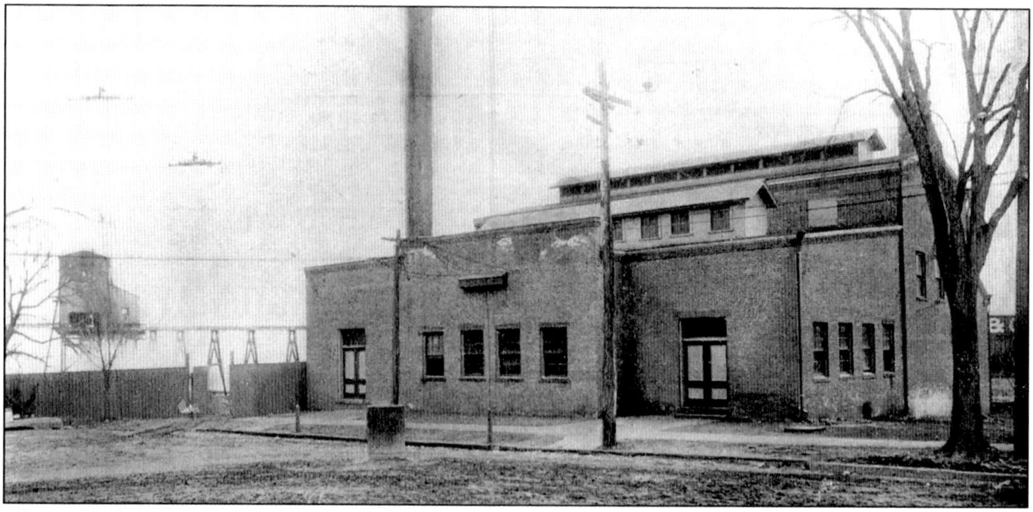

The Winchester Avenue Railroad power station is pictured here. When the Fairhaven and Westville Railroad first started running electric streetcars in New Haven, the company used power from this station until its own facility on Grand Avenue was working. During the Connecticut Company's operation of the streetcars in the area, this was know as Station C. The facility produced 1,175 kilowatts of direct current power using five coal-fired boilers. (Courtesy Fred Bennett collection.)

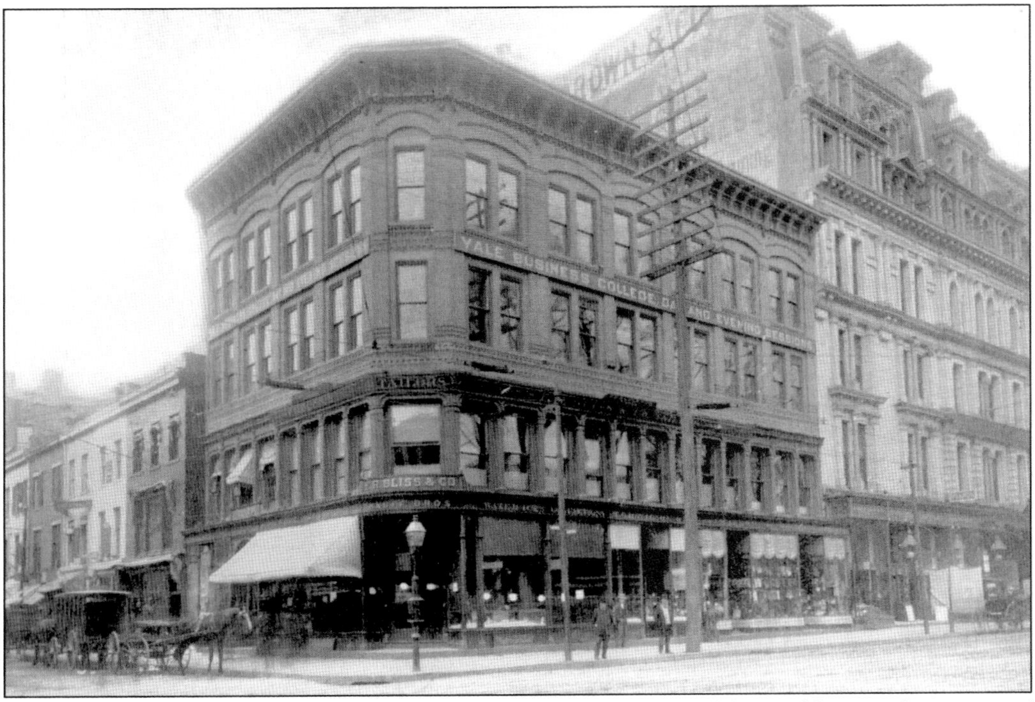

Almost all the streetcar lines serving New Haven passed by the Glebe Building, at the corner of Church and Chapel Streets. (Courtesy Fred Bennett collection.)

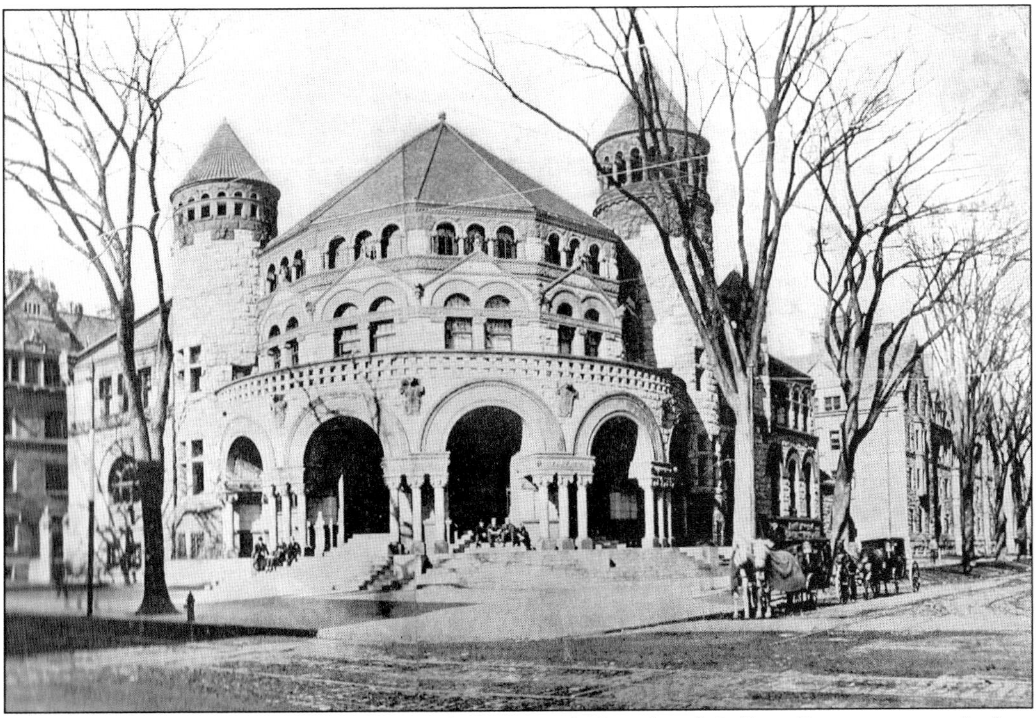

Yale University's Osborn Hall, located at the corner of Chapel and College Streets, was no doubt a source of much traffic for the Winchester Avenue Railroad. (Courtesy Fred Bennett collection.)

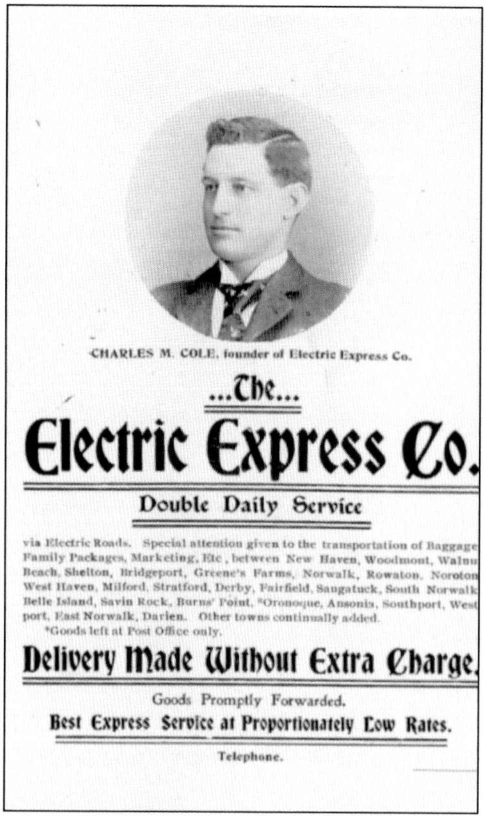

The Electric Express Company was formed in 1899 to handle package delivery, a service similar to that of today's UPS and FedEx. Winchester Avenue Railroad cars and crews delivered the shipments to drop-off points in New Haven for final delivery by horse and wagon. (Courtesy Connecticut Motor Coach Museum Archives.)

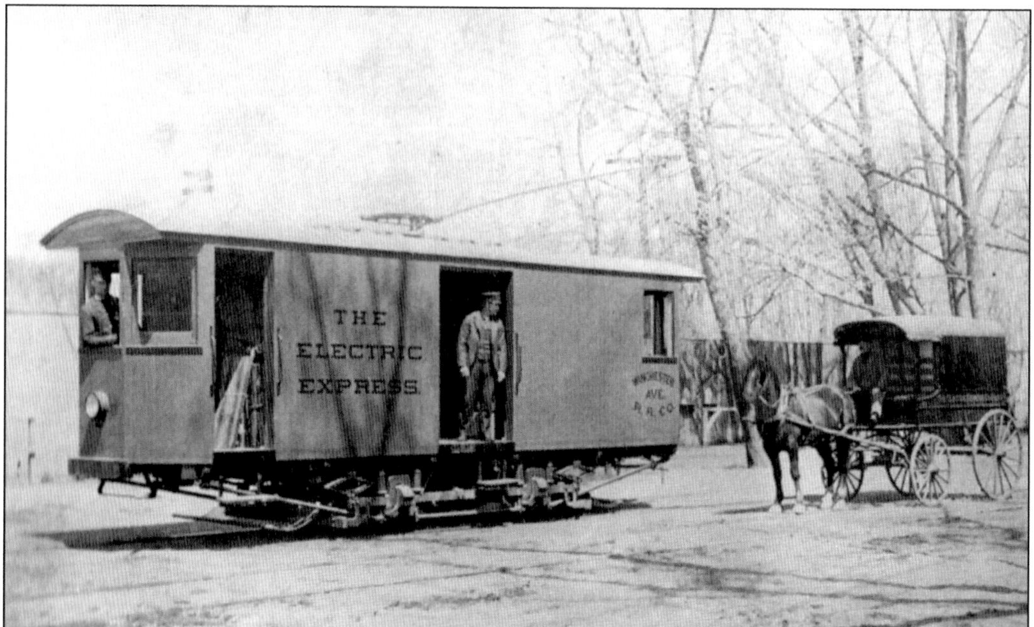

Winchester Avenue Railroad express car No. 20 transported freight around the New Haven area for the Electric Express Company. Built in the company shops in 1894, the car was scrapped by the Connecticut Company in April 1917. (Courtesy Connecticut Motor Coach Museum Archives.)

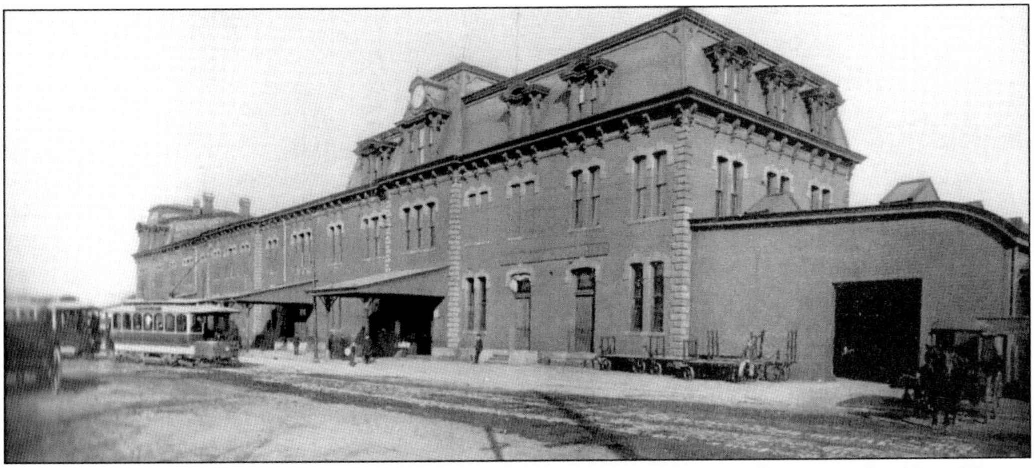

In 1900, the Winchester Avenue Railroad had a shuttle car that ran between the New Haven railroad station and the New Haven Green. Once at the green, passengers could transfer to one of their other routes or to a Fairhaven and Westville Railroad streetcar. This station building burned in a spectacular fire on May 8, 1918. (Courtesy Fred Bennett collection.)

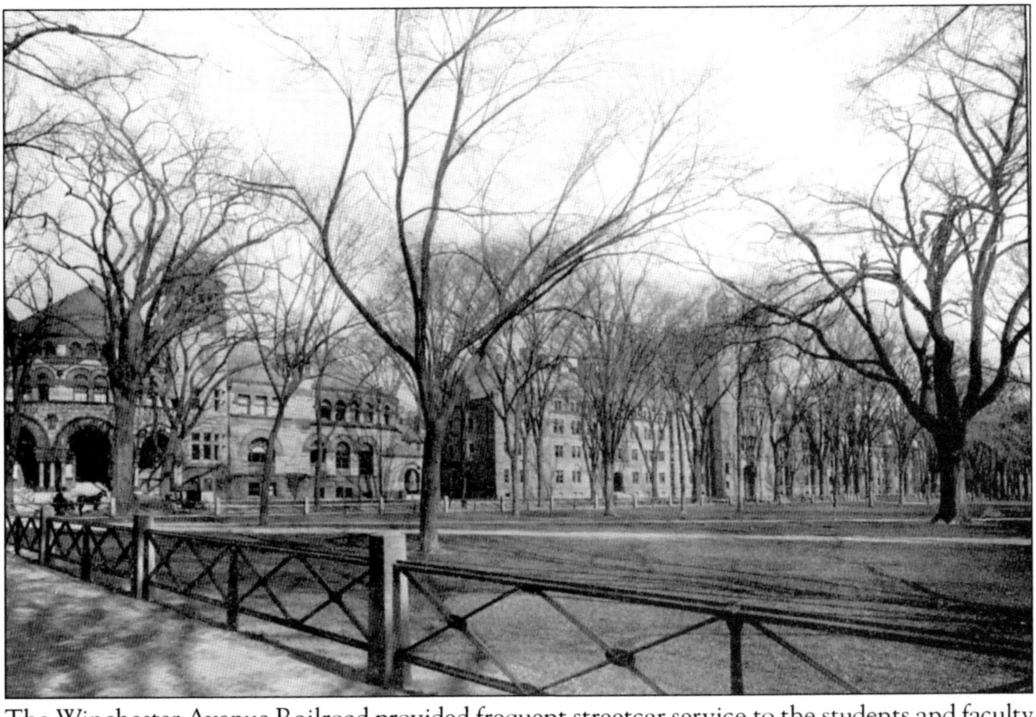

The Winchester Avenue Railroad provided frequent streetcar service to the students and faculty of Yale University on College Street in 1900. (Courtesy Fred Bennett collection.)

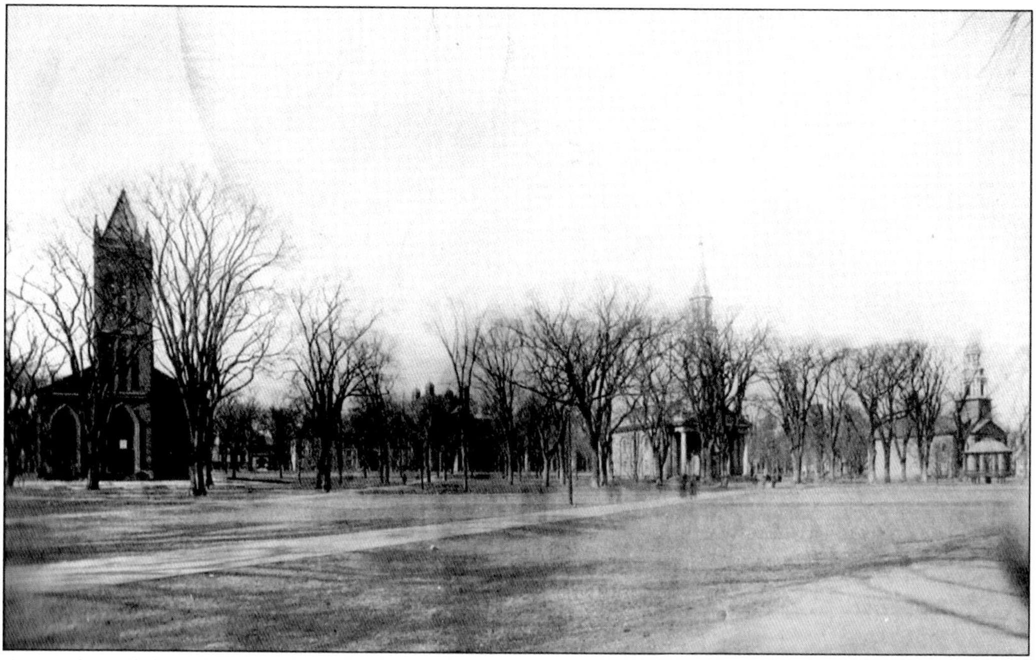

A number of churches stood on the New Haven Green in 1900. With the location of the streetcar line, getting to church on Sunday became easier. (Courtesy Fred Bennett collection.)

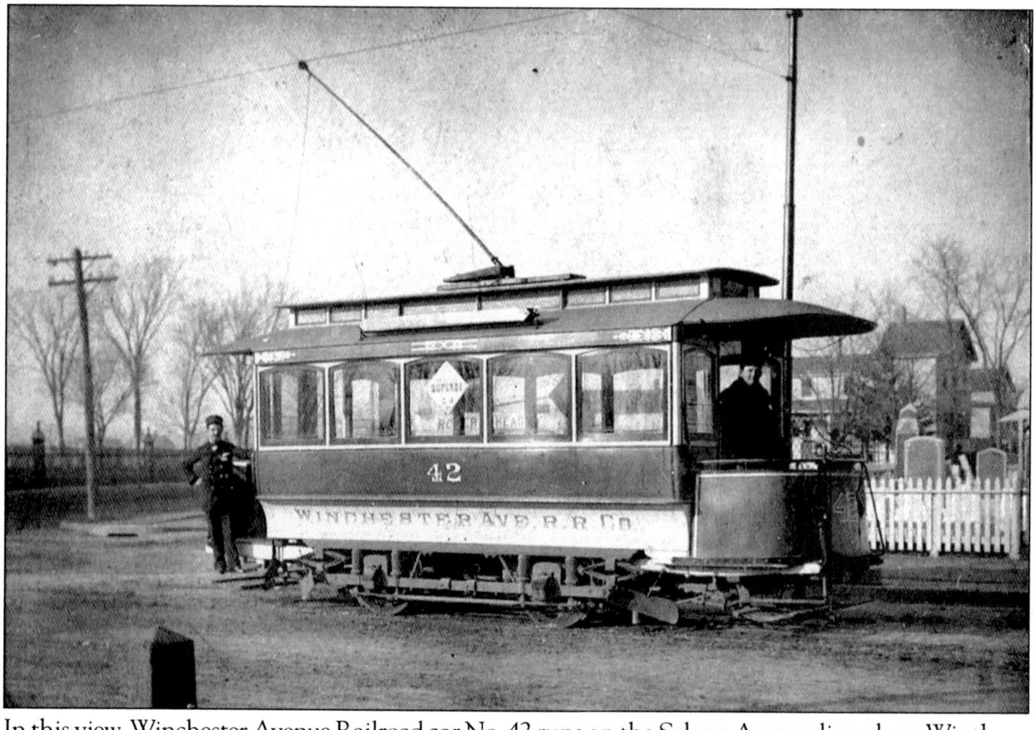

In this view, Winchester Avenue Railroad car No. 42 runs on the Sylvan Avenue line along Winthrop Avenue at Evergreen Cemetery. (Courtesy Branford Electric Railway Association Archives.)

George W. Warner's Choice Family Groceries was the equivalent of Super Stop and Shop in 1900. Everyone knew everyone else's name, and the clerk added up one's grocery bill on a brown paper bag using a pencil. When people were done shopping, they caught the next streetcar for home. (Courtesy Fred Bennett collection.)

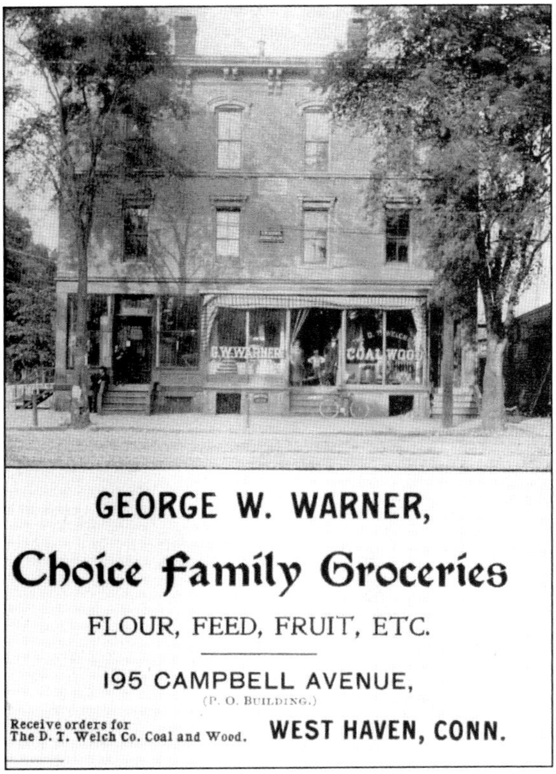

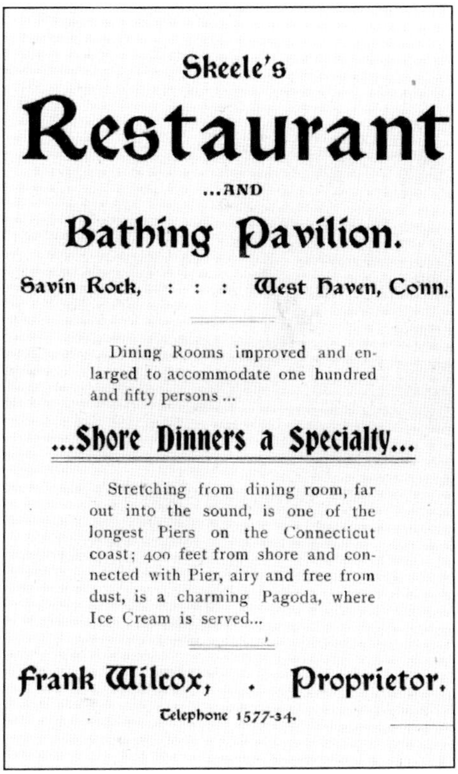

If passengers were hungry when they got off the streetcar at Savin Rock Park, they could get a full-course shore dinner at Skeele's Restaurant for about 40¢. (Courtesy Fred Bennett collection.)

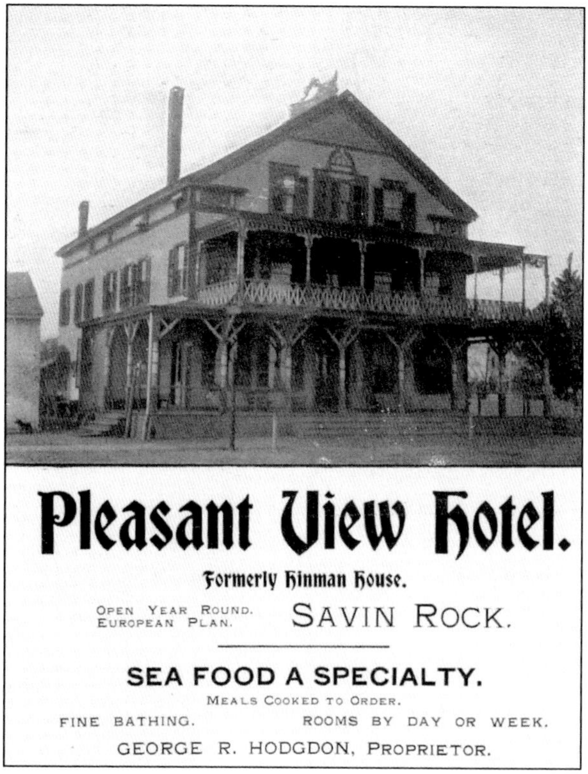

If people wanted to stay overnight at Savin Rock Park, they would go to the Pleasant View Hotel. (Courtesy Fred Bennett collection.)

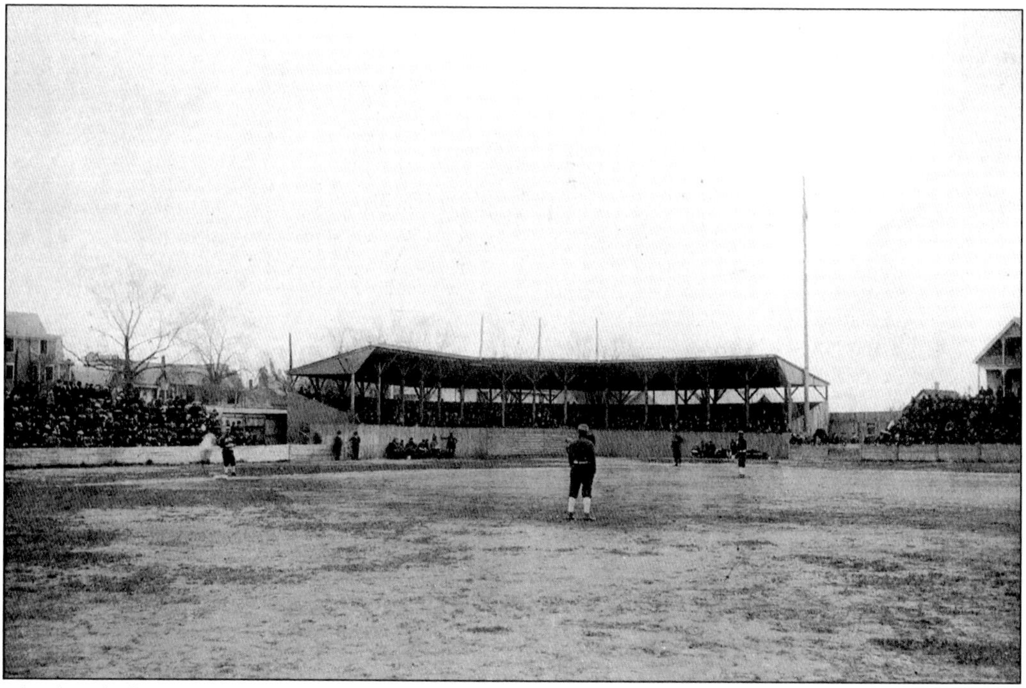

The baseball grounds, where the New Haven league team played its home games in 1899, were located next to Savin Rock Park. The streetcar line made it easier for fans to access the park. (Courtesy Fred Bennett collection.)

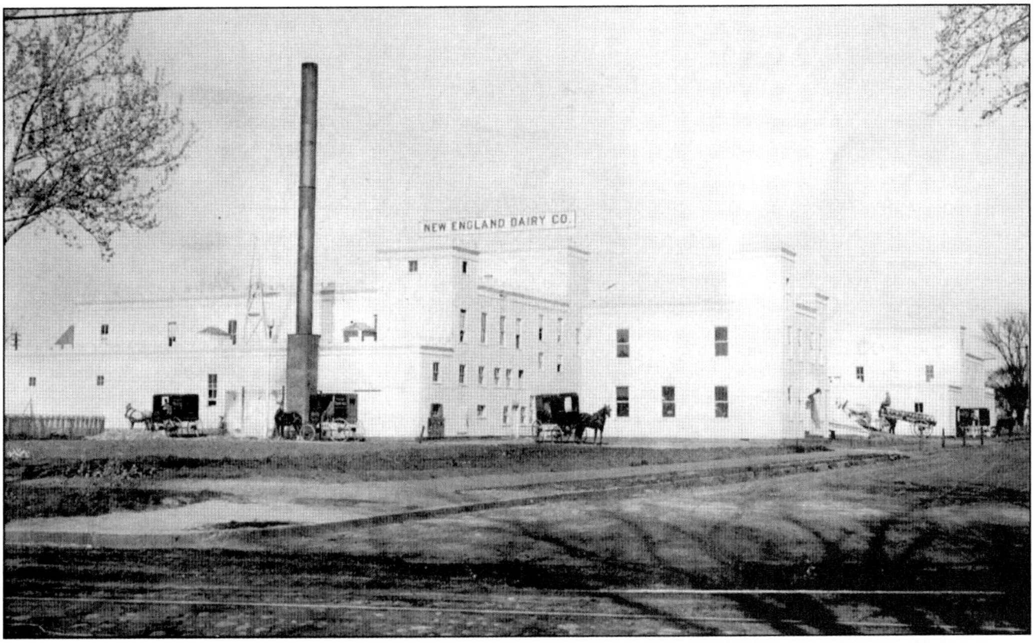

The New England Dairy Company's large creamery stood between Shelton and Dixwell Avenues, a short distance from the Winchester Avenue Railroad. This model creamery was built in 1899 to give the citizens of New Haven a clean, pure milk supply. (Courtesy Fred Bennett collection.)

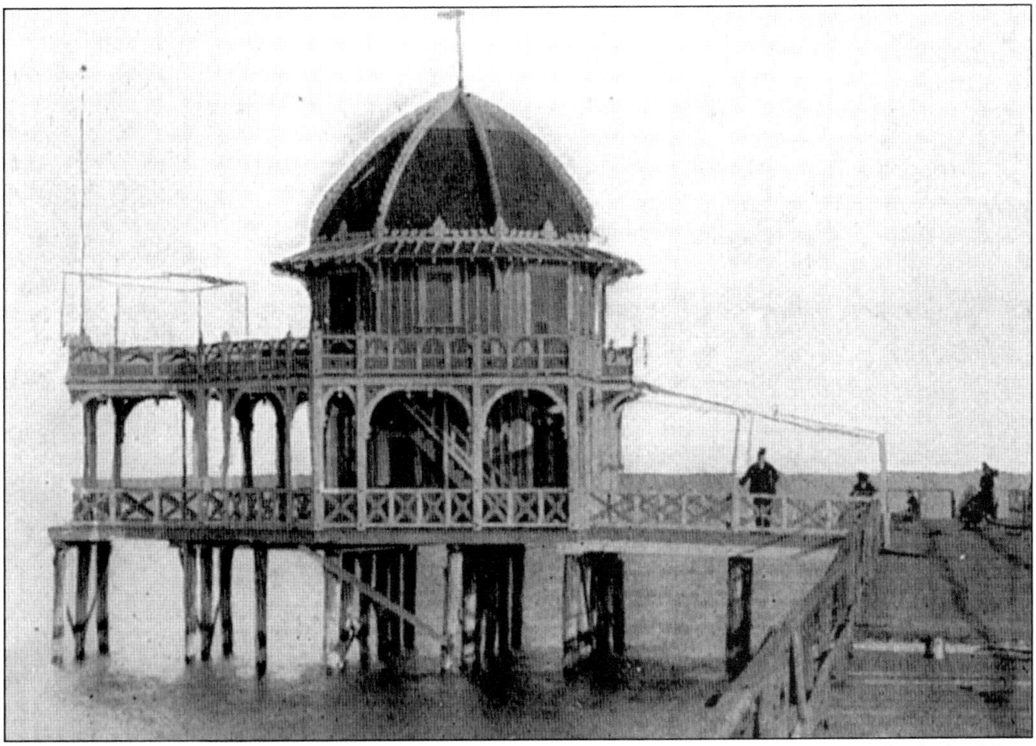

A. M. Hammer's Ice Cream Parlor was located at Savin Rock Park in this neat little building that sat out over the water. (Courtesy Fred Bennett collection.)

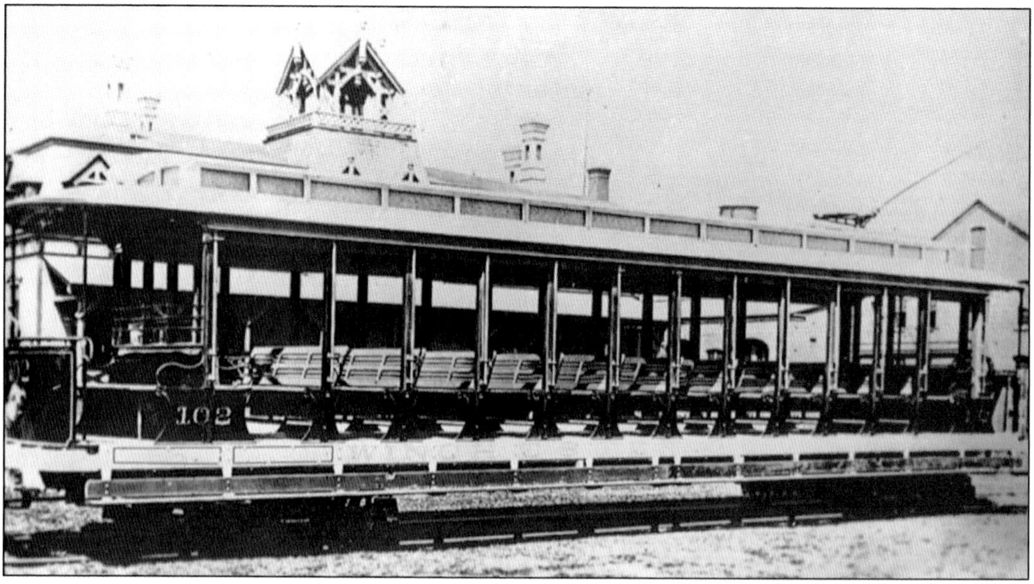

This builder's photograph of Winchester Avenue Railroad open car No. 102 was taken in 1900 at the Wason Manufacturing Company plant in Springfield. The car later became Connecticut Company car No. 564 and was scrapped in New Haven in 1926. (Courtesy Fred Bennett collection.)

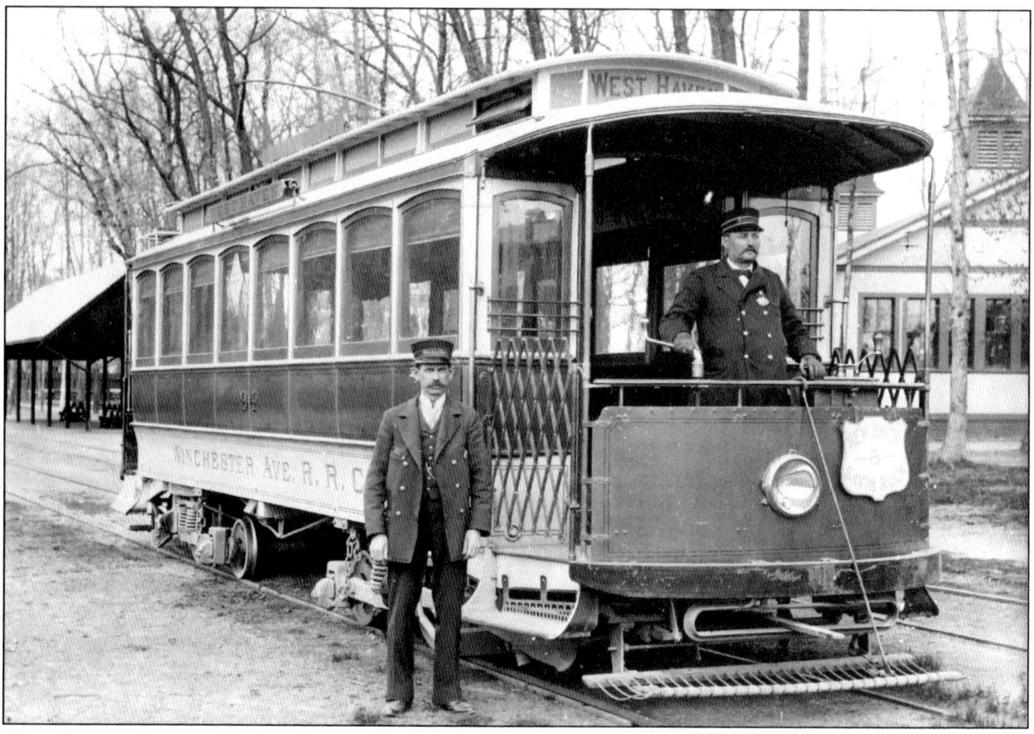

Winchester Avenue Railroad car No. 92 was built by the J. G. Brill Company of Philadelphia in 1898. In 1915, when many cars were renumbered, it became Connecticut Company car No. 484 and ran in Derby until being scrapped in the early 1920s. In its later days, the front vestibule was closed in to protect the motorman from the weather. (Courtesy Fred Bennett collection.)

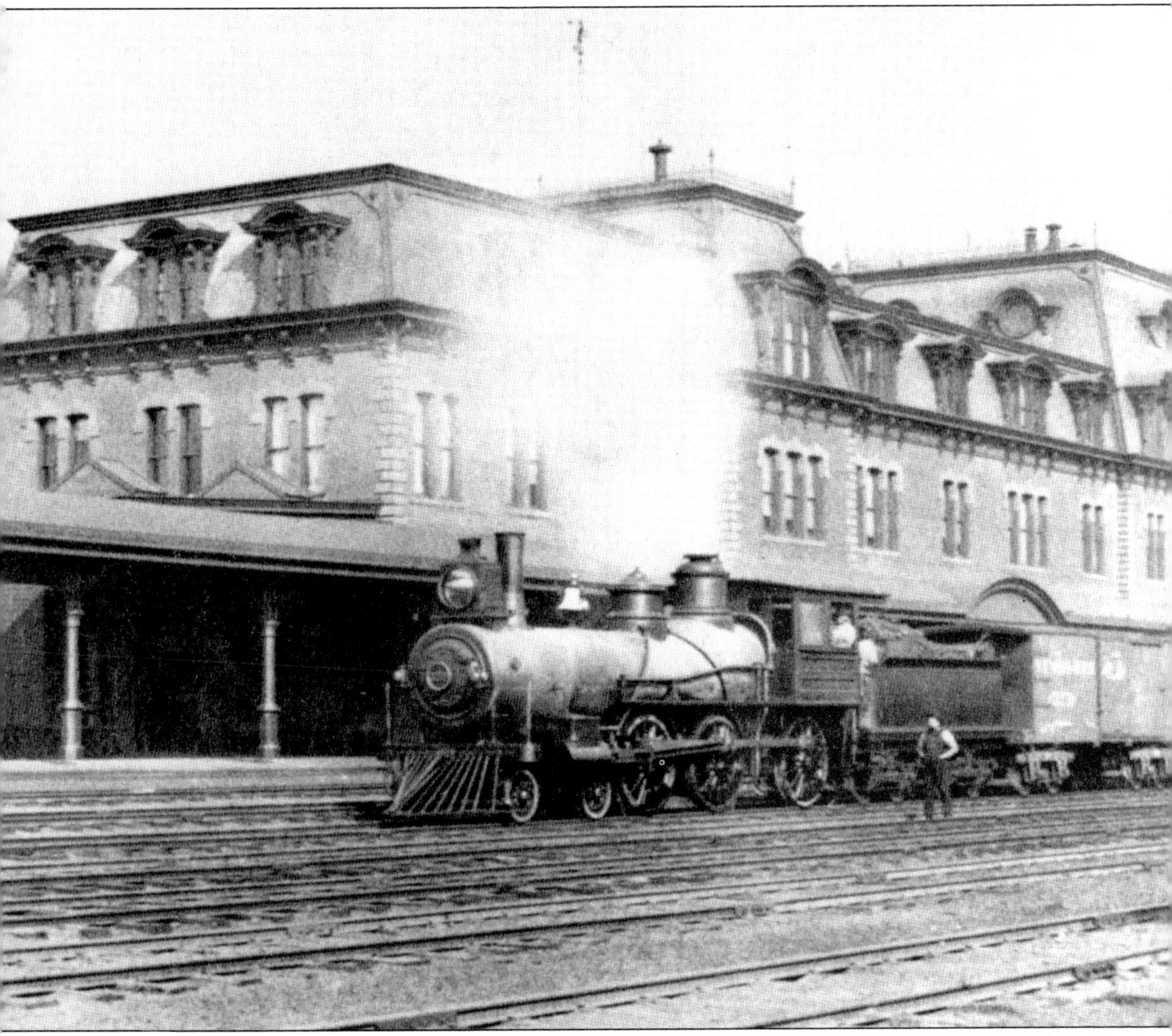

In 1905, the New Haven Railroad still ran steam passenger trains like this one, pictured in the rear of the New Haven station. By 1914, the New Haven Railroad had electrified its line between here and Grand Central Station in New York. (Courtesy Connecticut Motor Coach Museum Archives.)

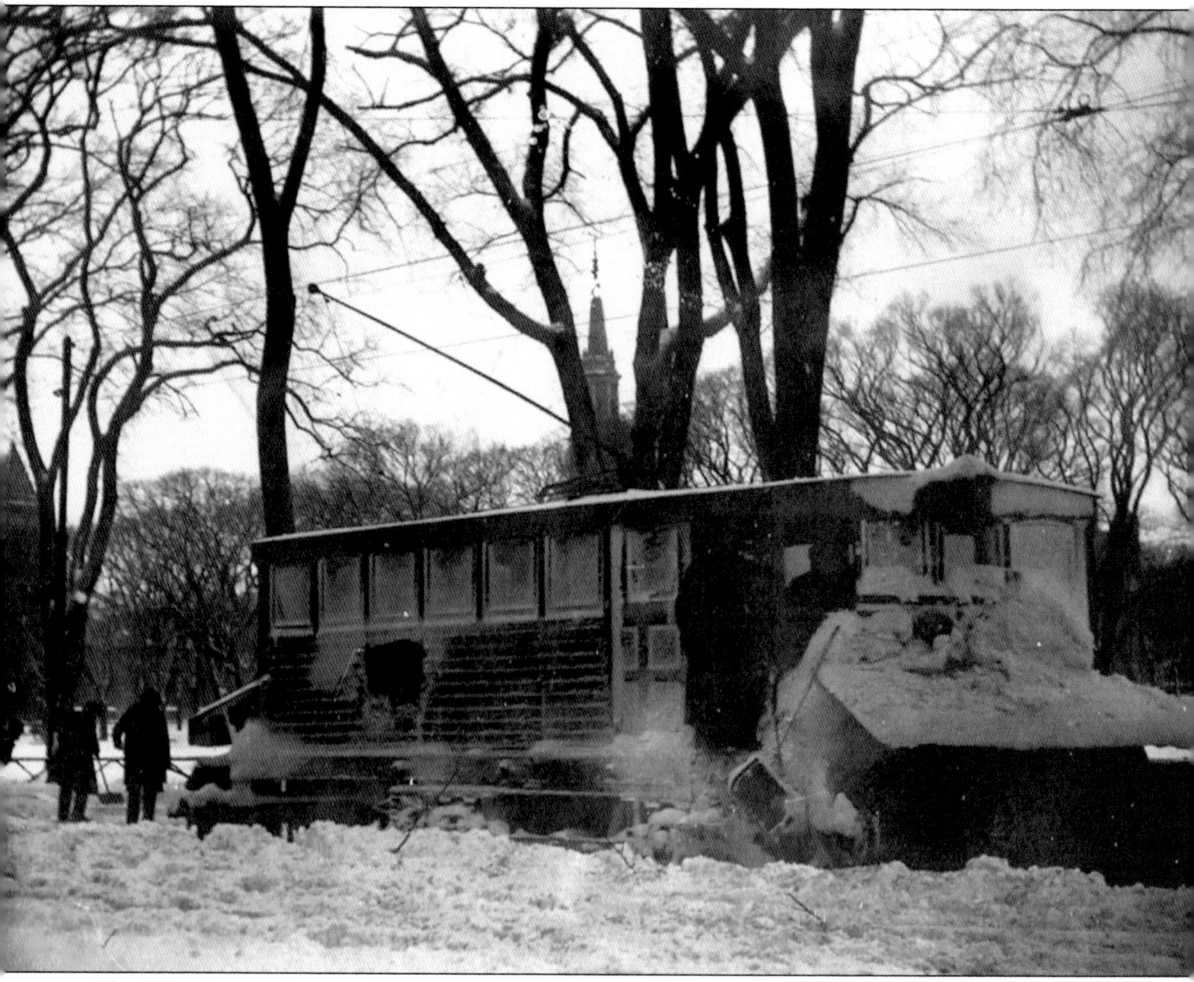

The Winchester Avenue Railroad plow, cleaning snow from Chapel Street, was one of many designs of snow removal equipment used in 1901. (Courtesy Fred Bennett collection.)

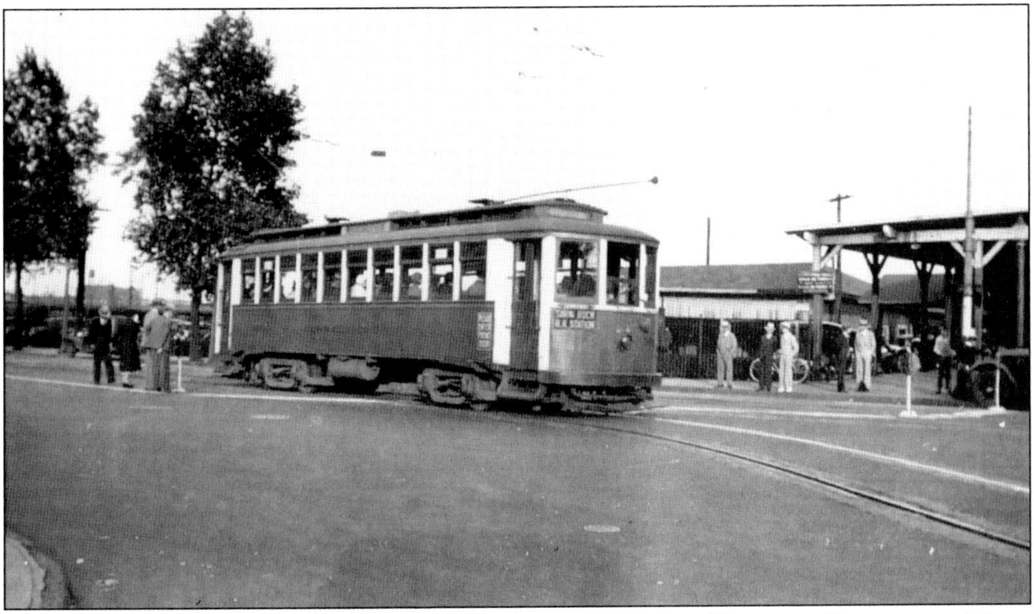

A Savin Rock Park car approaches the railroad station in 1914. (Courtesy Connecticut Motor Coach Museum Archives.)

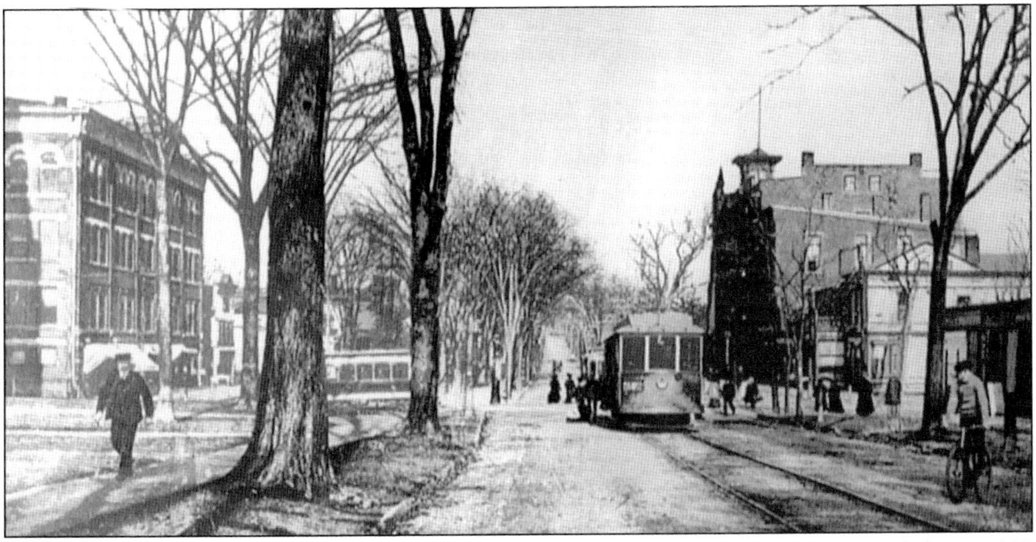

This line to New Haven, running down Main Street in Wallingford, operated from 1907 until 1937. There was also a short local car that traveled Central Avenue. Another line came down from Meriden but did not cross the New Haven Railroad main line; it was abandoned in September 1929. (Courtesy Connecticut Motor Coach Museum Archives.)

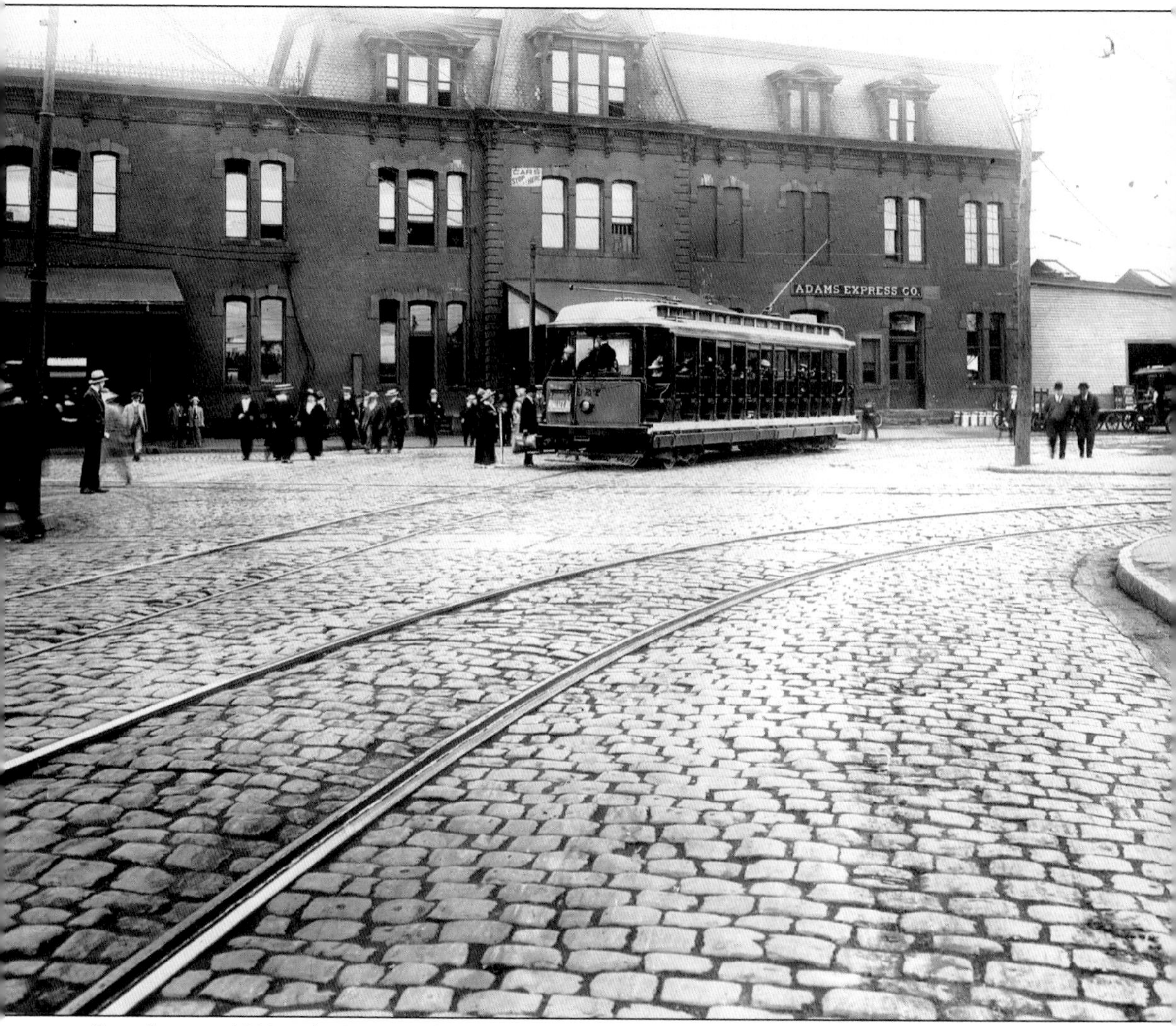

Seen here in 1914 is the New York, New Haven and Hartford Railroad passenger station in New Haven. The station burned in 1918 in a spectacular fire. It was replaced by the present building, which continues to serve thousands of Metro North and Amtrak rail passengers daily. (Courtesy Fred Bennett collection.)

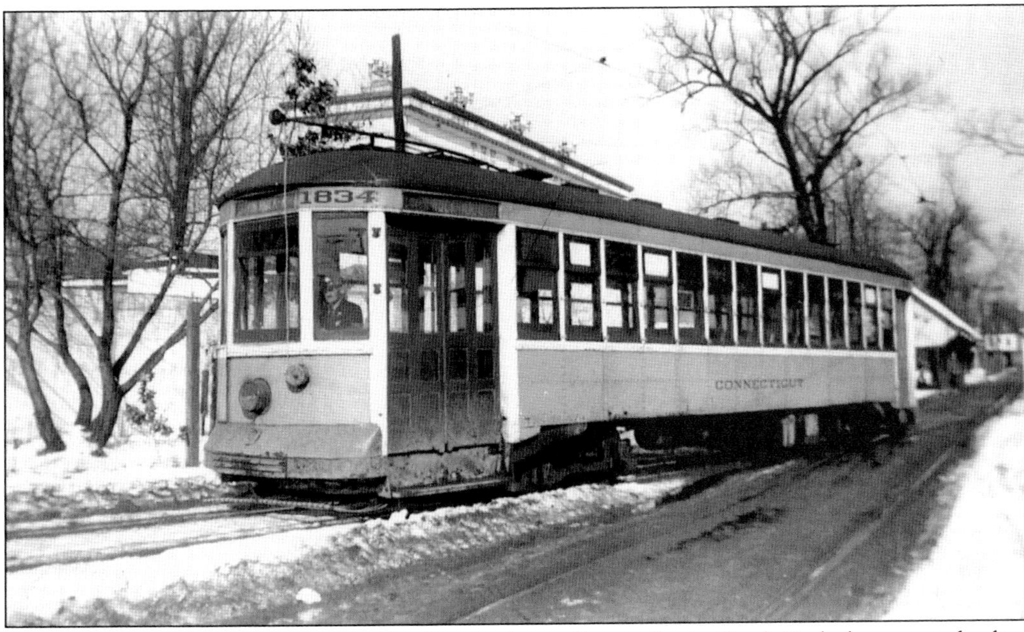

In the early 1940s, passengers could still ride the trolley to Savin Rock Park; however, the line was converted to motor coach on September 25, 1948. (Courtesy Connecticut Motor Coach Museum Archives.)

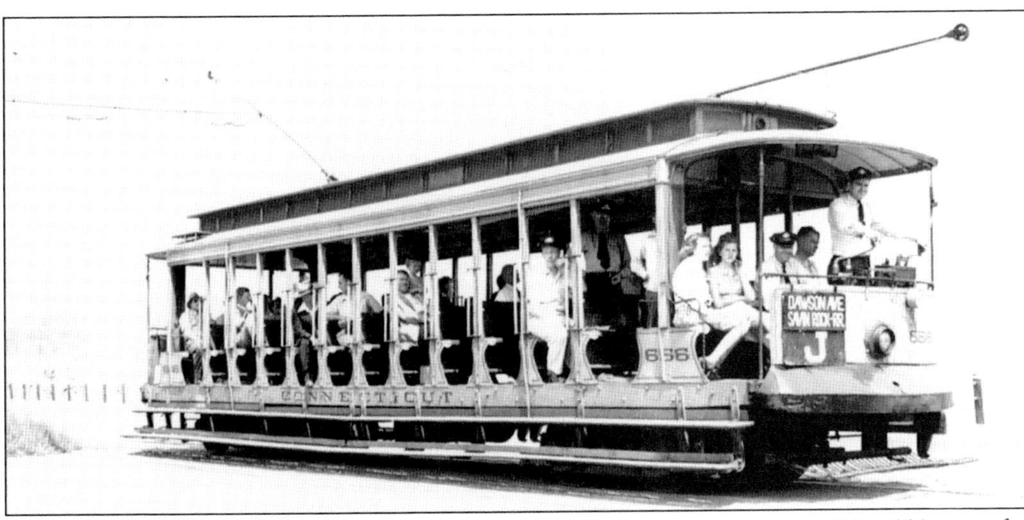

Streetcar historian and photographer Horace Bromley operates open car No. 656 on a fan trip to Savin Rock in 1948. Bromley worked as a streetcar and then motor coach operator for the Hartford Division of the Connecticut Company from 1941 until he retired in 1984. He donated his entire collection of streetcar and railroad photographs to the Connecticut Motor Coach Museum Archives before he passed away in 1991. (Courtesy Connecticut Motor Coach Museum Archives.)

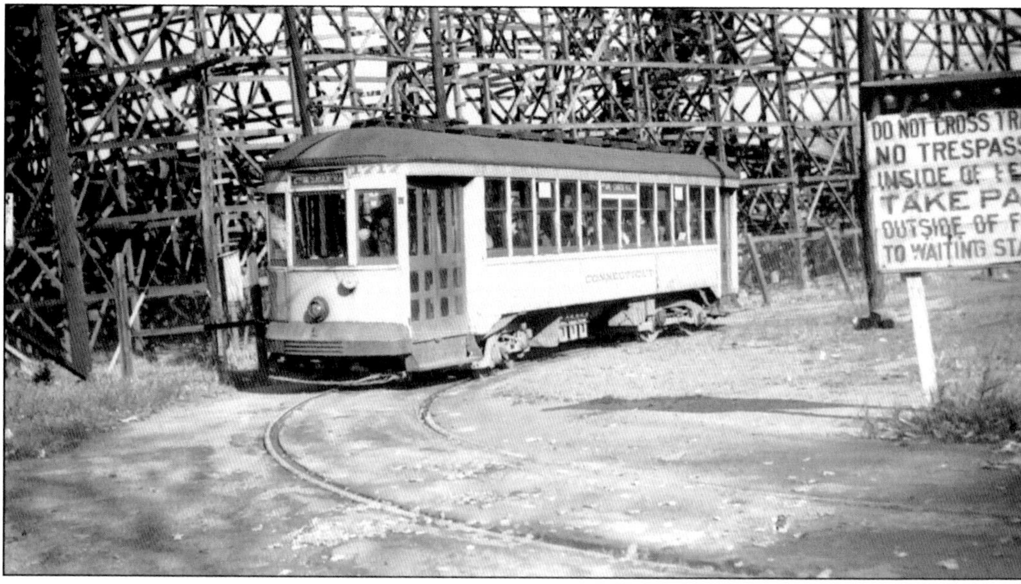

This view of the loop track at Savin Rock reveals a wooden roller coaster in the background. (Courtesy Connecticut Motor Coach Museum Archives.)

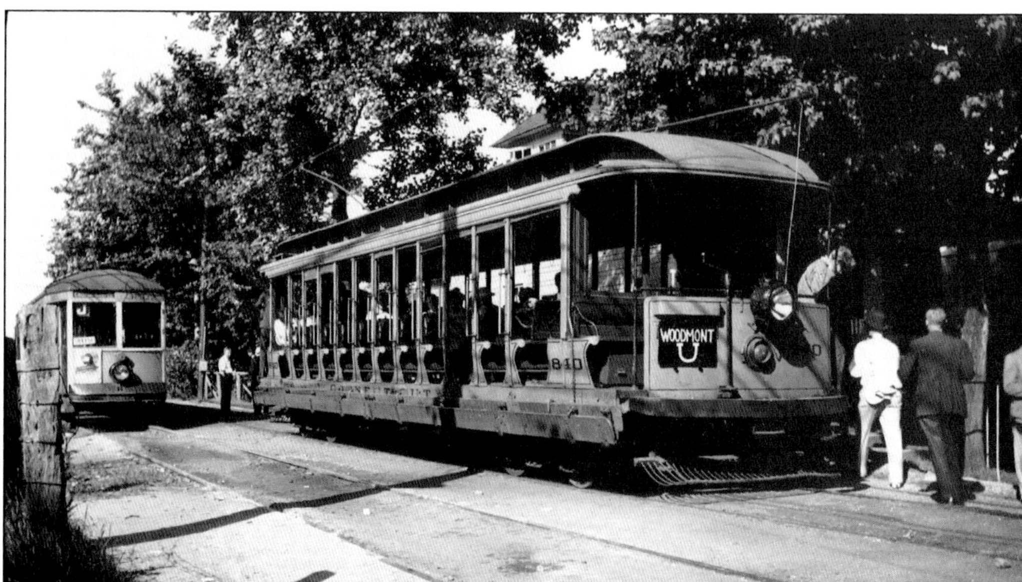

Connecticut Company car No. 840 runs on the Savin Rock line during a fan trip in the 1940s. This car has been preserved at the Connecticut Trolley Museum in East Windsor. (Courtesy Connecticut Motor Coach Museum Archives.)

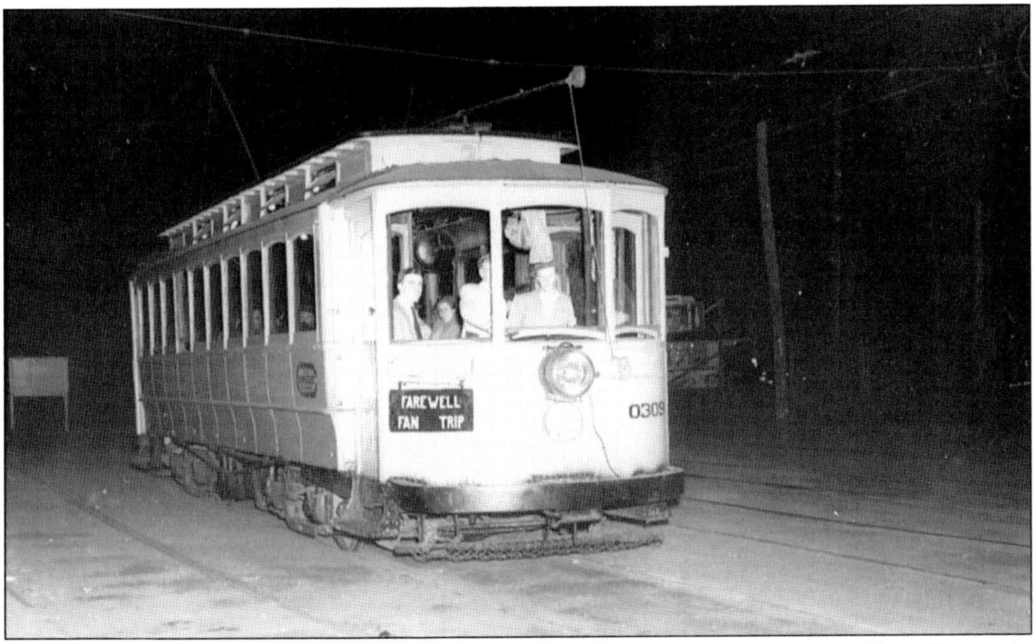

Work car No. 0309 is pictured on the last night of streetcar operation in New Haven in September 1948. This car was originally built as Fairhaven and Westville Railroad car No. 152 in 1902. It too has been preserved at the Connecticut Trolley Museum. (Courtesy Connecticut Motor Coach Museum Archives.)

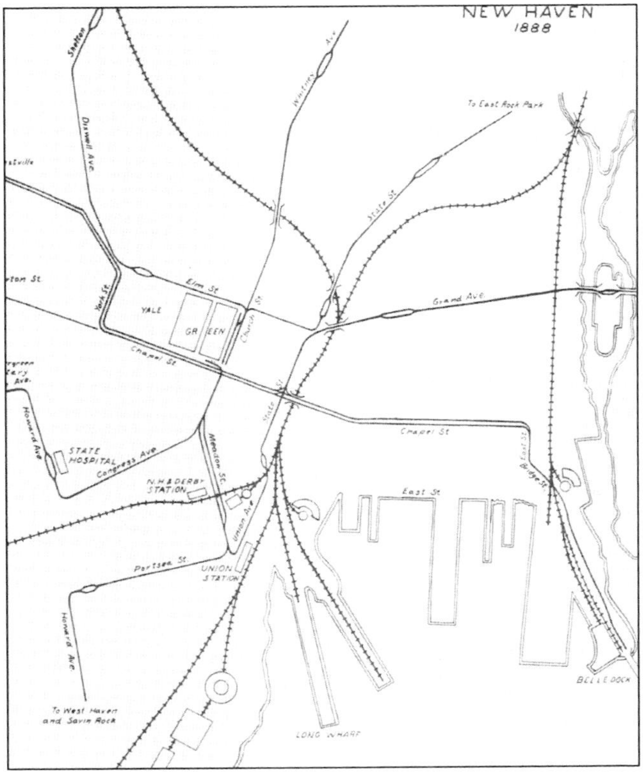

Shown here is a map of the horsecar lines operating in New Haven in 1888. (Courtesy Fred Bennett collection.)

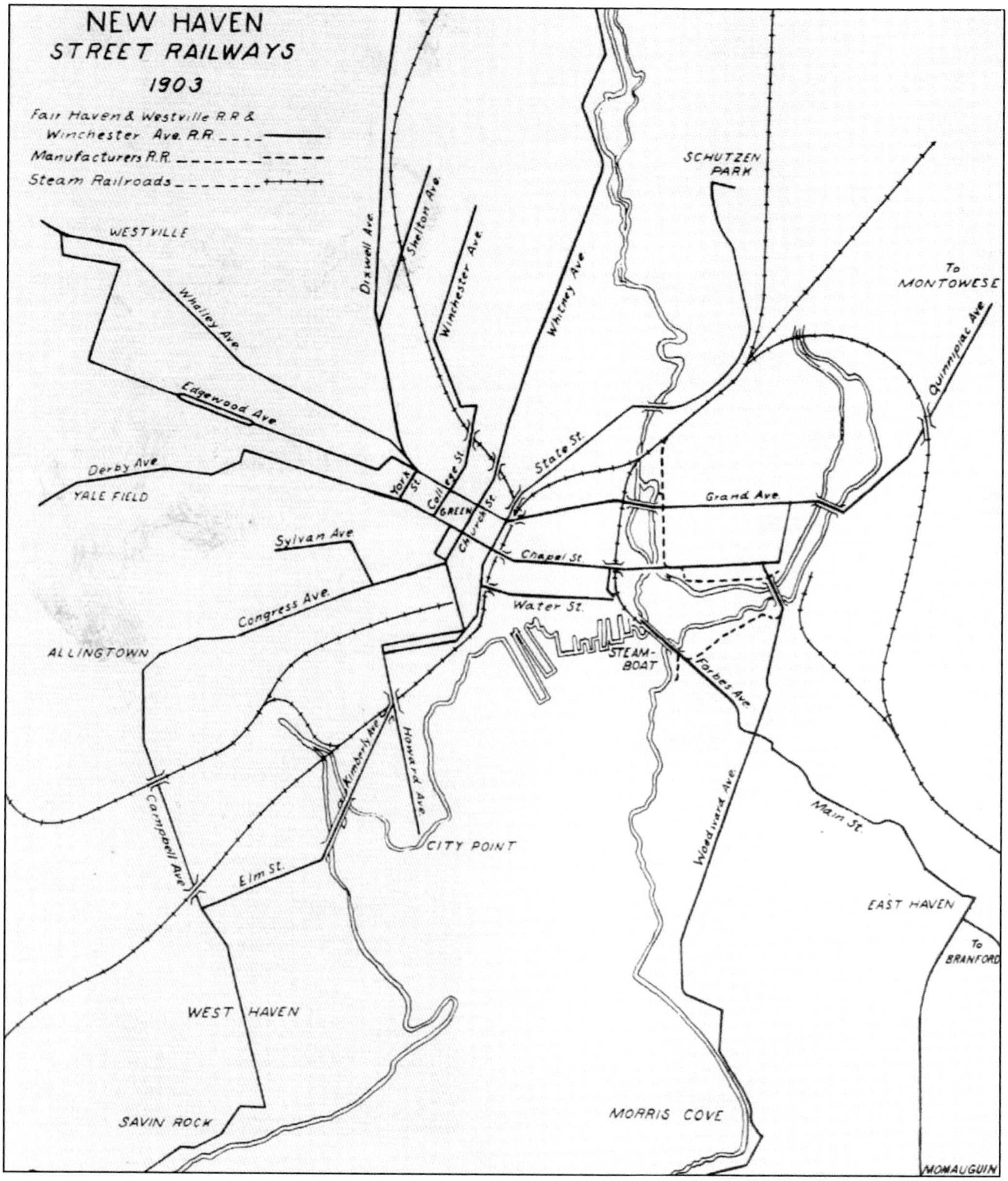

This image displays the New Haven streetcar lines during the year 1903. (Courtesy Fred Bennett collection.)

Six

NORWALK LINES

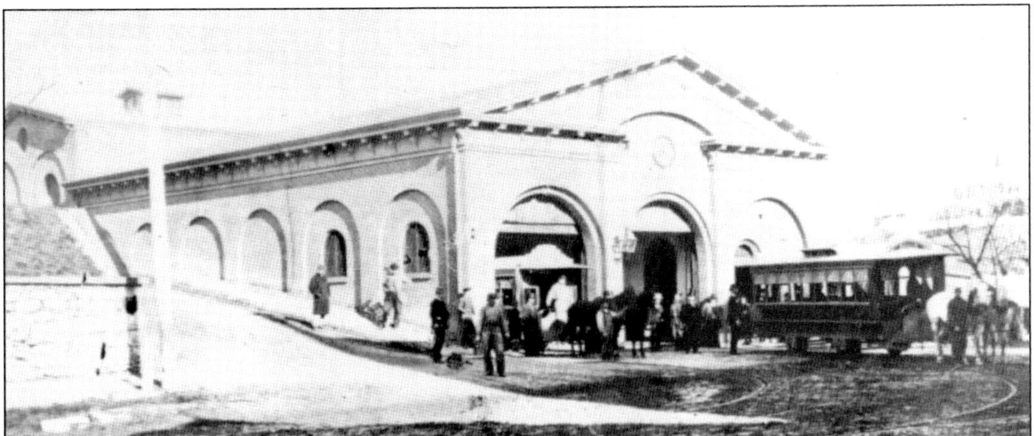

Public transportation started in Norwalk in 1863 with the opening of the Norwalk Horse Railroad. The horsecar stable is shown here in 1870. This building became a carbarn in 1894, when the company electrified its lines and changed its name to the Norwalk Street Railway. (Courtesy Fred Bennett collection.)

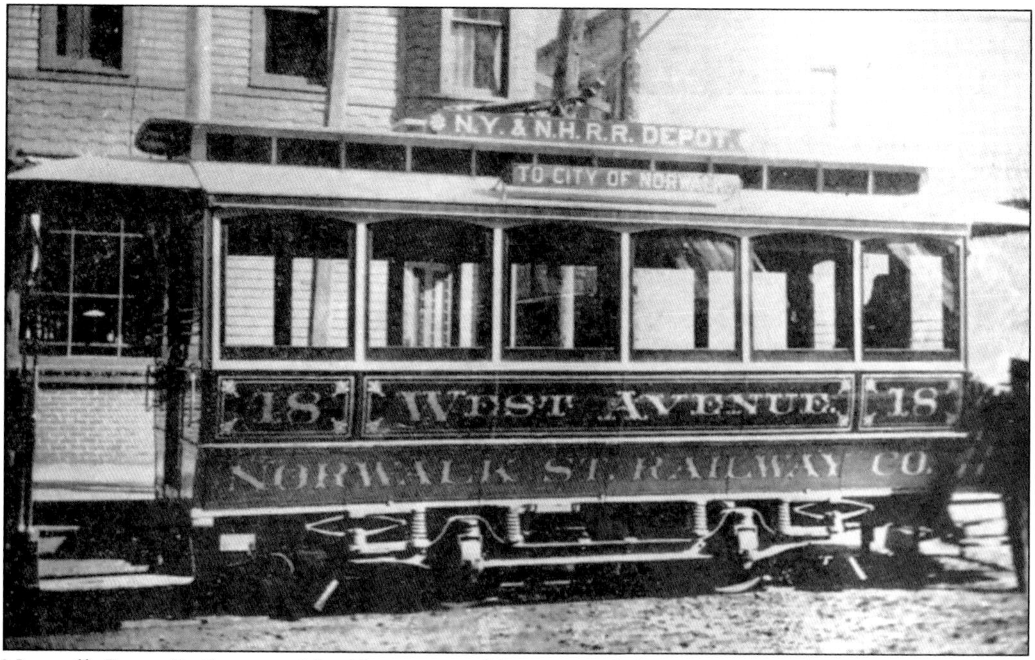

Norwalk Street Railway car No. 18 was one of the original electric cars purchased when the lines were electrified in Norwalk. (Courtesy Fred Bennett collection.)

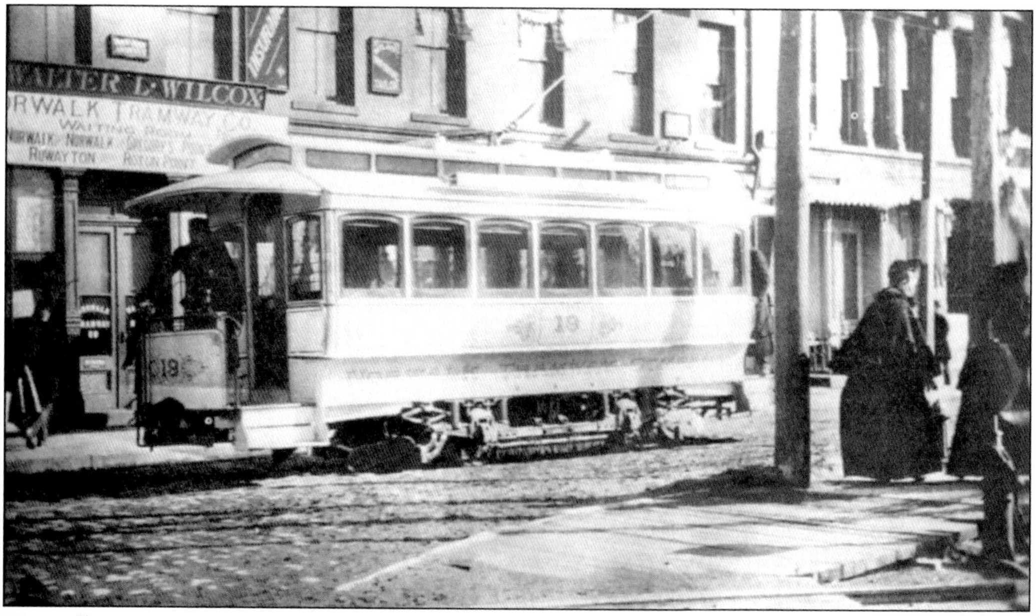

Norwalk Tramway was the first company to electrify its lines in Norwalk, in 1893. The Connecticut Railway and Lighting Company acquired Norwalk Tramway and the Norwalk Street Railway between 1899 and 1900. In 1906, Connecticut Railway and Lighting leased its entire streetcar system to the Consolidated Railways, a New Haven Railroad subsidiary, for 99 years. The Connecticut Company began running all streetcar lines owned and leased by the New Haven Railroad in 1910. From 1910 until November 16, 1936, the Connecticut Company was the primary operator of street railways in Connecticut. (Courtesy Fred Bennett collection.)

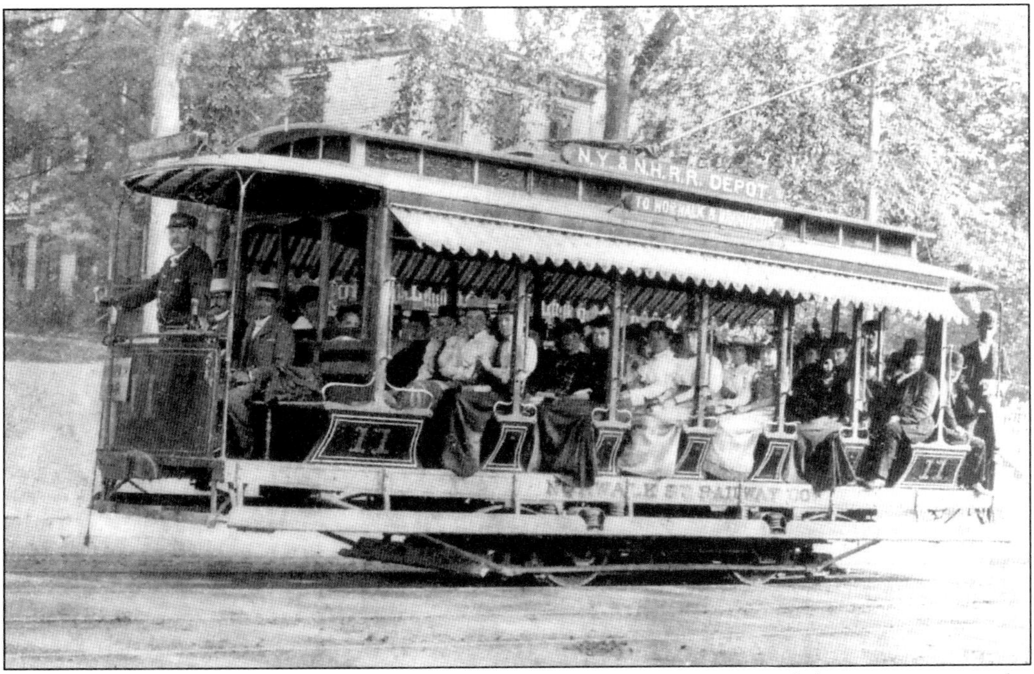

Open cars had great popular appeal with the riding public in 1900, and this open car on the Norwalk Street Railway was no exception. That year, there were over 25,000 in use in the United States and Canada. (Courtesy Fred Bennett collection.)

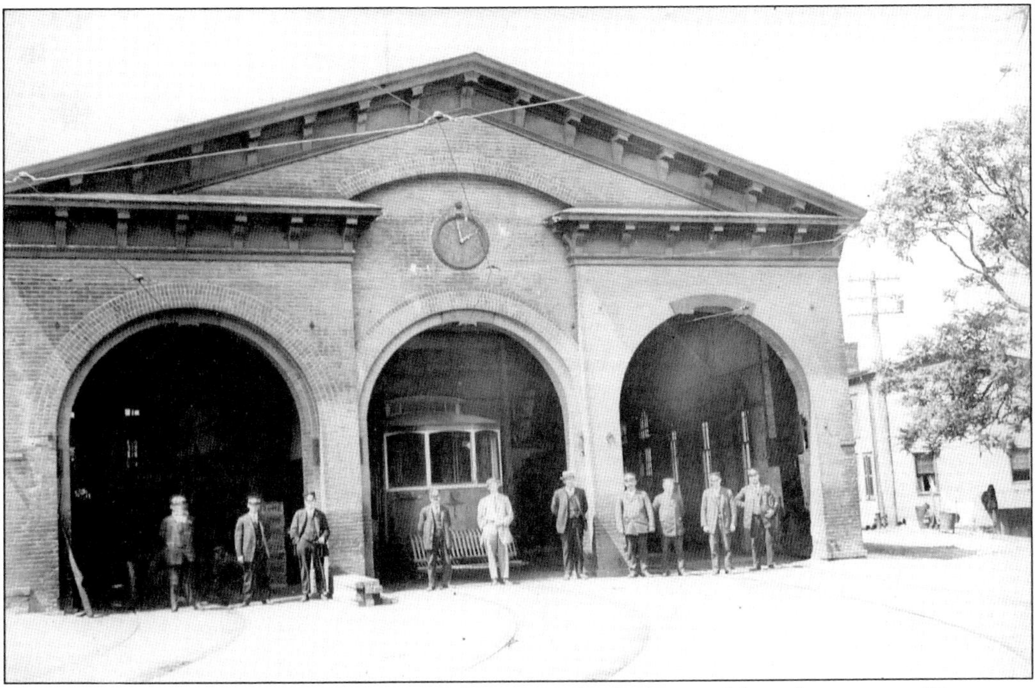

The Norwalk carbarn was rather unique because it looked more like a fire station. Disastrous blazes often occurred in streetcar barns, as they were typically made of wood rather than the brick shown here. (Courtesy Fred Bennett collection.)

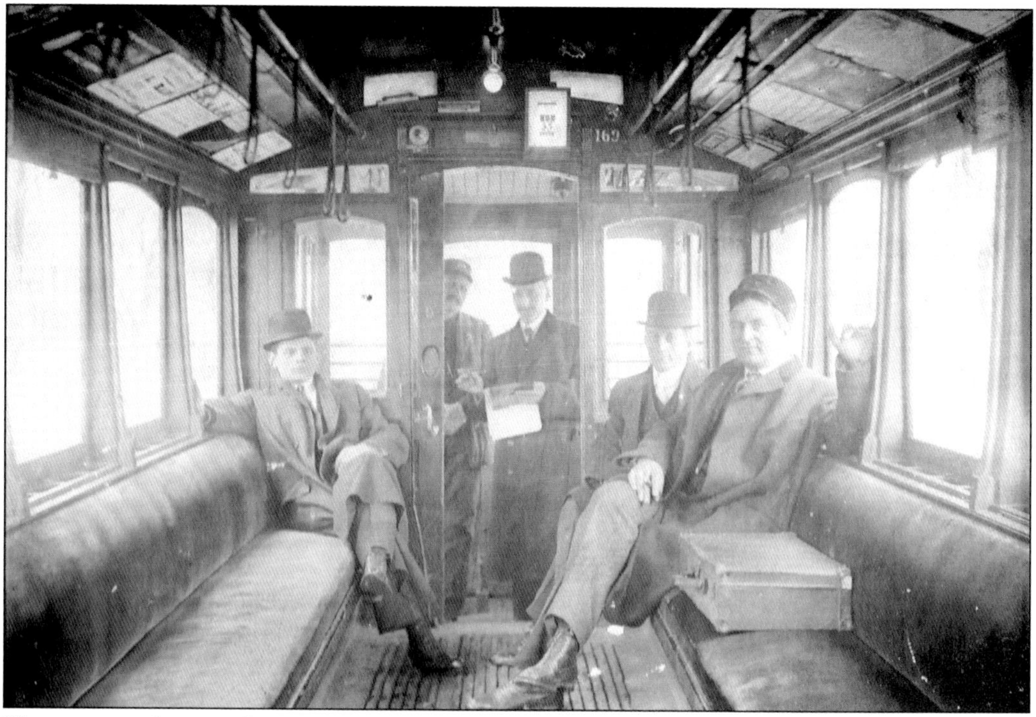

The crew and some Connecticut Company officials are pictured inside closed car No. 169. (Courtesy Fred Bennett collection.)

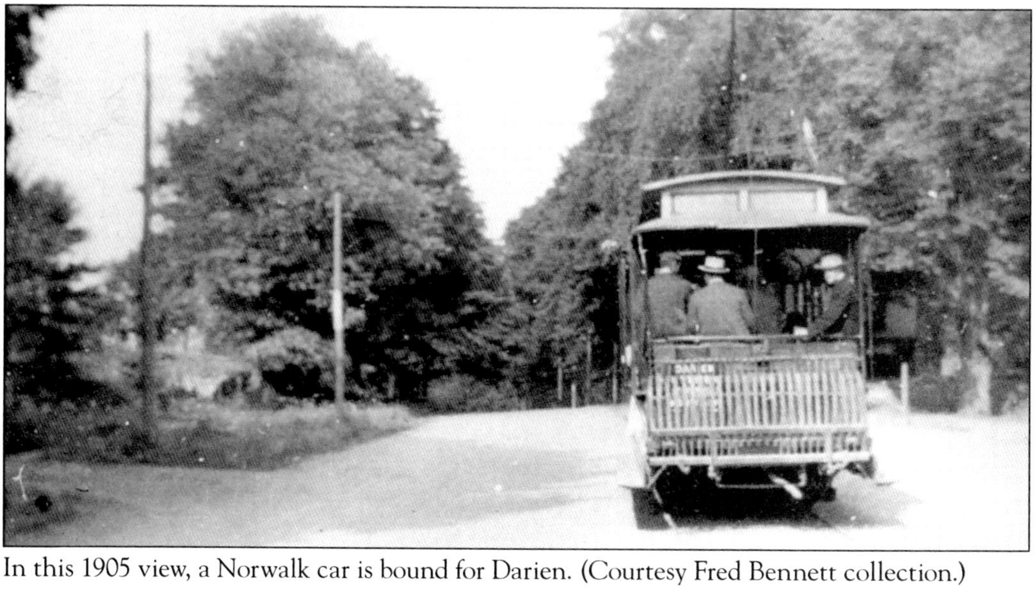

In this 1905 view, a Norwalk car is bound for Darien. (Courtesy Fred Bennett collection.)

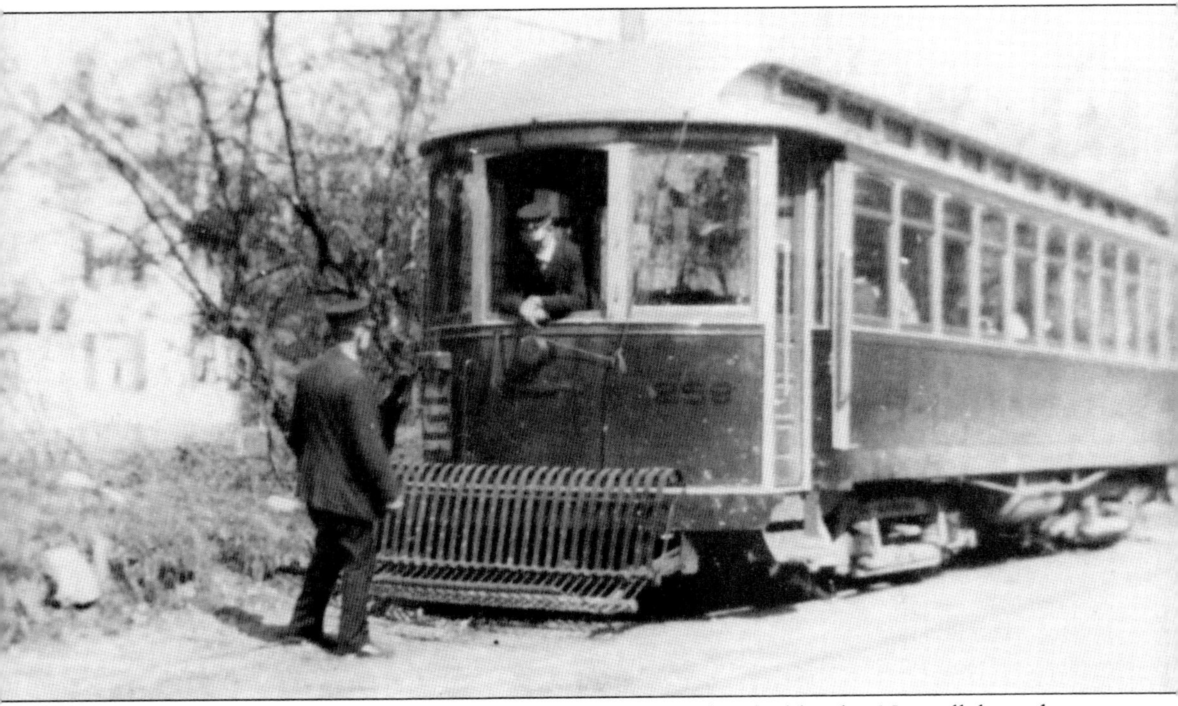

Maintaining a schedule sometimes meant that a car arrived early, like this Norwalk-bound car waiting at a passing siding for the outbound car to arrive. (Courtesy Fred Bennett collection.)

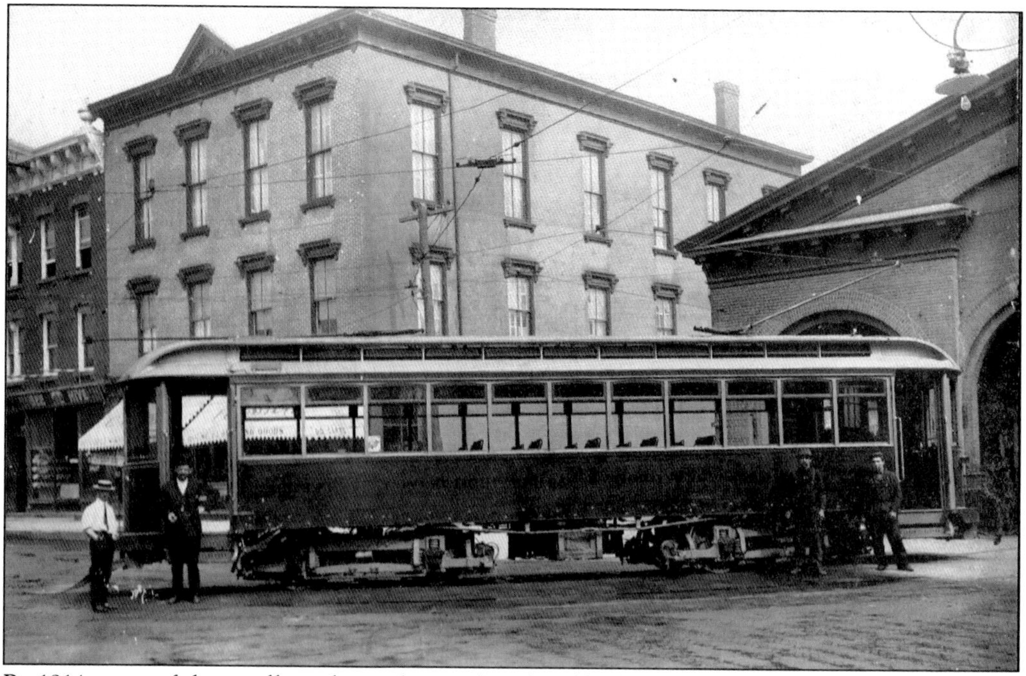

By 1914, most of the small single-truck cars that dated back to the 1890s were gone or had been made into work cars. This double-truck car is typical of a Connecticut Company car of 1914. (Courtesy Fred Bennett collection.)

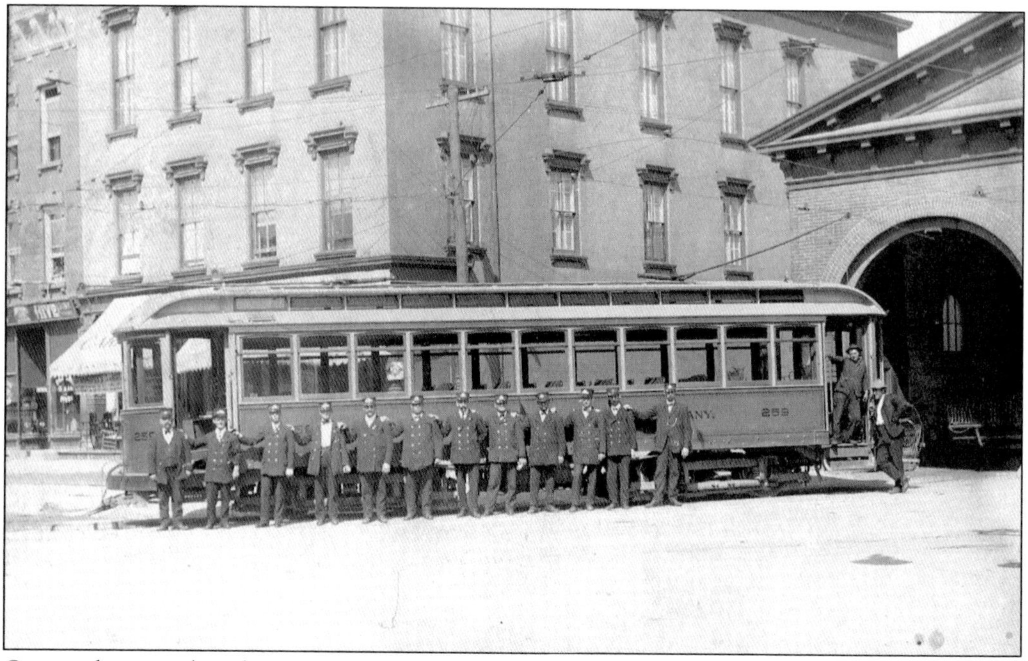

Group photographs of operating personnel were often taken. Some of the Norwalk Division operating personnel gather here for such a portrait. (Courtesy Fred Bennett collection.)

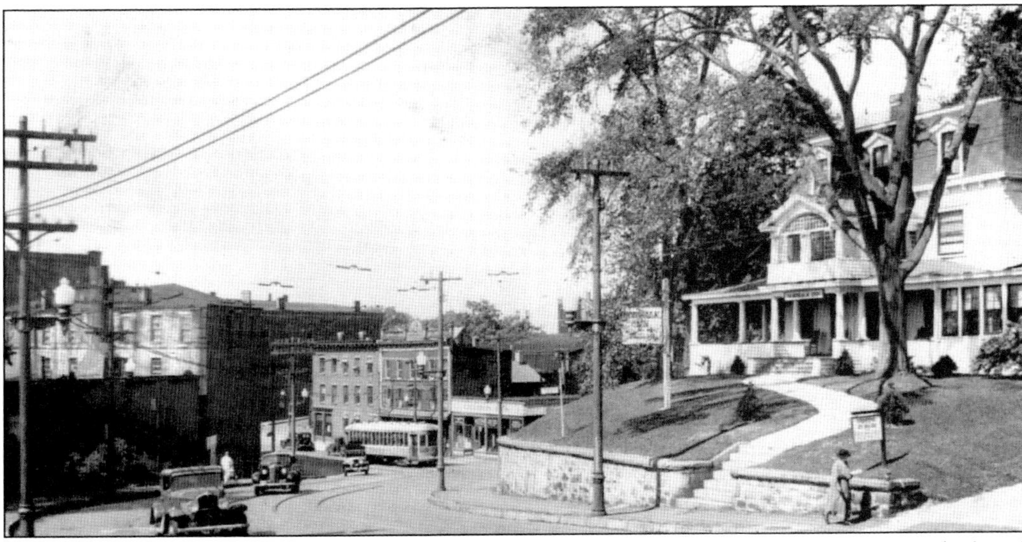

With the increase in the number of automobiles on the roads, the need for trolley cars declined. This photograph was taken only a few days before September 22, 1935, when the last streetcars ran in Norwalk. (Courtesy Fred Bennett collection.)

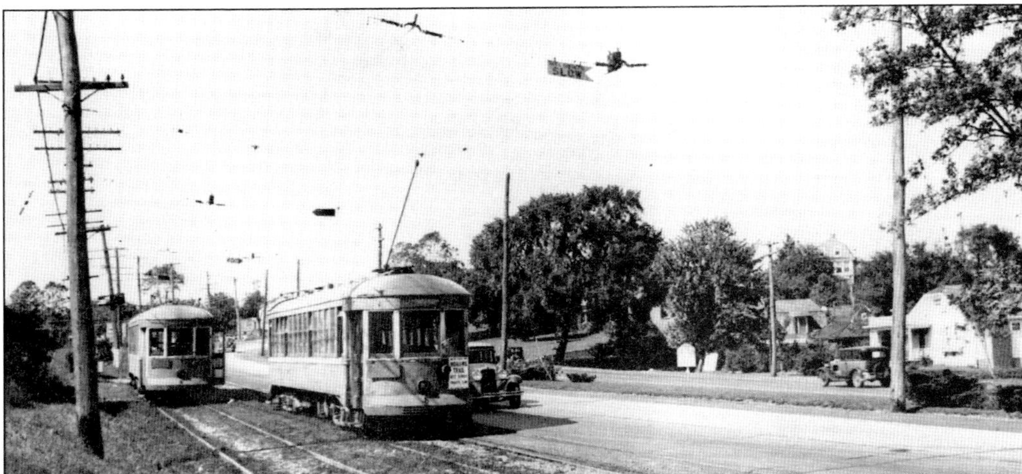

Automobiles share the street with trolley cars on Boston Post Road in Westport just a few months before streetcar operation ended. (Courtesy Fred Bennett collection.)

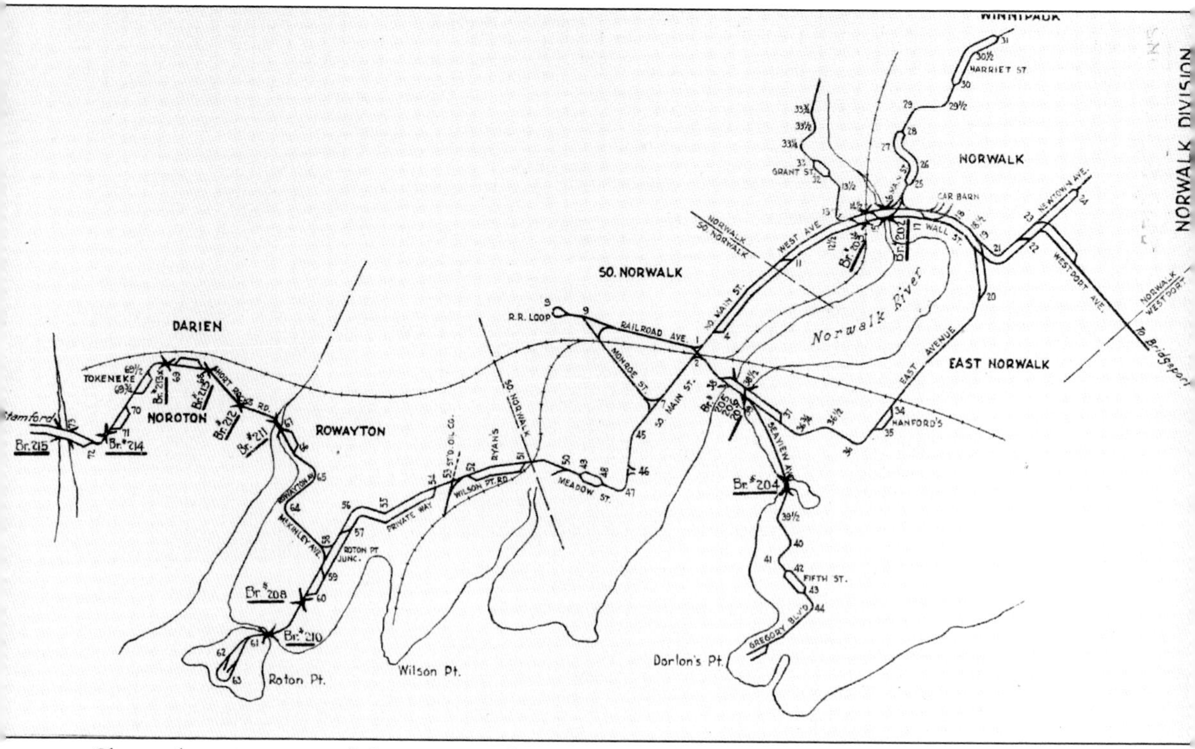

Shown here is a map of the streetcar lines in Norwalk. (Courtesy Connecticut Motor Coach Museum Archives.)

Seven

Shore Line Electric Railway

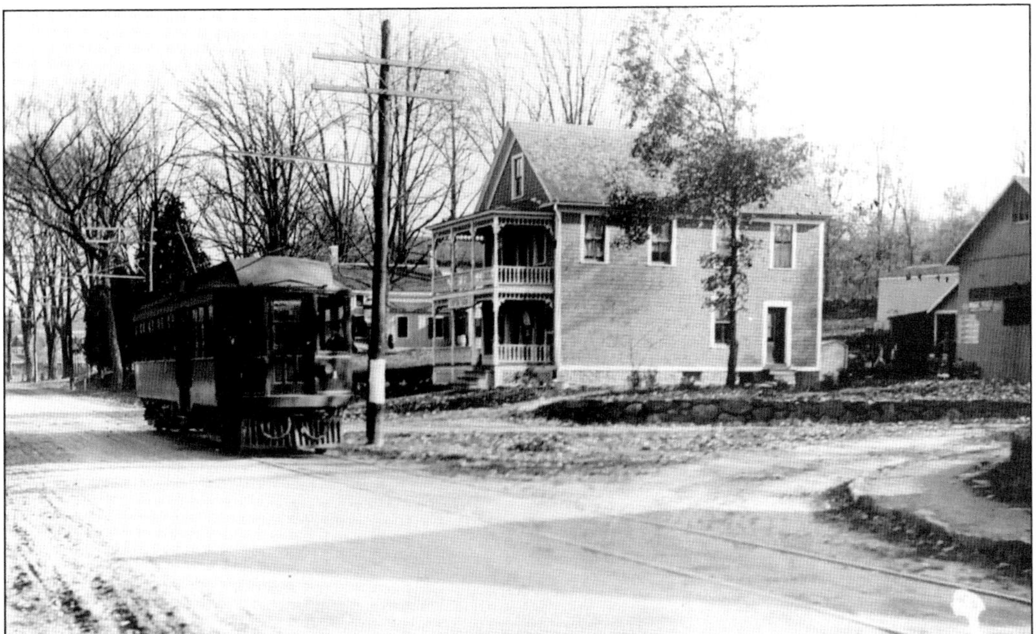

Track on the side of the road was typical on the Shore Line Electric, as it ran through the small shoreline towns of Connecticut. The Shore Line Electric was constructed between Old Saybrook and Stony Creek Village in Branford in 1910. In 1911, a more direct line was built into New Haven through North Branford using Connecticut Company tracks from Middletown Avenue to the railroad station. In 1912, a branch was built to Deep River and extended to Chester in 1914. (Courtesy Connecticut Motor Coach Museum Archives.)

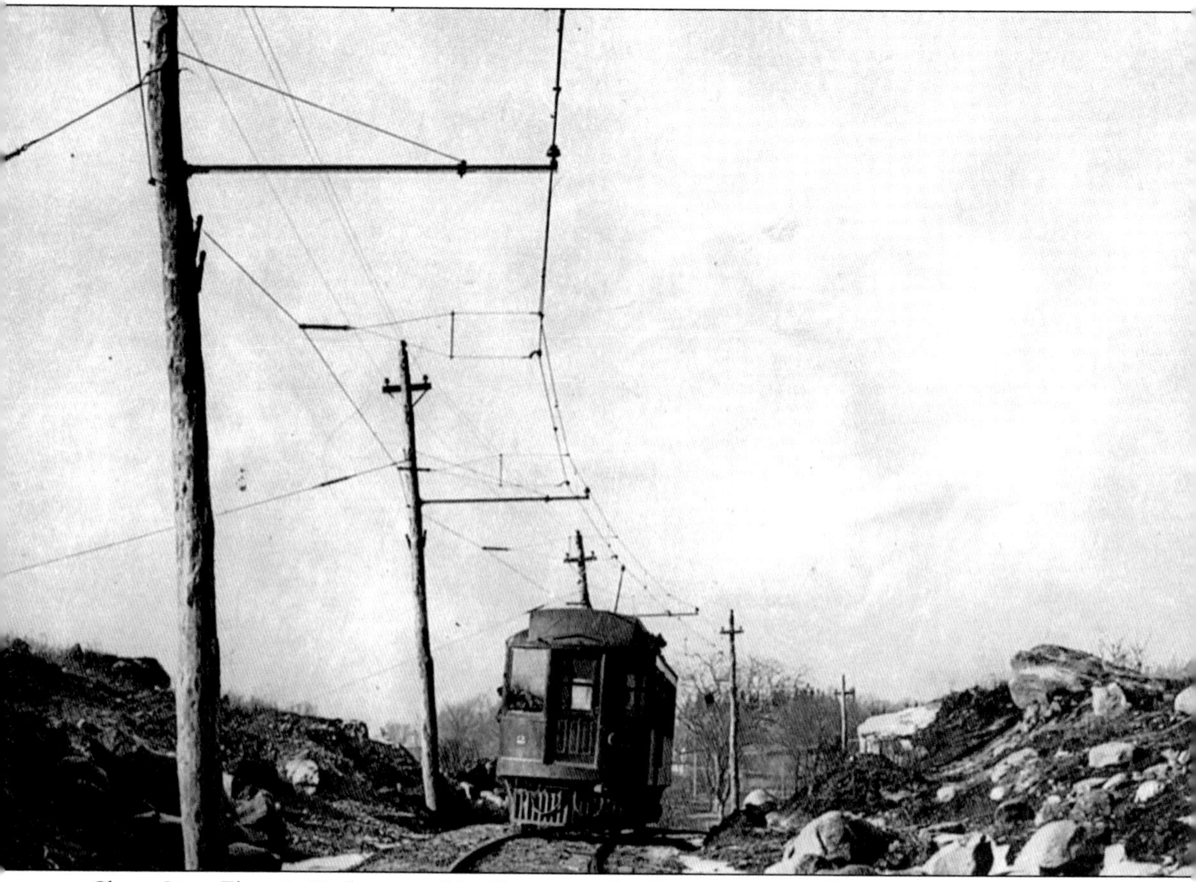

Shore Line Electric Railway car No. 2 runs in the Foxon section of East Haven in 1912. This line was built to very high standards and used 1,200 volts direct current to power the cars, as opposed to the conventional 600 volts used by all other lines in Connecticut. Shore Line Electric Railway cars ran on Connecticut Company tracks from the end of their line on Middletown Avenue via State Street to the railroad station in New Haven. In order to run into New Haven, the motorman threw a switch in the cab that allowed the Shore Line car to run on 600 volts. (Courtesy Connecticut Motor Coach Museum Archives.)

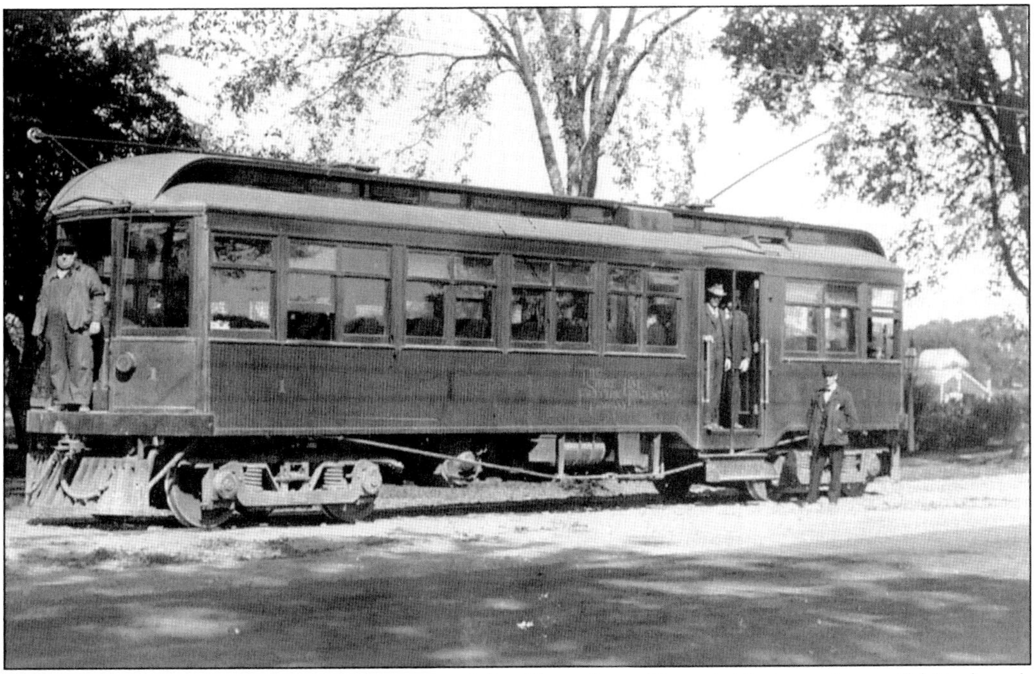

This image captures the historic first trip of the Shore Line Electric Railway from Old Saybrook at its stop in Madison. The motorman on car No. 1, Harry Morris, was killed in an accident in North Branford in 1918. (Courtesy Connecticut Motor Coach Museum Archives.)

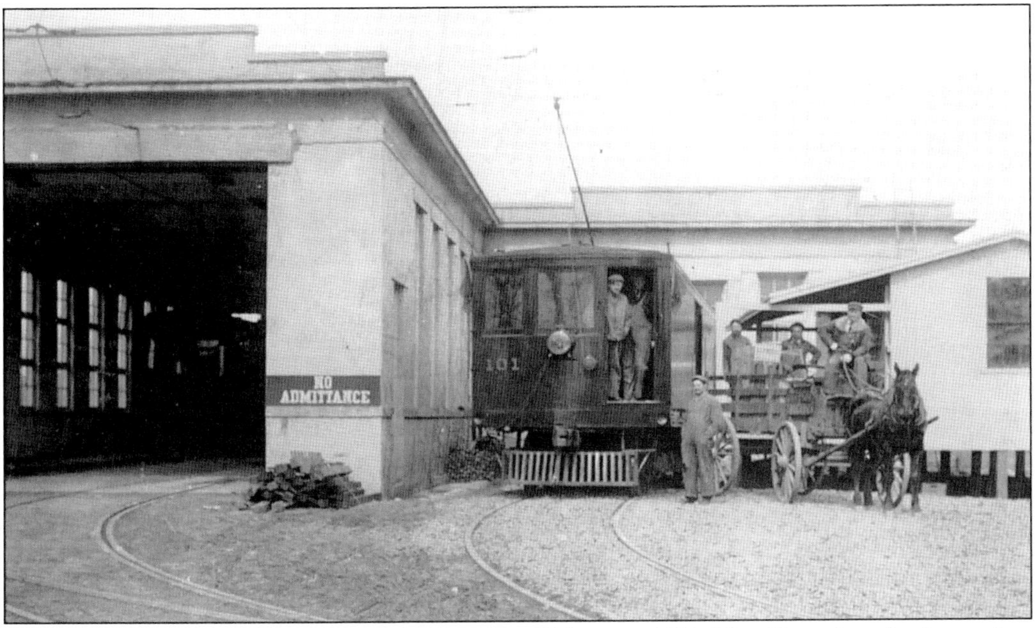

The Guilford carbarn and freight depot is pictured here in 1914. The Shore Line had a modest freight business carrying milk from outlying farms to New Haven, some of which most likely went to the New England Dairy Company (see page 81). The Guilford carbarn was a substantial cement structure that held four cars and was located off Water Street on the line to Stony Creek Village. (Courtesy Connecticut Motor Coach Museum Archives.)

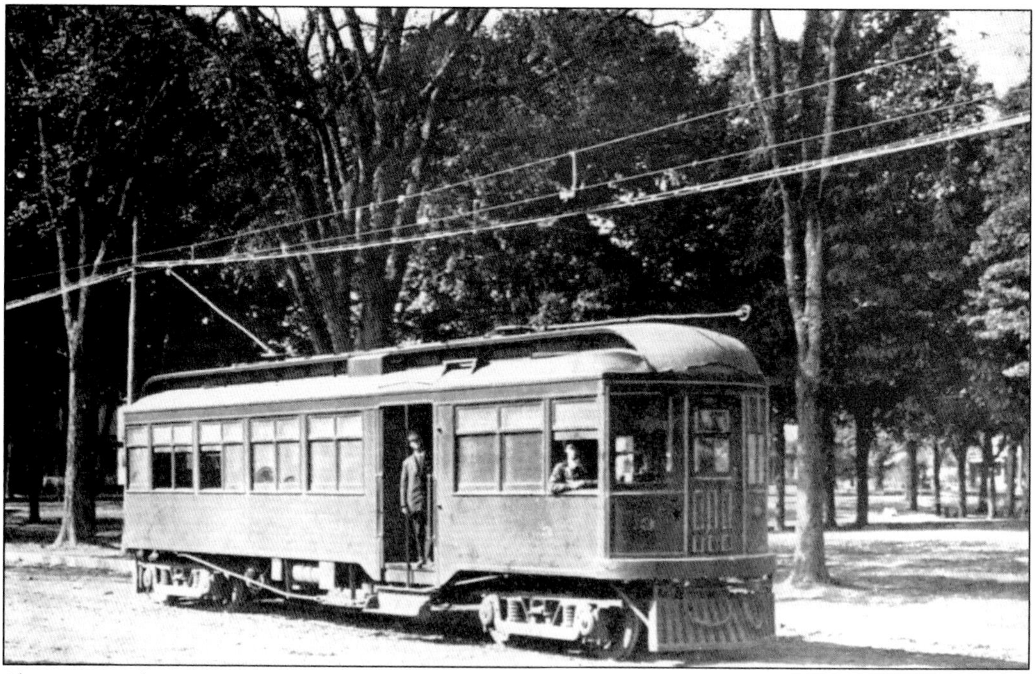

Shore Line Electric cars were more like midwestern interurban cars because of their size and the center entrance door. Cars No. 1 to 10 were built by the Jewett Car Company of Newark, Ohio, in 1911 and were equipped to run in trains of two or three cars. In 1912, Jewett delivered cars No. 11, 12, 14, 15, and 16. There never was a car No. 13; maybe the management was superstitious! (Courtesy Connecticut Motor Coach Museum Archives.)

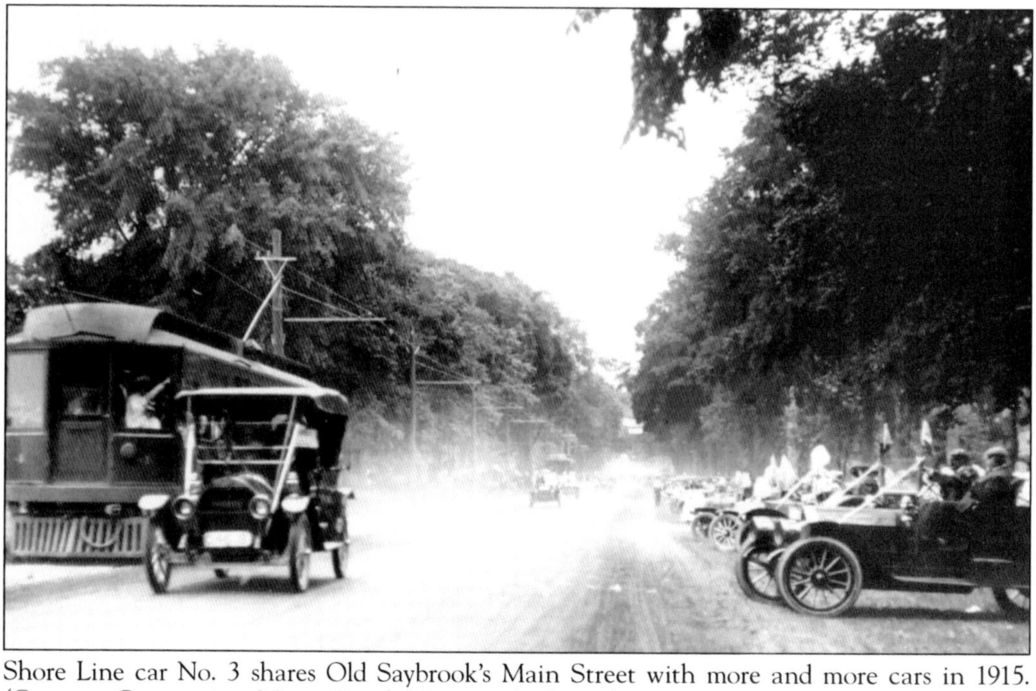

Shore Line car No. 3 shares Old Saybrook's Main Street with more and more cars in 1915. (Courtesy Connecticut Motor Coach Museum Archives.)

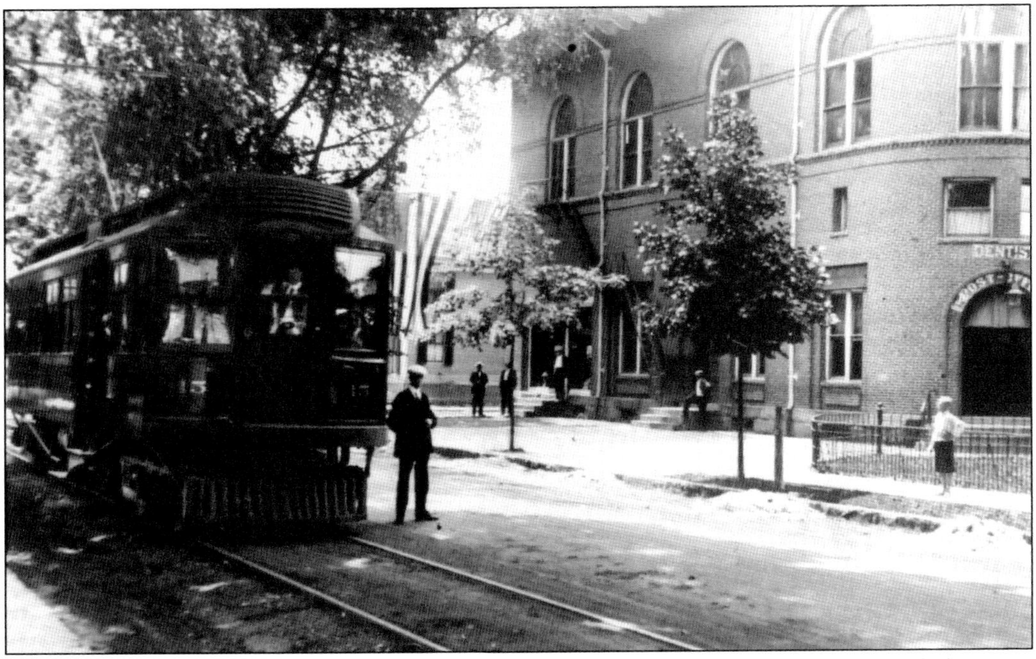

In 1914, Shore Line Electric car No. 15 runs past the Deep River Town Hall on its daily route. (Courtesy Connecticut Motor Coach Museum Archives.)

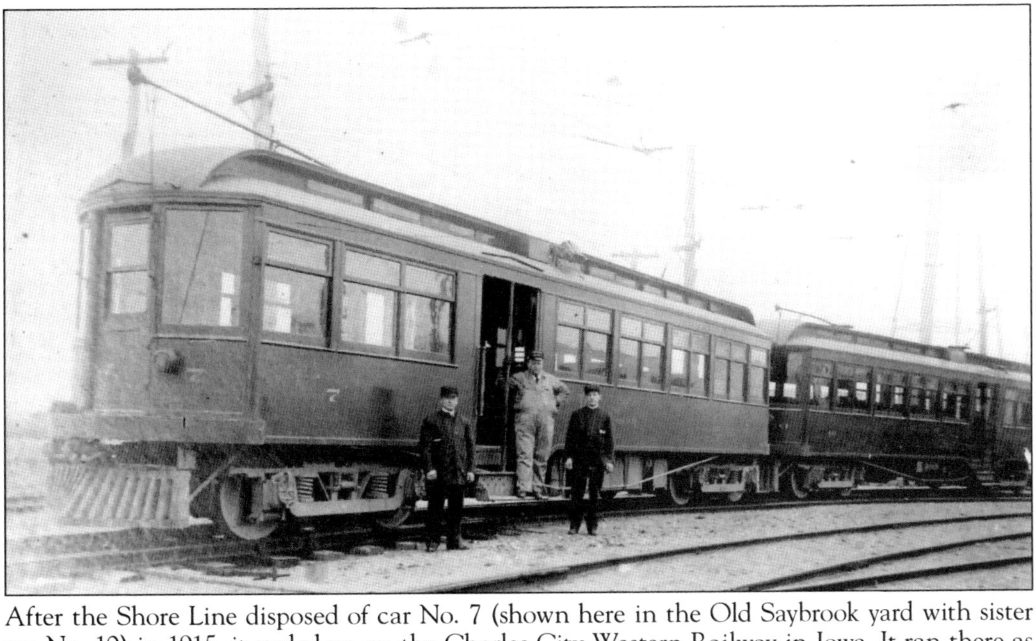

After the Shore Line disposed of car No. 7 (shown here in the Old Saybrook yard with sister car No. 10) in 1915, it ended up on the Charles City Western Railway in Iowa. It ran there as car No. 53 until 1952, when passenger service was discontinued on the Charles City Western. Trains were seldom operated on the Shore Line because of the amount of power they drew. This run is most likely an extra train to bring employees up from Old Saybrook to the piano factory in Ivoryton. (Courtesy Connecticut Motor Coach Museum Archives.)

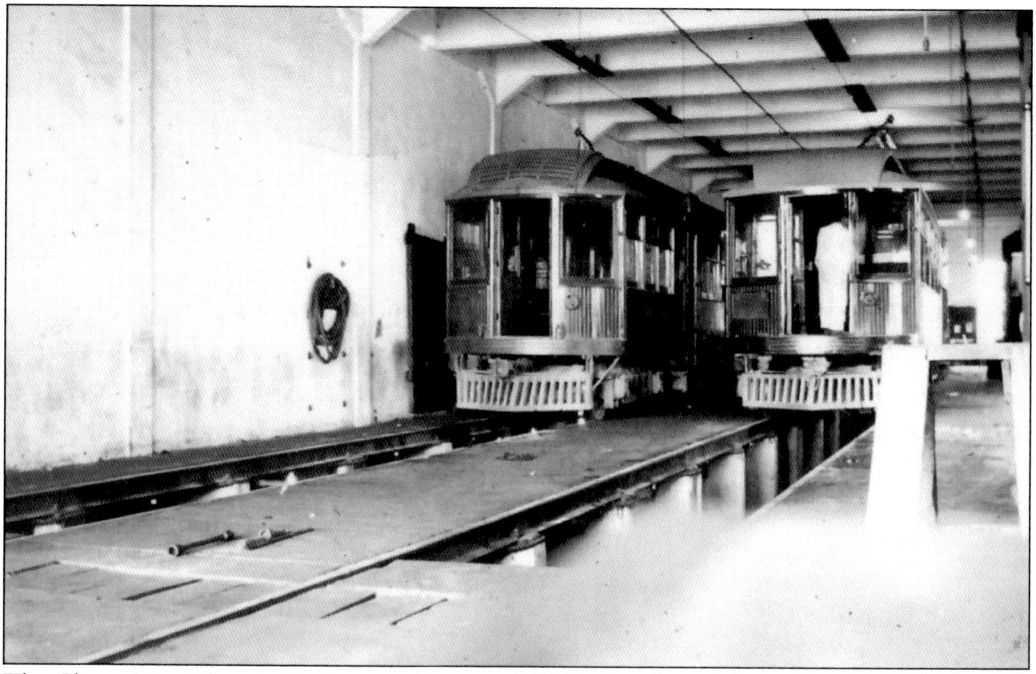

The Shore Line Electric Railway carbarn in Old Saybrook was the main repair facility for the railway as well as the location of the powerhouse. (Courtesy Connecticut Motor Coach Museum Archives.)

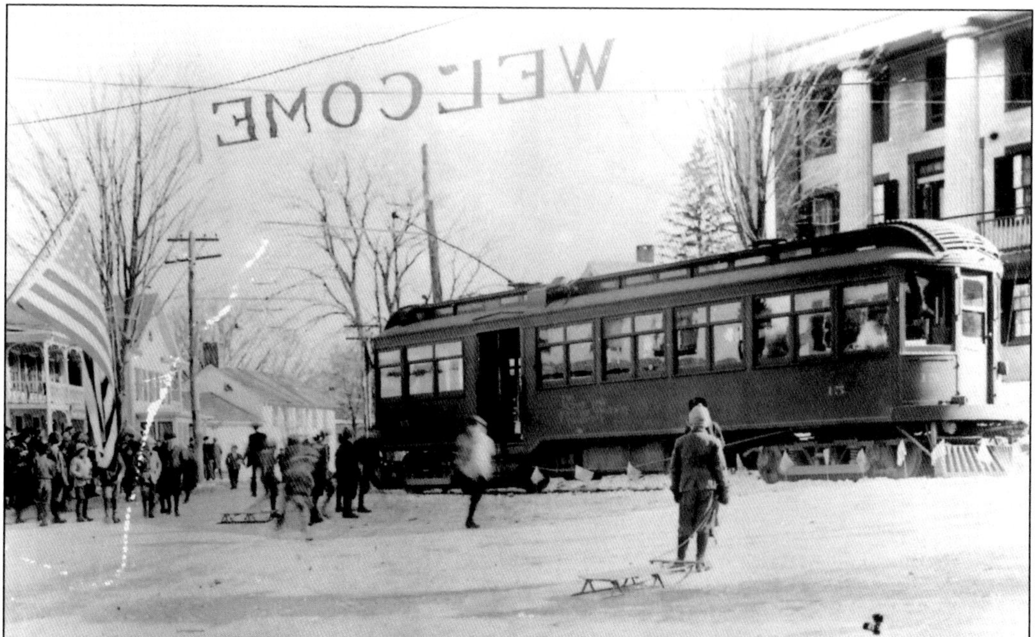

On January 23, 1914, the first car operated in Chester. The large welcome sign is no doubt to receive the railway in town. (Courtesy Connecticut Motor Coach Museum Archives.)

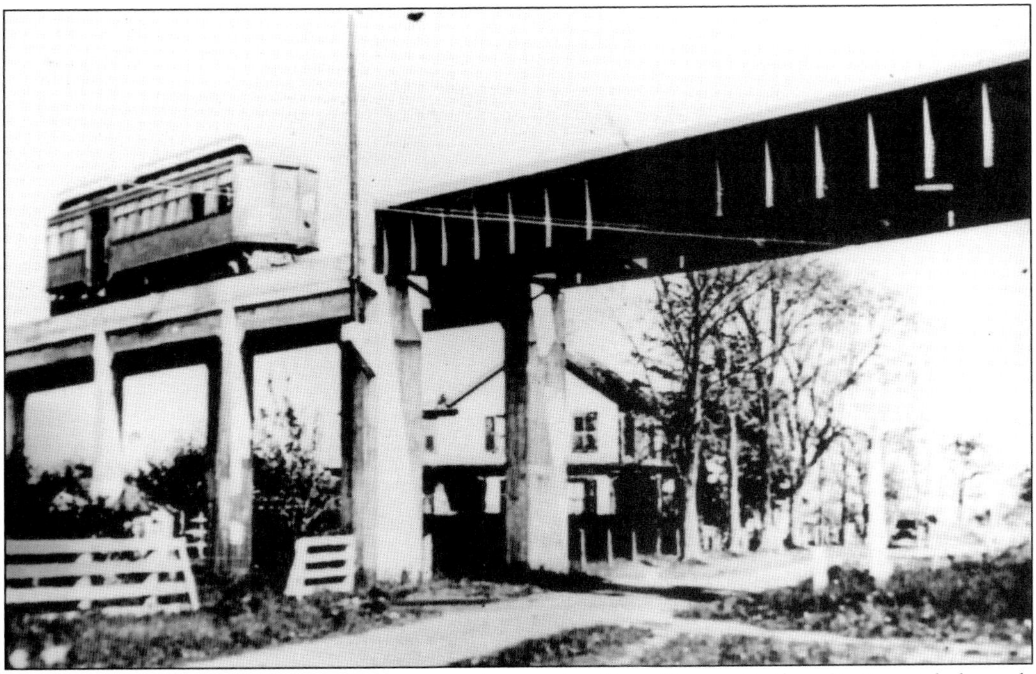

The Shore Line Electric main line crossed over the New Haven Railroad's Fenwick branch line on this very massive concrete viaduct in Old Saybrook. This structure was not torn down until the 1970s even though rail service ended in 1919. (Courtesy Connecticut Motor Coach Museum Archives.)

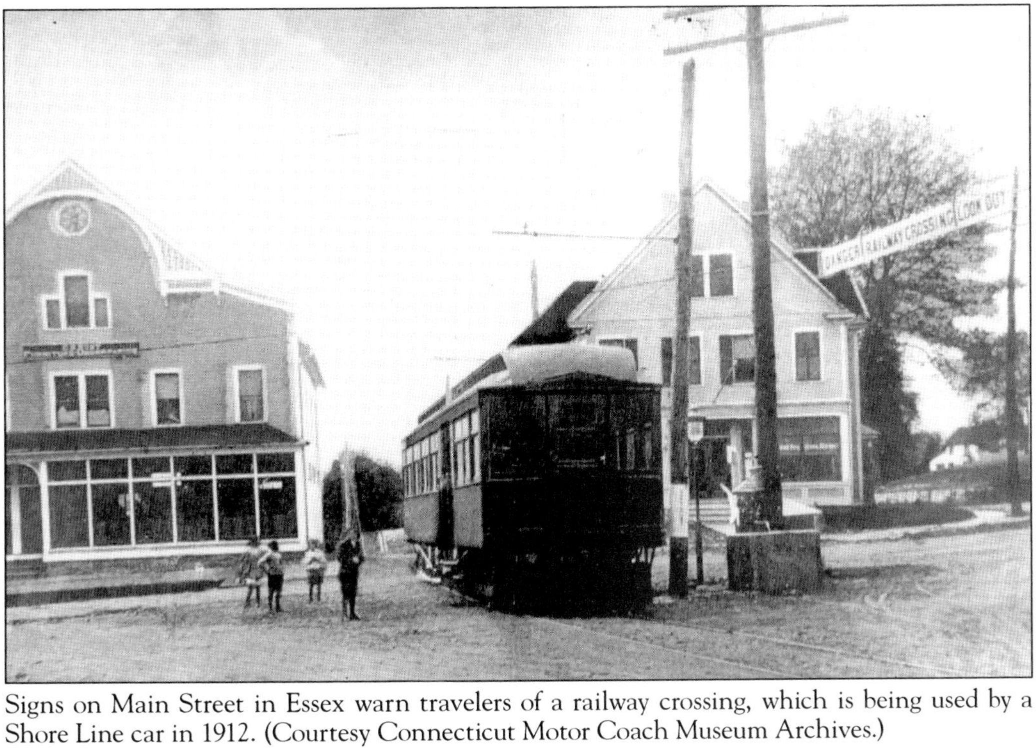

Signs on Main Street in Essex warn travelers of a railway crossing, which is being used by a Shore Line car in 1912. (Courtesy Connecticut Motor Coach Museum Archives.)

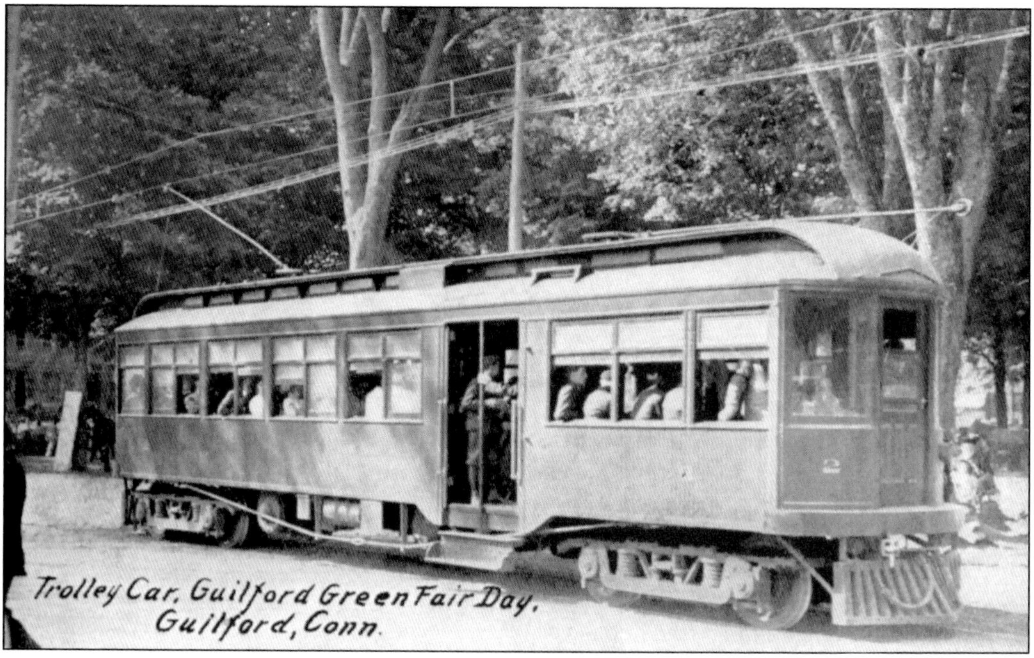

Shore Line car No. 2 is pictured on the Guilford Green during the Guilford Fair in 1915. (Courtesy Connecticut Motor Coach Museum Archives.)

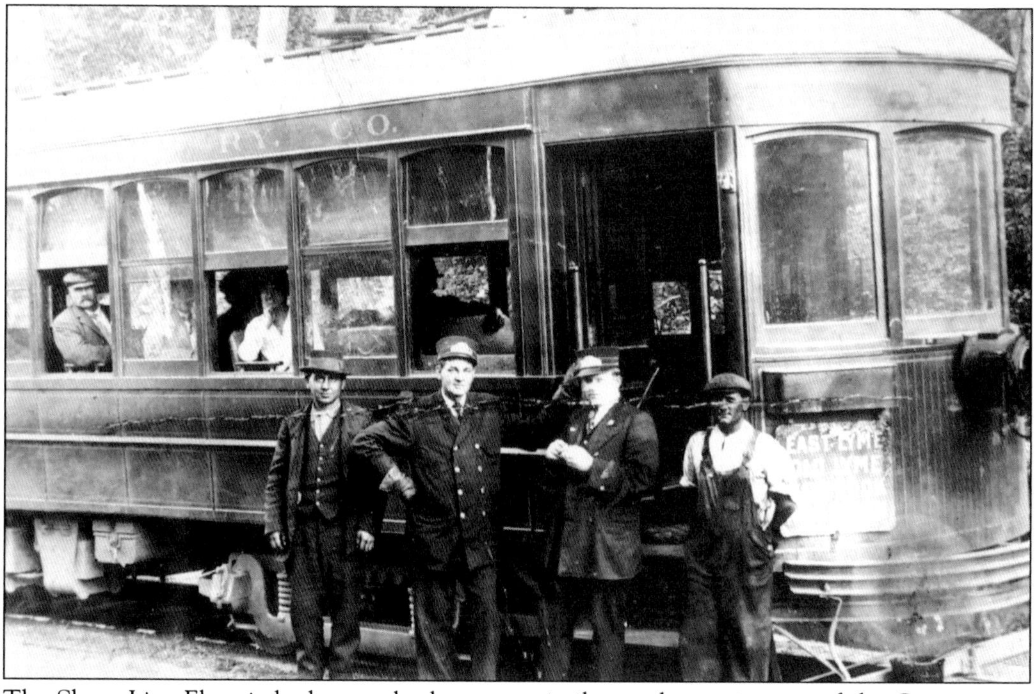

The Shore Line Electric had two suburban cars, similar to the equipment of the Connecticut Company, that ran between Guilford and Stony Creek Village. (Courtesy Connecticut Motor Coach Museum Archives.)

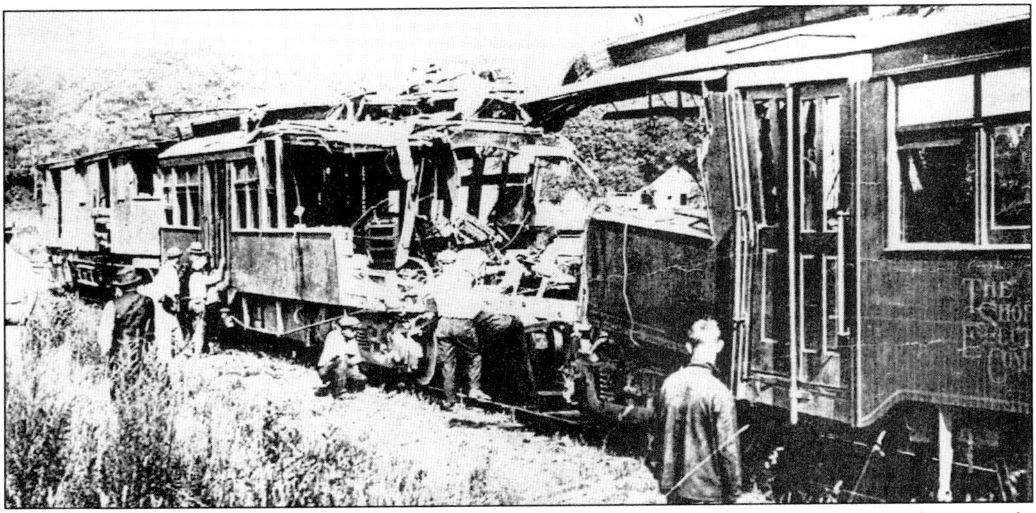

On August 3, 1917, the Shore Line Electric suffered a serious accident that was subsequently attributed to the primitive operating conditions and poor discipline on the line. The track between New Haven and Chester had over 44 regular trains running every day with no signals and only verbal orders that the operators were expected to remember. The collision between cars No. 3 and 16 killed 19 people and severely injured 35 after the motorman of an "extra" unscheduled car overrode the safety device on his car and fell asleep at the controller. While asleep, he ran past a meeting point with the regularly scheduled car. This accident resulted in many damage claims, which eventually contributed to the line's closing in 1919. (Courtesy Connecticut Motor Coach Museum Archives.)

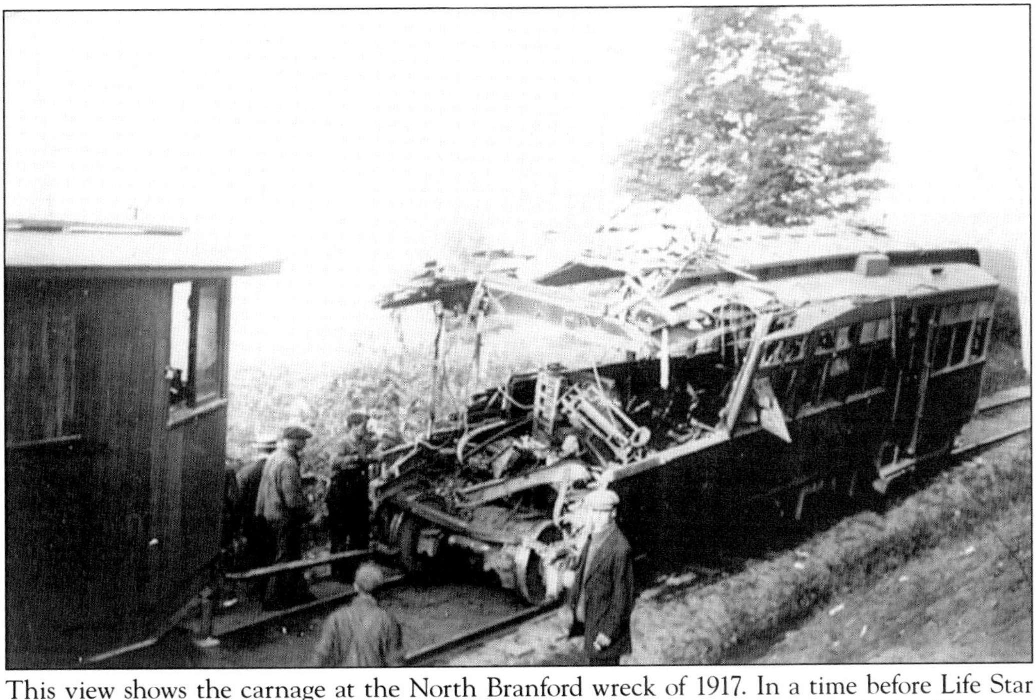

This view shows the carnage at the North Branford wreck of 1917. In a time before Life Star helicopters and EMTs, medical services were very primitive by today's standards. (Courtesy Connecticut Motor Coach Museum Archives.)

WAR PRICES ARE HIGH BECAUSE WAR COSTS ARE HIGH

Unless the butcher could get for his meat more money than the meat costs him, he would have to stop selling meat. His customers understand this, they know his high costs, and they pay his high prices without grudge against him, realizing that his predicament is identical with their own. The struggle with us all is to get money enough to cover our heavy bills of expense.

The street railroad rates of Eastern Connecticut are about to be increased as a matter of public necessity.

STREET RAILROAD TRANSPORTATION is as VITAL TO THE COMMUNITY as the railroad and the telephone. Without it business would be paralyzed.

STREET RAILROAD TRANSPORTATION CANNOT BE MAINTAINED EXCEPT AS ITS REVENUES MEET ITS COSTS.

STREET RAILROAD TRANSPORTATION COSTS HAVE BECOME PROHIBITIVE on the basis of former revenues. THIS CONDITION IS TRUE EVERYWHERE and it cannot be altered by change of ownership or management. It has created a street railroad crisis as desperate in New York, Massachusetts and Pennsylvania as it has in Connecticut. THE MOVEMENT TOWARD INCREASE OF RATES IS A UNIVERSAL ONE.

In two years the operating cost of our street railroads has increased more than 30 per cent.

The cost of supplies has doubled.

Overhead charges have increased. Taxes have increased. Labor costs have increased. Every enumerable item of costs has startlingly increased.

EXISTING REVENUES ARE HOPELESSLY INADEQUATE. STREET RAILWAY CREDIT IS SADLY IMPERILLED.

Continuation of this disparity between costs and revenues means the quick collapse of street raiload transportation. SERVICE, ALREADY SERIOUSLY IMPAIRED BY THE TASK OF HAULING PEAK LOADS WITH INSUFFICIENT FACILITIES OF POWER AND CARS AND MEN must come to calamitous breakdown, replacing deplorable inconvenience with downright hardship. Upon Eastern Connecticut there would be forced a ruinous decade of BUSINESS AND SOCIAL DISADVANTAGE out of which there could be but SLOW, PAINFUL AND MOST COSTLY EMERGENCE through any means of restoration imaginable.

THE TRUTH OF THESE STATEMENTS IS INCONTROVERTIBLY EVIDENBED by the books of our railways, and the figures of street railroad transportation, frankly open to any reasonable inquiry.

The Shore Line Electric Railway Company.

The fare increase sought by the Shore Line Electric in 1918 was very unpopular with the riding public due to the poor service provided by the company. This advertisement ran in the *New London Day* in 1918. (Courtesy Connecticut Motor Coach Museum Archives.)

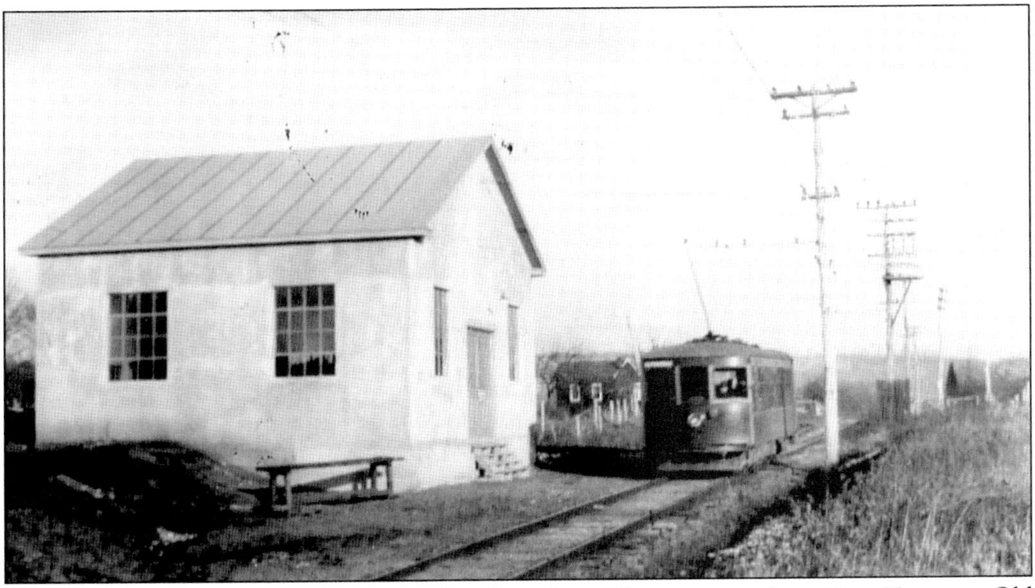

In 1923, after being idle for four years, the Shore Line Electric route from New Haven to Old Saybrook was reopened by a new company, the New Haven and Shore Line Railway. The company purchased five new lightweight cars from the Wason Manufacturing Company, along with some surplus equipment from the Hartford and Springfield Street Railway. Here a car passes the Totoket substation in East Haven. By 1929, this operation had ended and the company had become a charter bus operator. (Courtesy Connecticut Motor Coach Museum Archives.)

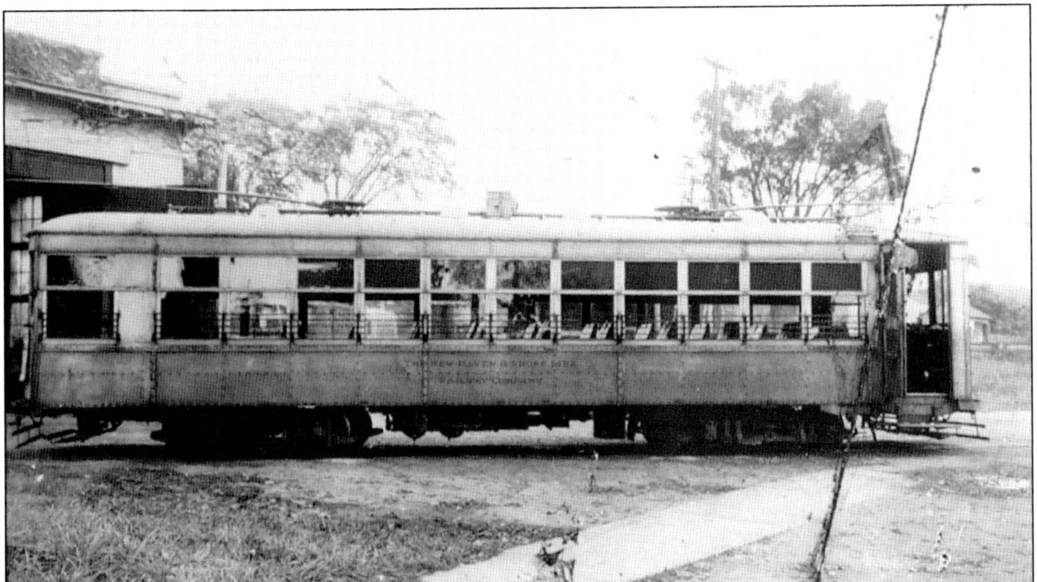

A route traveled by the New Haven and Shore Line started at the Guilford carbarn, a building located on the old Shore Line Electric to Stony Creek Village. The line started at the Guilford Green at the intersection of Whitfield and Boston Streets, extended westerly through Water Street, and then ran over a private right-of-way past Sachem's Head, Shell Beach, and Leete's Island to the Connecticut Company connection at Stony Creek Village. (Courtesy Connecticut Motor Coach Museum Archives.)

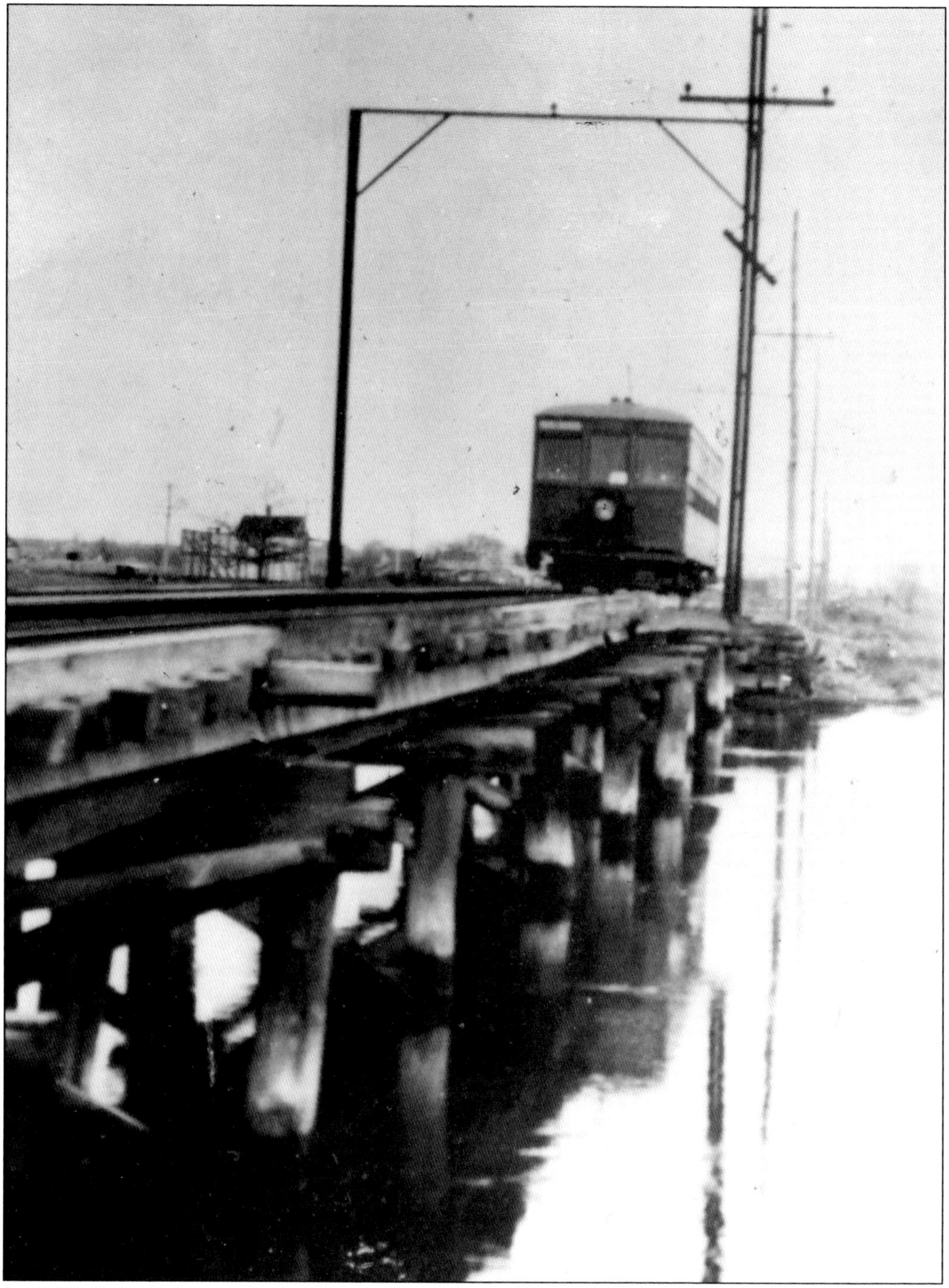

In 1925, the New Haven and Shore Line crossed the Quinnipiac River. The line then cut across the meadows on a private right-of-way to Quinnipiac Avenue, where it crossed the Connecticut Company line to Wallingford. It then continued east through Foxon and Totoket to North Branford. Much of Route 80 in East Haven is built on the right-of-way of this line. (Courtesy Connecticut Motor Coach Museum Archives.)

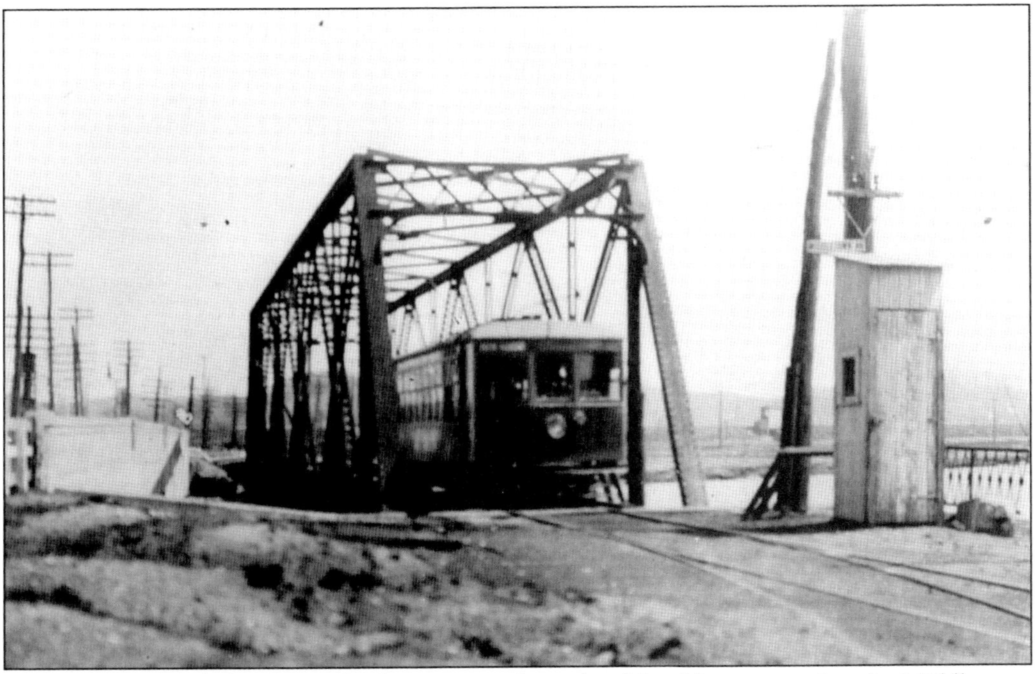

A New Haven and Shore Line Railway car is inbound to New Haven, crossing the Middletown Avenue Bridge in 1926. (Courtesy Connecticut Motor Coach Museum Archives.)

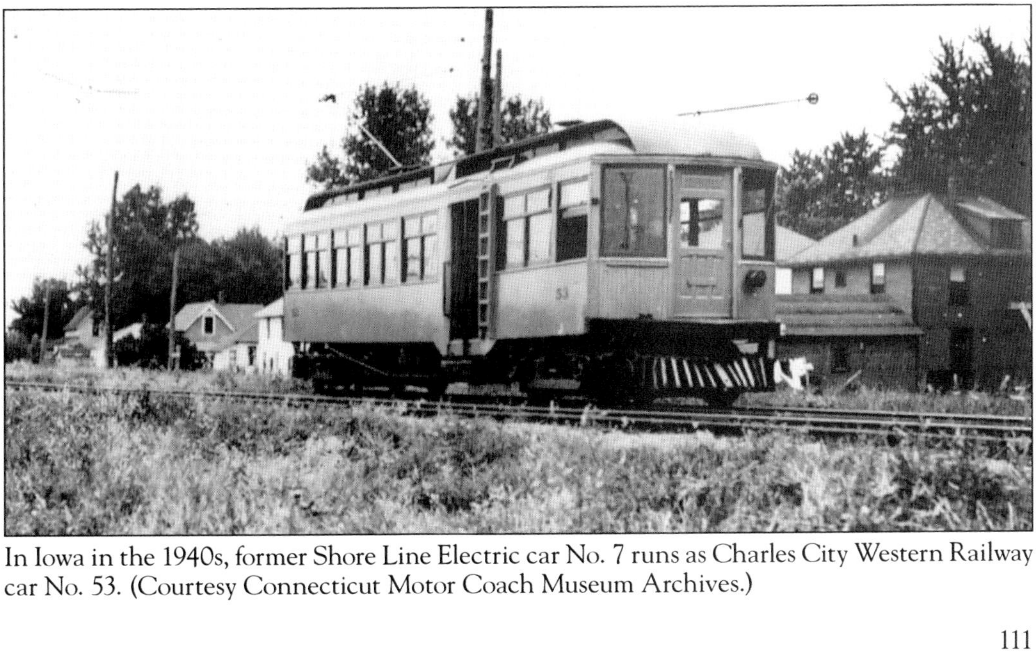

In Iowa in the 1940s, former Shore Line Electric car No. 7 runs as Charles City Western Railway car No. 53. (Courtesy Connecticut Motor Coach Museum Archives.)

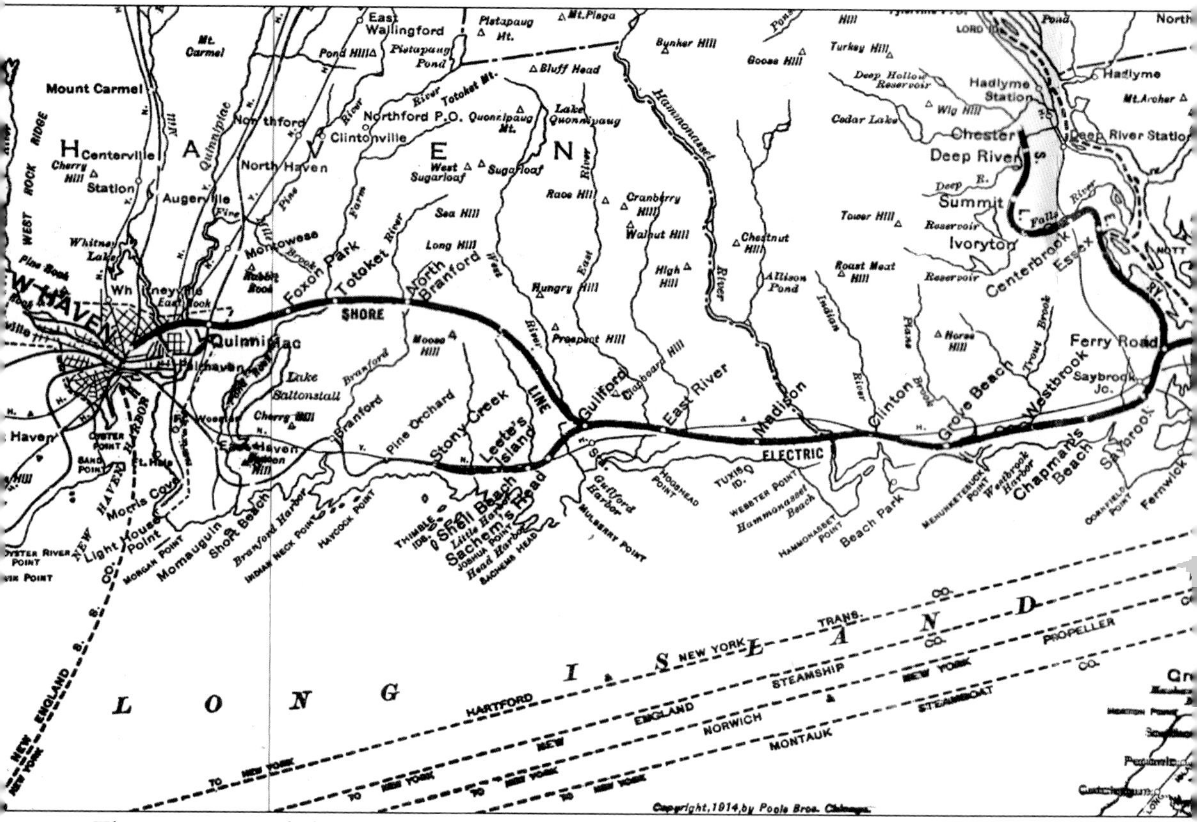

This is a map of the Shore Line Electric Railway. (Courtesy Connecticut Motor Coach Museum Archives.)

Eight

Stamford Lines

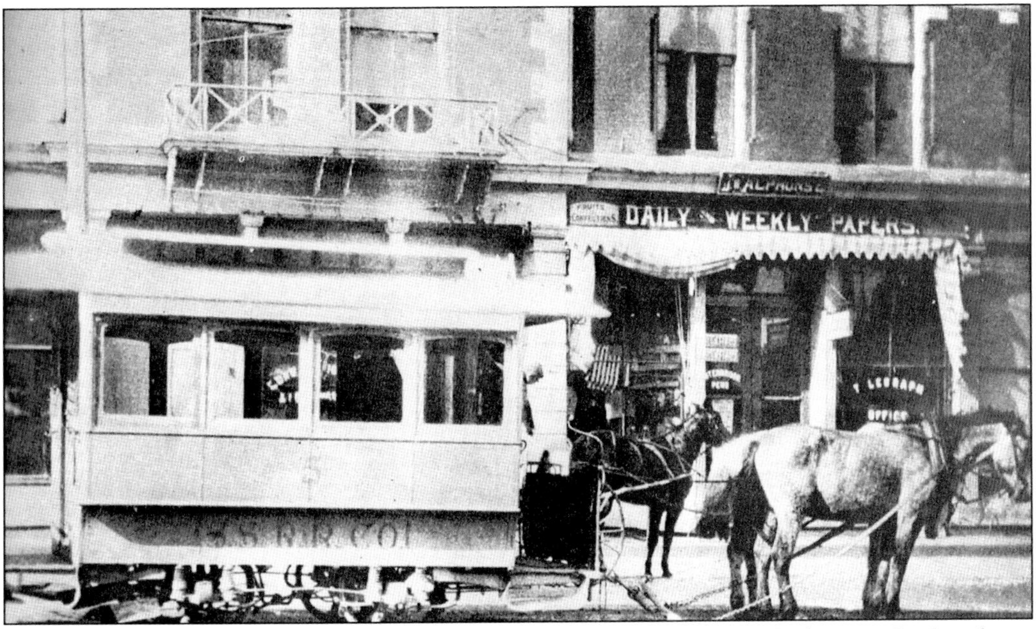

Public transportation came to Stamford in July 1870 when the Stamford Horse Railroad was organized by a group of local businessmen. However, it was not until January 1887 that tracks were laid and cars started to operate. The company never made money, and by 1888, it had entered bankruptcy. (Courtesy Fred Bennett collection.)

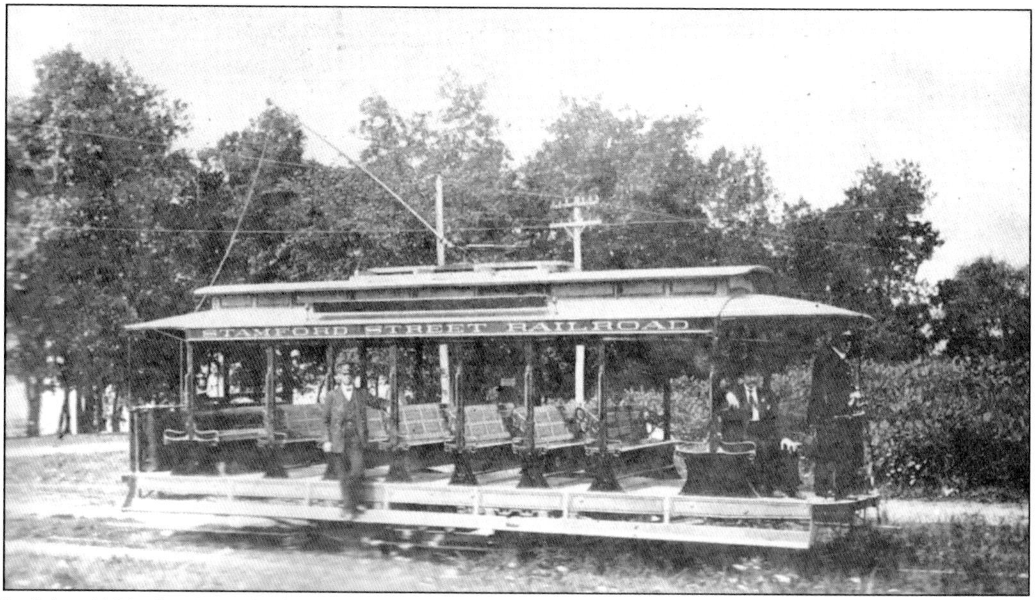

In May 1889, the Stamford Street Railway was organized to buy and operate the property of the Stamford Horse Railroad. In 1895, the New Haven Railroad made its first purchase of a street railway property when it obtained a controlling interest in the Stamford Street Railway. Electric cars first operated in Stamford in 1894. Car No. 7, one of the first, sits on Fairview Avenue at Ocean Drive at the end of the Shippan Point line in 1900. It was purchased secondhand from the Norwalk Tramway Company. (Courtesy Fred Bennett collection.)

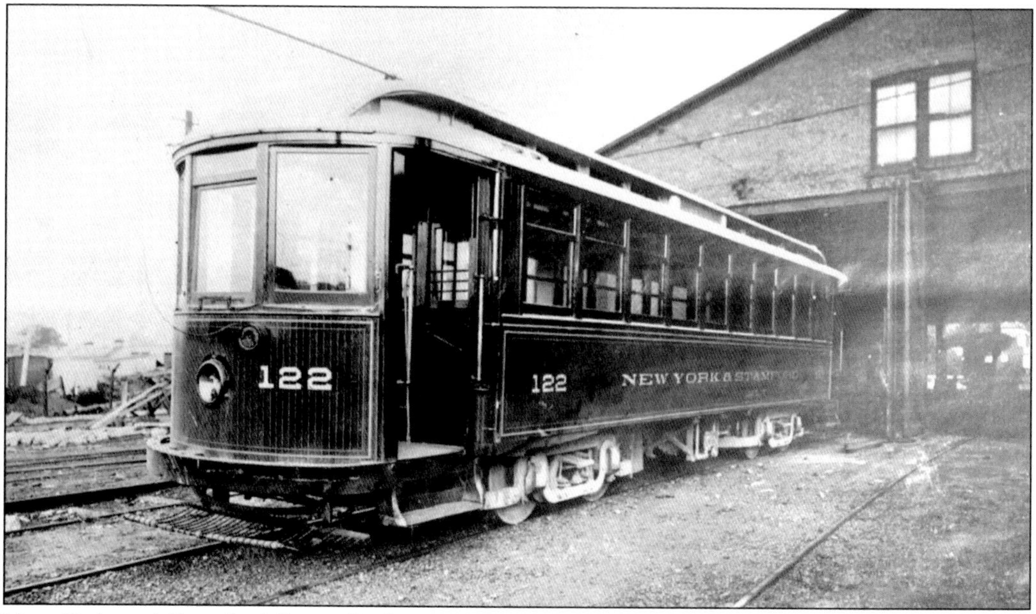

New York and Stamford Street Railway car No. 122 is shown at the Port Chester, New York, carbarn. Opening in 1905 and closing in 1927, this line ran from Atlantic Square in Stamford to New Rochelle, New York. These cars were very similar to those of the Connecticut Company, although they were painted maroon. The New York and Stamford was also under the control of the New Haven Railroad. (Courtesy Connecticut Motor Coach Museum Archives.)

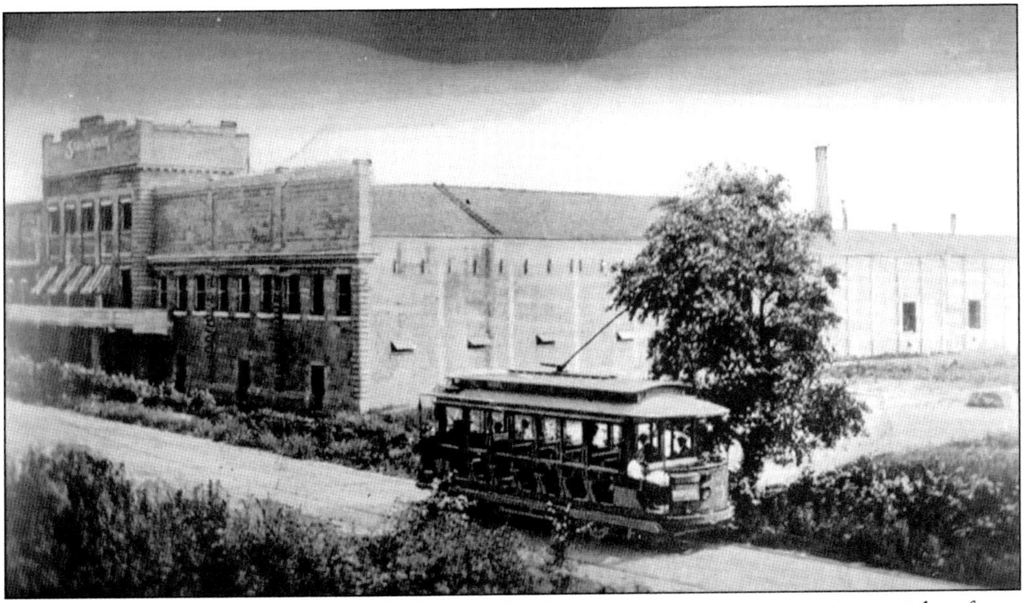

In this 1900 postcard view, a Stamford Street Railway open car runs on a private right-of-way alongside the New Haven Railroad main line. (Courtesy Fred Bennett collection.)

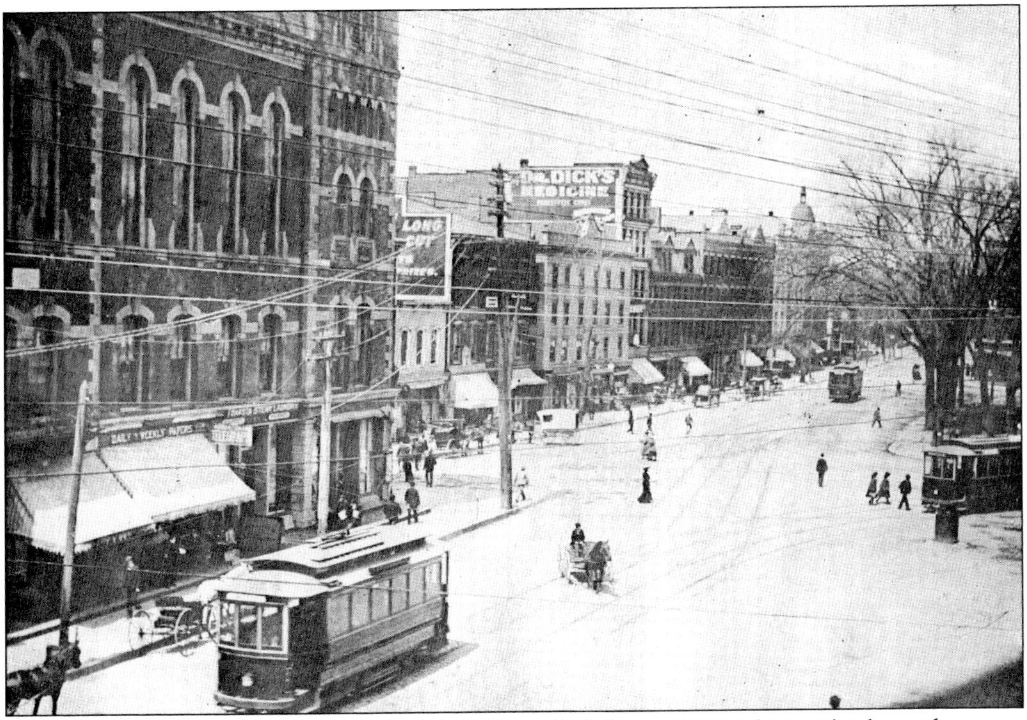

This winter 1904 scene of Central Square in Stamford depicts horse-drawn sleighs and wagons alongside trolley cars. (Courtesy Fred Bennett collection.)

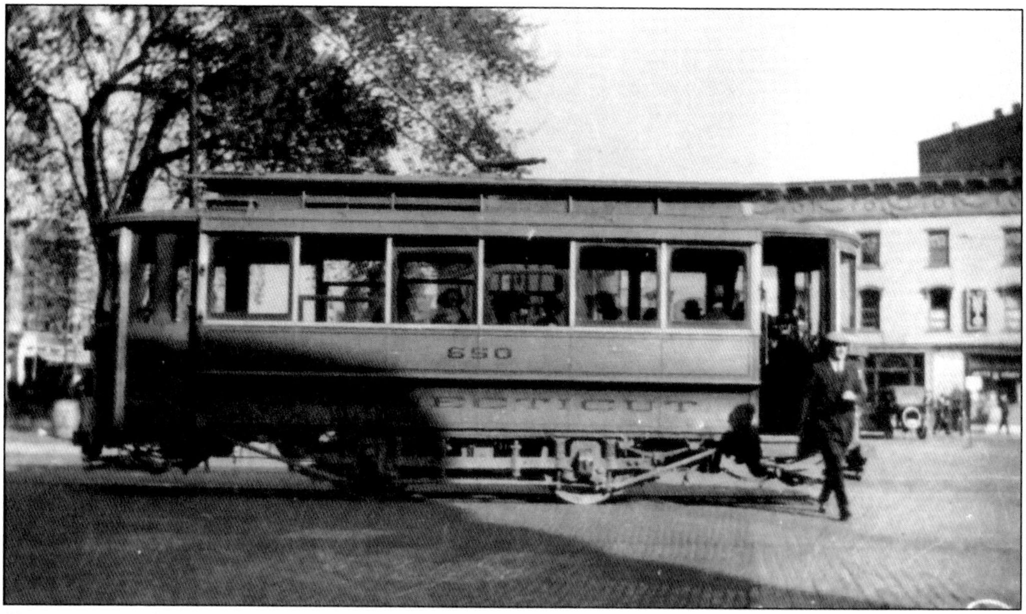

Connecticut Company car No. 650 is pictured after being converted to man operation, which by this time was well past its prime. Originally car No. 22 of the Stamford Street Railway, it was scrapped in 1926. (Courtesy Fred Bennett collection.)

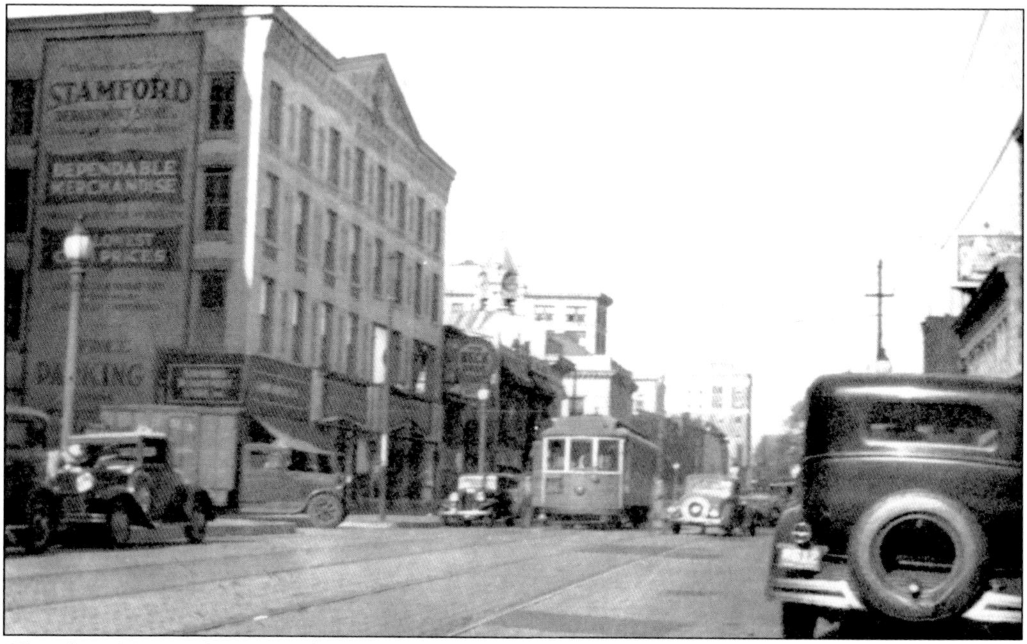

Closed car No. 1495 stops at the intersection of Atlantic Avenue and Bell Street on November 12, 1933, the last day of streetcar operation in Stamford. (Courtesy Fred Bennett collection.)

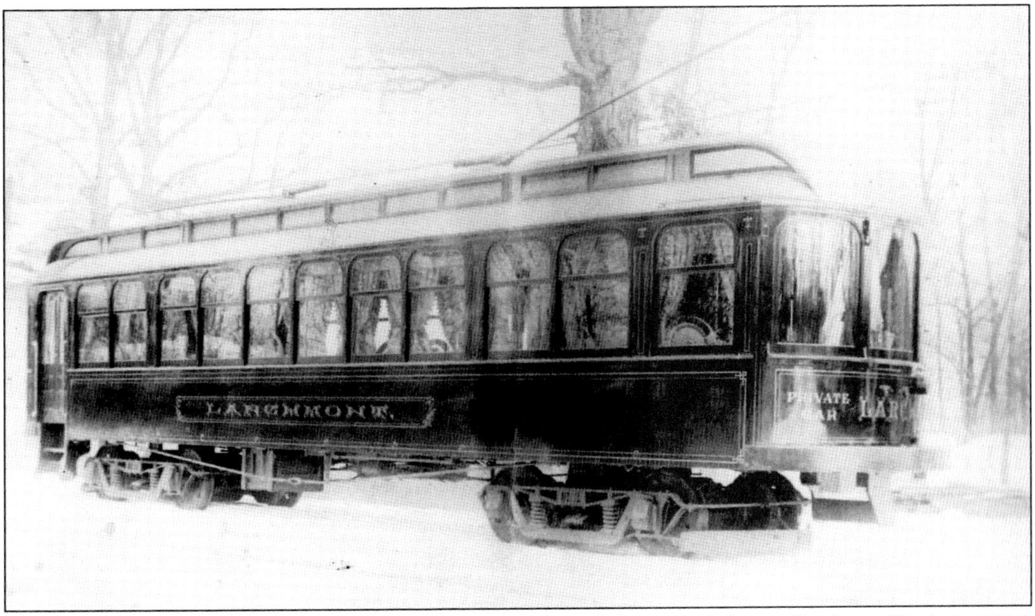

The *Larchmont* was the parlor car of the New York and Stamford Street Railway. Built in 1901 by the St. Louis Car Company of St. Louis, Missouri, it was eventually sold to the Connecticut Company and renumbered 1606. It was used as an instruction car for training new motormen in New Haven until being retired in 1921. The car's body was sold and is now part of a house in the Momauguin section of East Haven. (Courtesy Fred Bennett collection.)

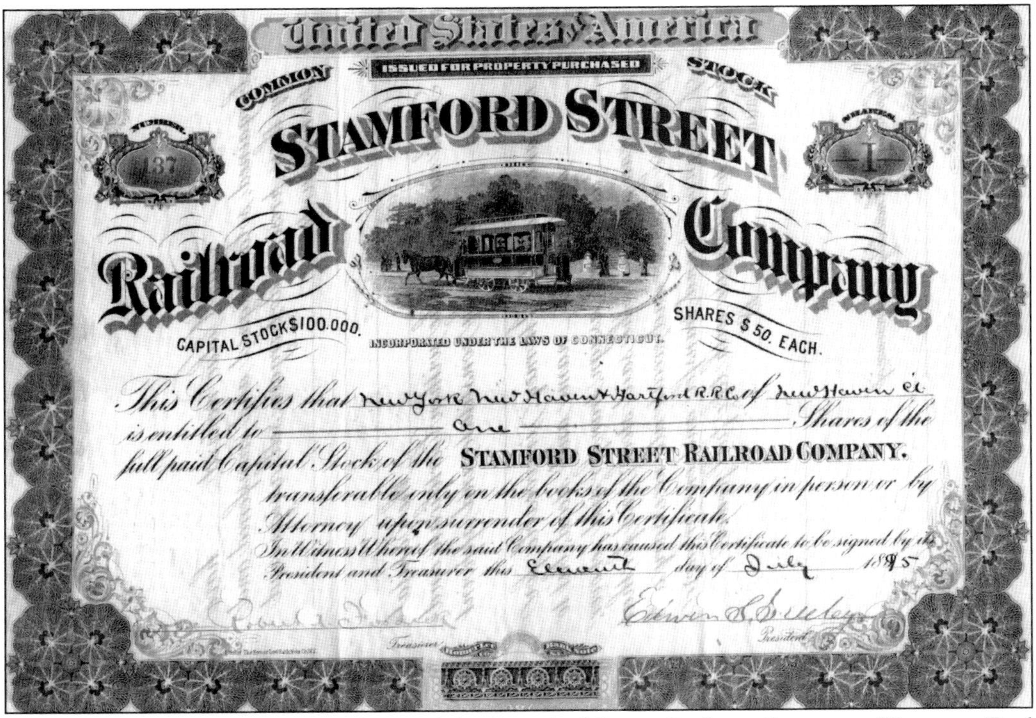
United States of America
ISSUED FOR PROPERTY PURCHASED
COMMON STOCK
STAMFORD STREET
137
1
Railroad Company
CAPITAL STOCK $100.000.
SHARES $ 50. EACH.
INCORPORATED UNDER THE LAWS OF CONNECTICUT.
This Certifies that New York New Haven & Hartford R.R. Co. of New Haven Ct
is entitled to One Shares of the full paid Capital Stock of the STAMFORD STREET RAILROAD COMPANY. transferable only on the books of the Company in person or by Attorney upon surrender of this Certificate.
In Witness Whereof the said Company has caused this Certificate to be signed by its President and Treasurer this Eleventh day of July 1895
Treasurer
President

This image displays a stock certificate of the Stamford Street Railway Company. (Courtesy Fred Bennett collection.)

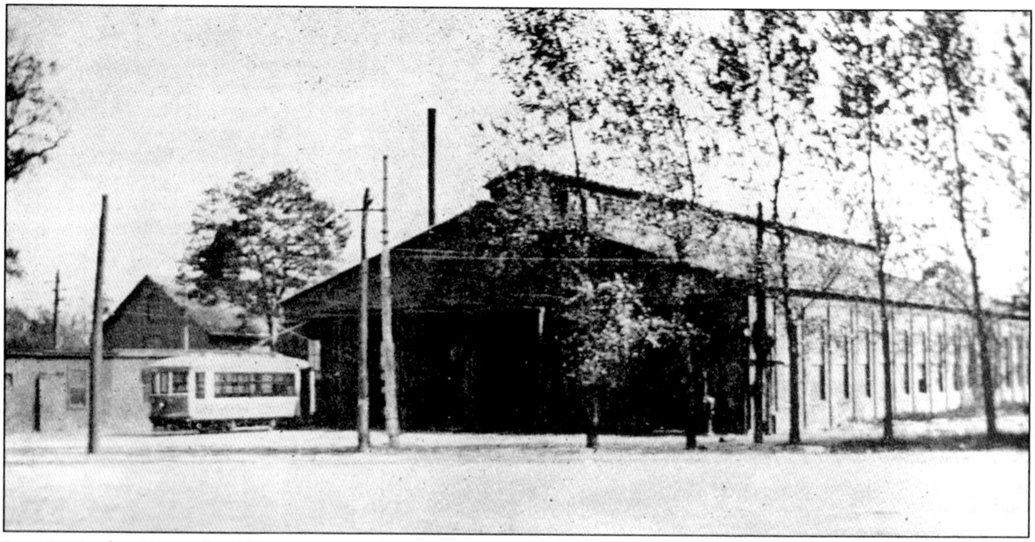

In 1925, the Stamford Division carbarn was used to store trolley cars like this safety car. After the lines in Stamford were converted to motor coach, this building was used as a bus garage. The barn was erected in 1902 and dismantled in the late 1980s. The Connecticut Trolley Museum in East Windsor houses the roof's structural steel with the hope of someday using the beams to construct a new carbarn. (Courtesy Fred Bennett collection.)

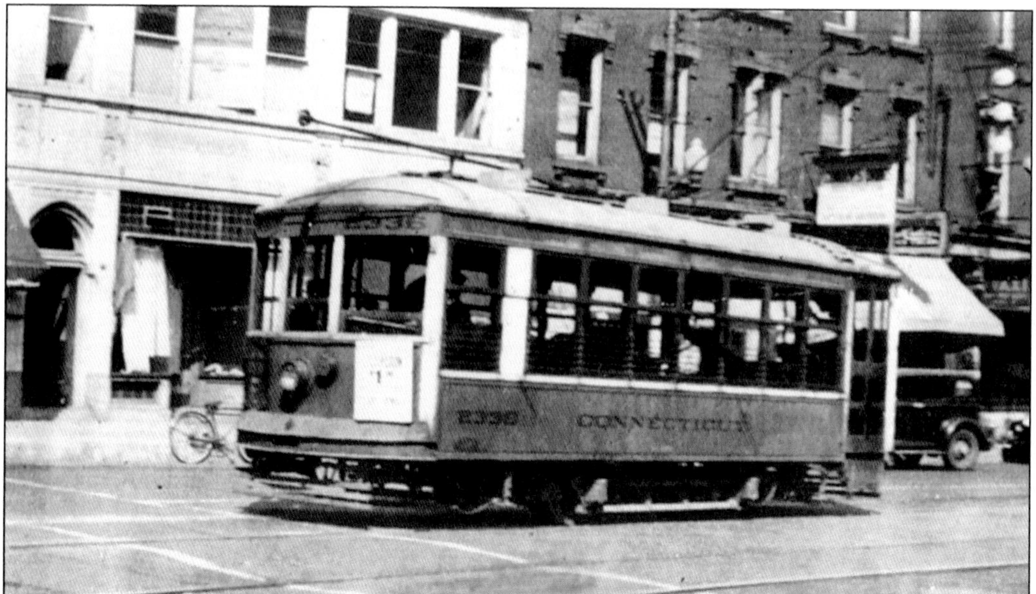

A single-truck Birney safety car runs on Atlantic Avenue sometime in the 1920s. (Courtesy Fred Bennett collection.)

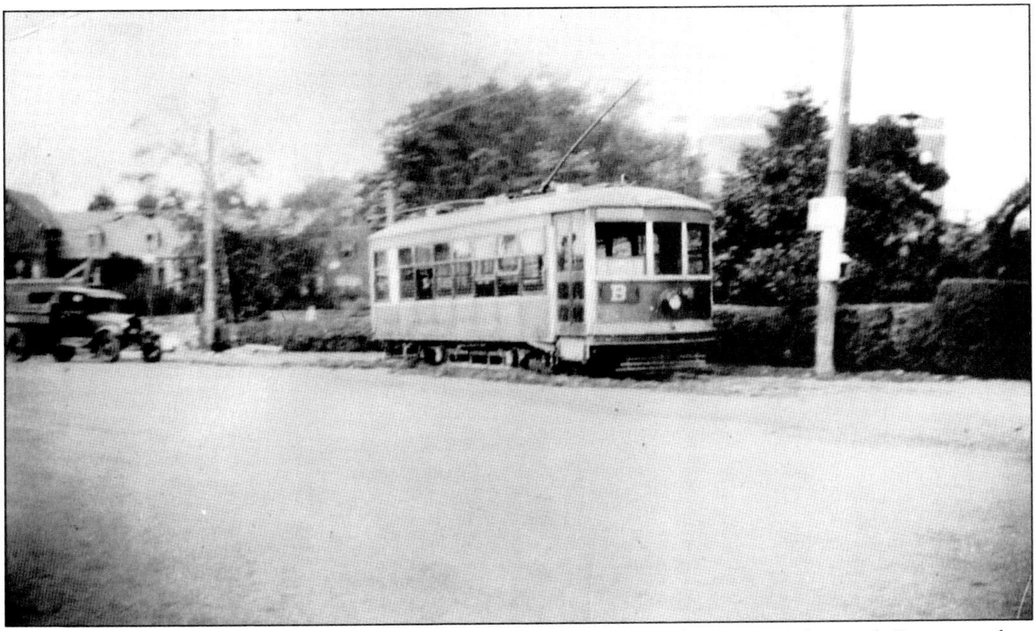

The Stamford Division of the Connecticut Company operated many single-truck Birney safety cars. (Courtesy Fred Bennett collection.)

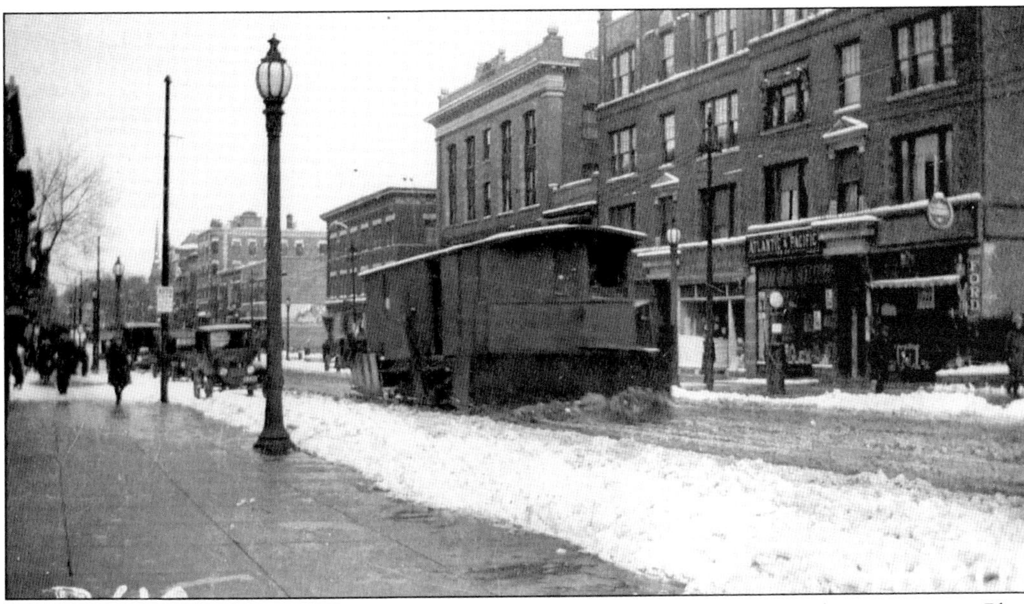

Road maintenance, including snow removal, was often the chore of the trolley companies. Plow No. 0144 clears snow from Atlantic Avenue during March 1923. (Courtesy Connecticut Motor Coach Museum Archives.)

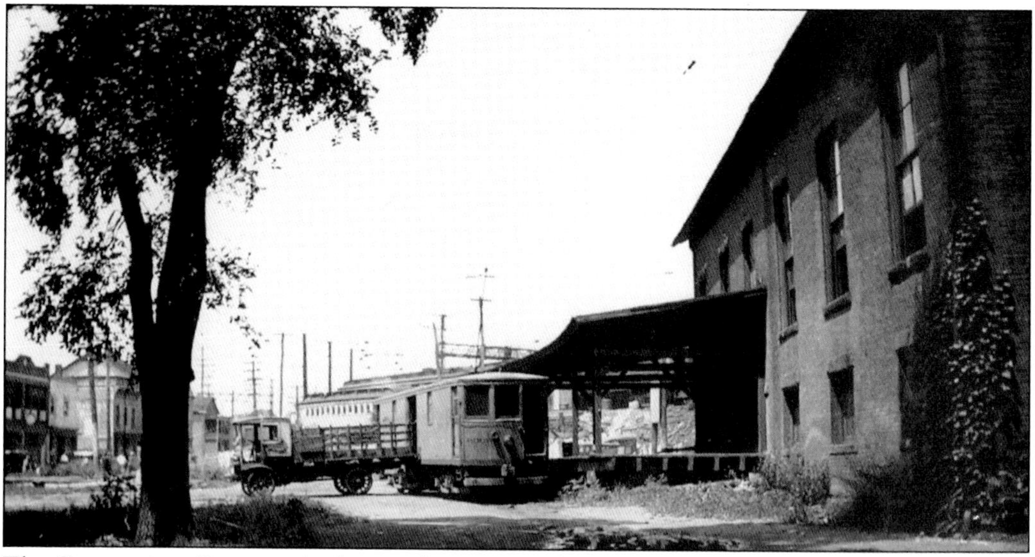

The Connecticut Company had a very lucrative package and freight business with freight depots in all major cities. A business in Stamford could ship a package via trolley freight and have it delivered the next morning in New York City, Hartford, or Springfield, Massachusetts—something people take for granted today. The freight depot in Stamford, seen here, was converted from an old power station. (Courtesy Connecticut Motor Coach Museum Archives.)

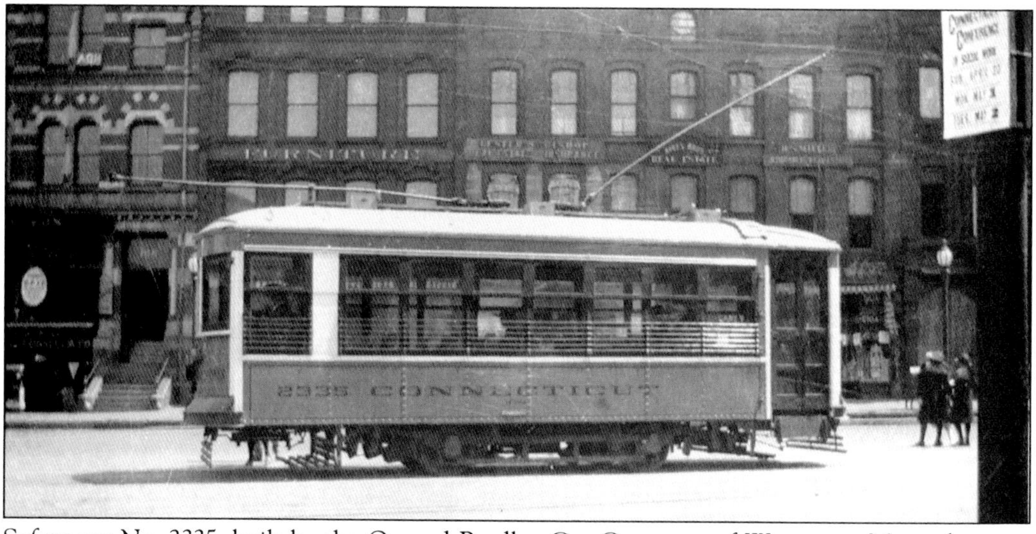

Safety car No. 2335, built by the Osgood Bradley Car Company of Worcester, Massachusetts, runs in Stamford in 1920. This car later served in New Haven and Bridgeport before being scrapped in 1936. (Courtesy Fred Bennett collection.)

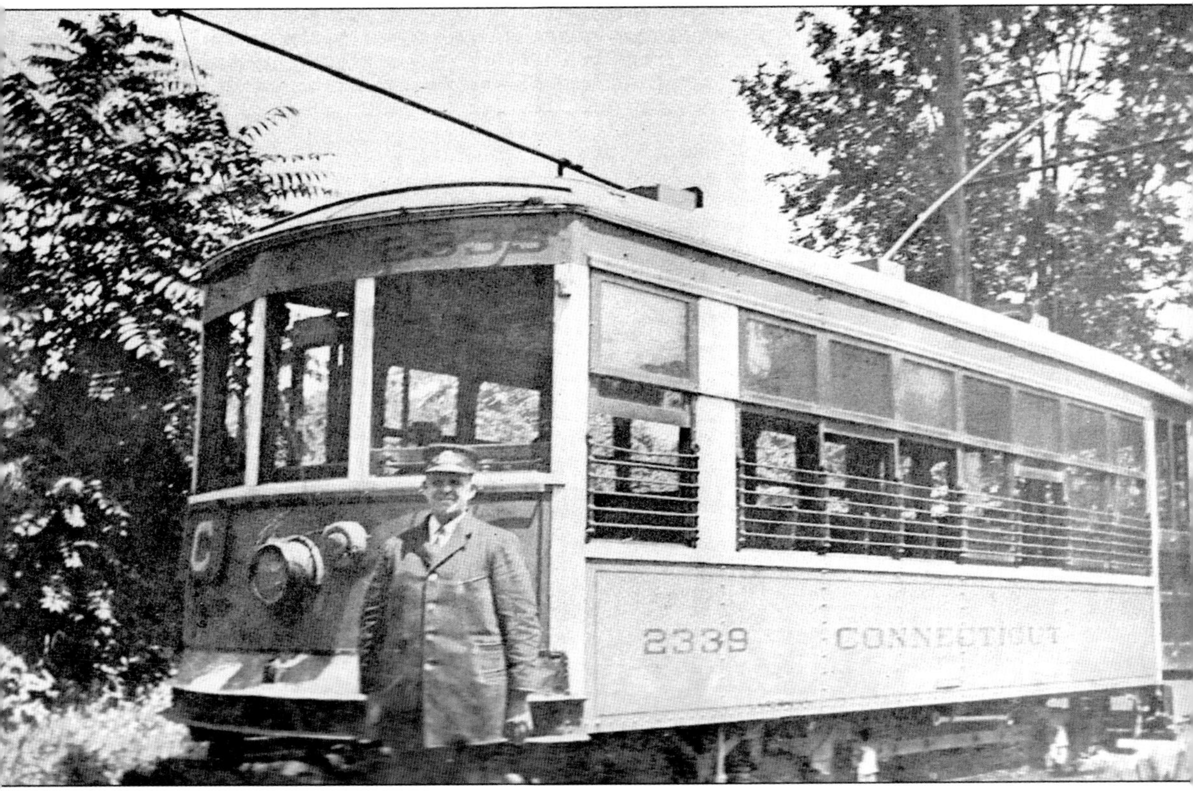

Motorman Harry Champion is pictured with car No. 2339 on July 25, 1931, the last day of streetcar operation in Stamford. (Courtesy Fred Bennett collection.)

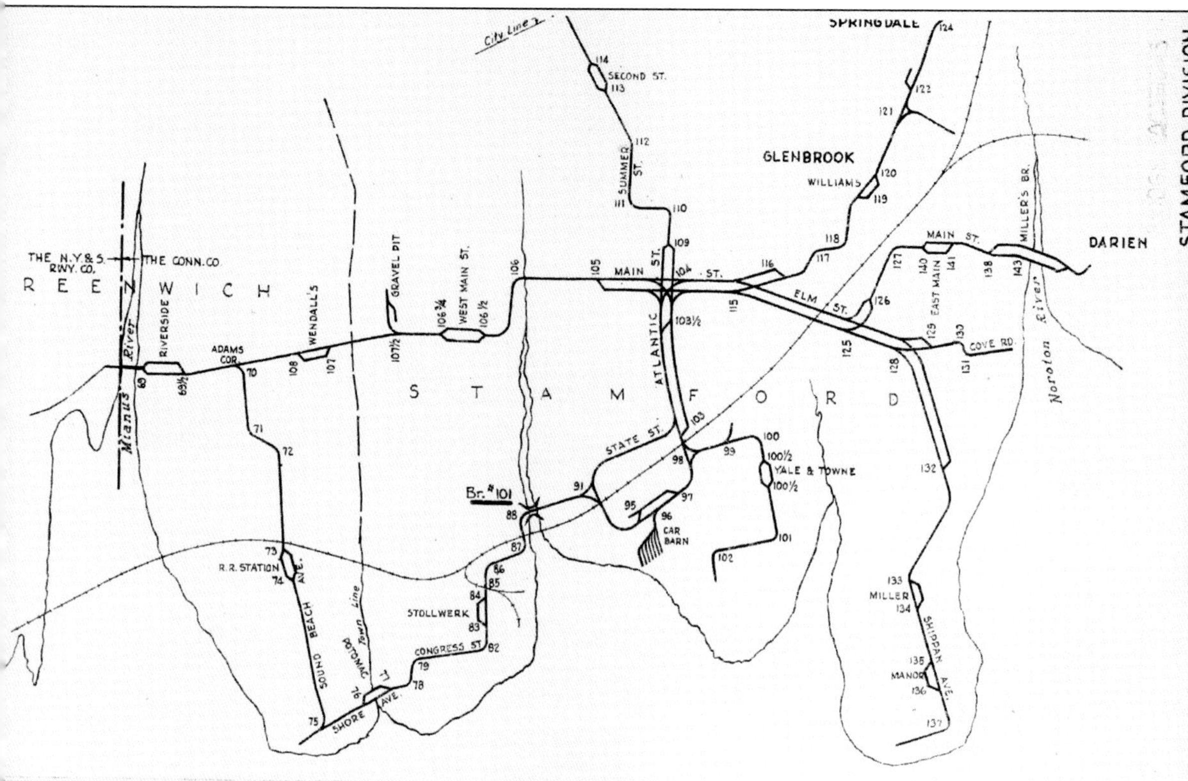

This map illustrates the streetcar lines in Stamford. (Courtesy Connecticut Motor Coach Museum Archives.)

Nine

ODDS AND ENDS

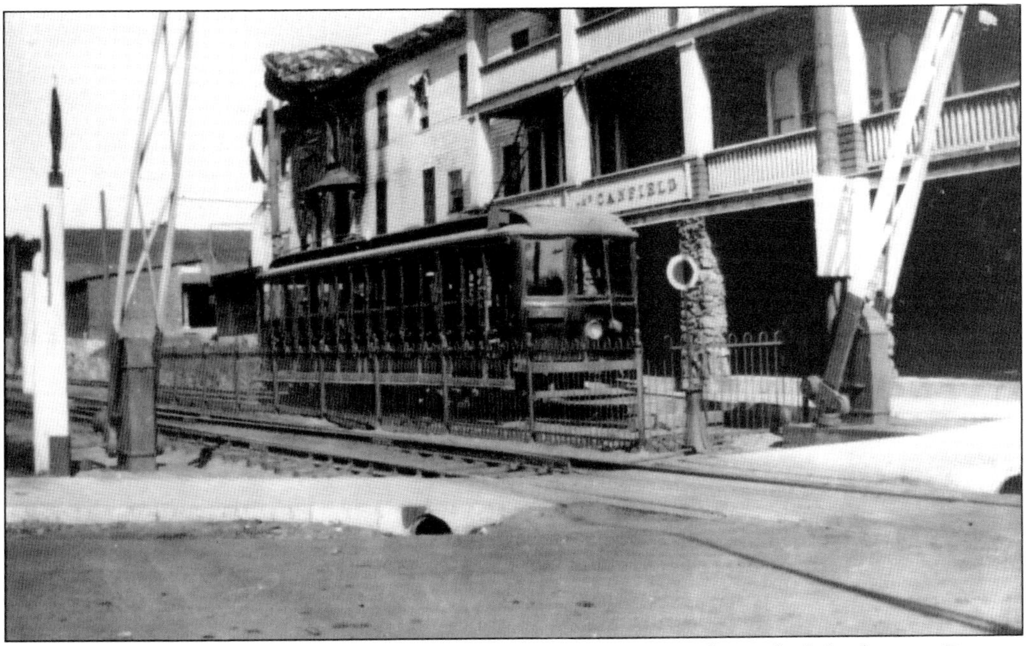

In 1914, one might find a Berkshire Street Railway car sitting at the end of the line in Canaan at the Hotel Canfield. The Berkshire Street Railway was the only street railway company in the country to operate in four states: Connecticut, Massachusetts, New York, and Vermont. Rail operations between Great Barrington, Massachusetts, and Canaan were abandoned in 1919, and the remainder of the system was abandoned piecemeal between 1922 and 1932, when the company became a motor coach service. The Berkshire Street Railway went out of business in 1958. (Courtesy Connecticut Motor Coach Museum Archives.)

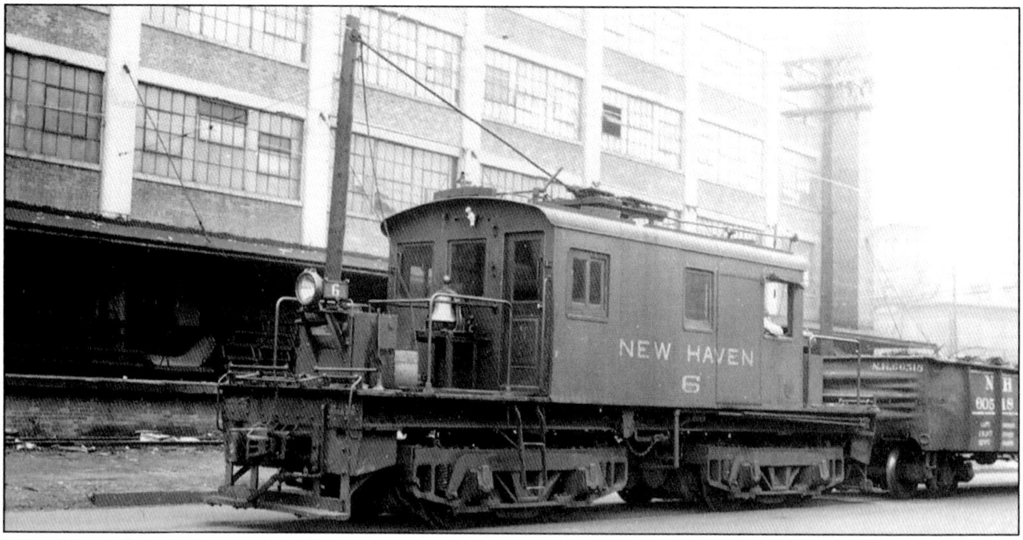

The Manufacturers Railroad in New Haven never carried passengers. It was still technically a streetcar line because it utilized electric locomotives designed to operate over street railway lines and in fact did use Connecticut Company tracks on Farren and Forbes Avenues. The line served over 45 shippers in New Haven. In September 1948, it was converted to a diesel operation when the Connecticut Company ended trolley service and the line lost its source of 600-volt direct current power. Locomotive No. 6, shown in 1940, was sold in 1948 to Capitol Traction of Washington, D.C., where it served a power station until being scrapped in 1955. (Courtesy Connecticut Motor Coach Museum Archives.)

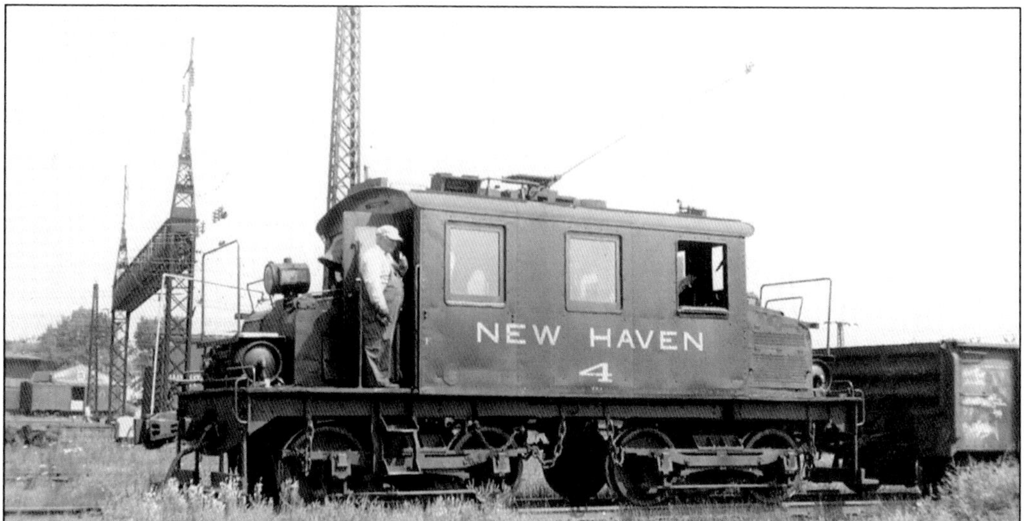

The New Haven Railroad operated a line in Bridgeport similar to the Manufacturers Railroad in New Haven. The Seaview Avenue Railroad served a number of freight customers on Stratford Avenue, the largest being the Stanley Works. Locomotive No. 4, originally running on the Manufacturers Railroad, was transferred to Bridgeport in 1931 along with its twin, No. 3. This line operated as an electric railway until 1953, when diesel engines were brought in to switch the freight customers. Both No. 3 and No. 4 were scrapped in 1953. (Courtesy Connecticut Motor Coach Museum Archives.)

Ten

Connecticut Trolleys in 2006

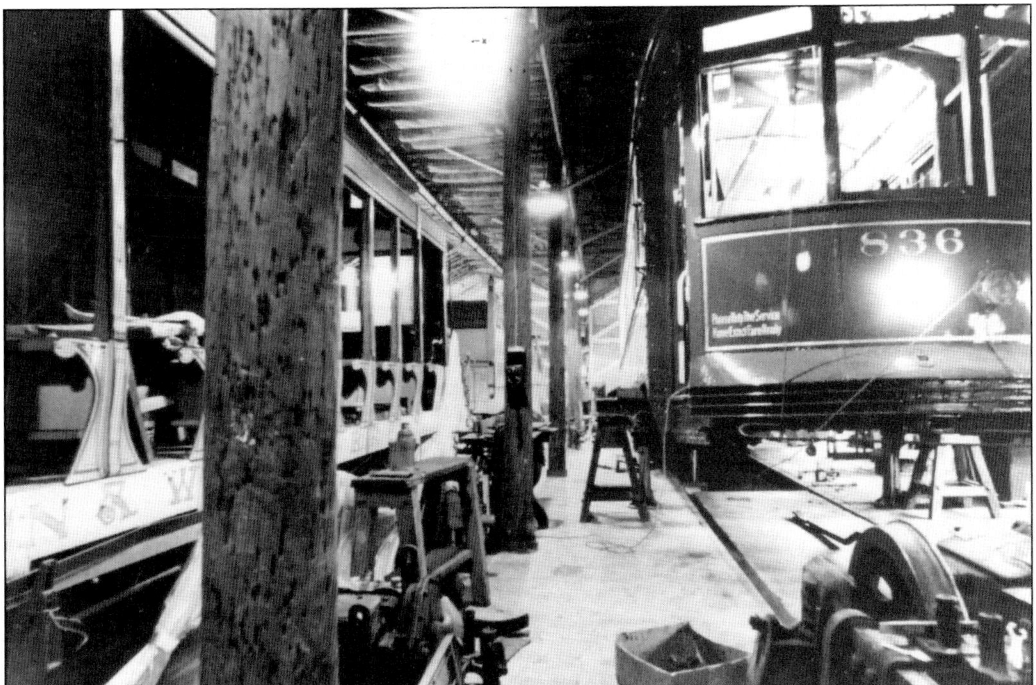

Heavy repairs of streetcars are still being performed in 2006. At the Connecticut Trolley Museum repair shop in East Windsor, New Orleans car No. 836 is having its wheels repaired. On the left is Connecticut Company open car No. 355, which was restored in the 1950s by Fred Bennett, one of the best streetcar restorers in the country. (Courtesy Connecticut Electric Railway Association Archives.)

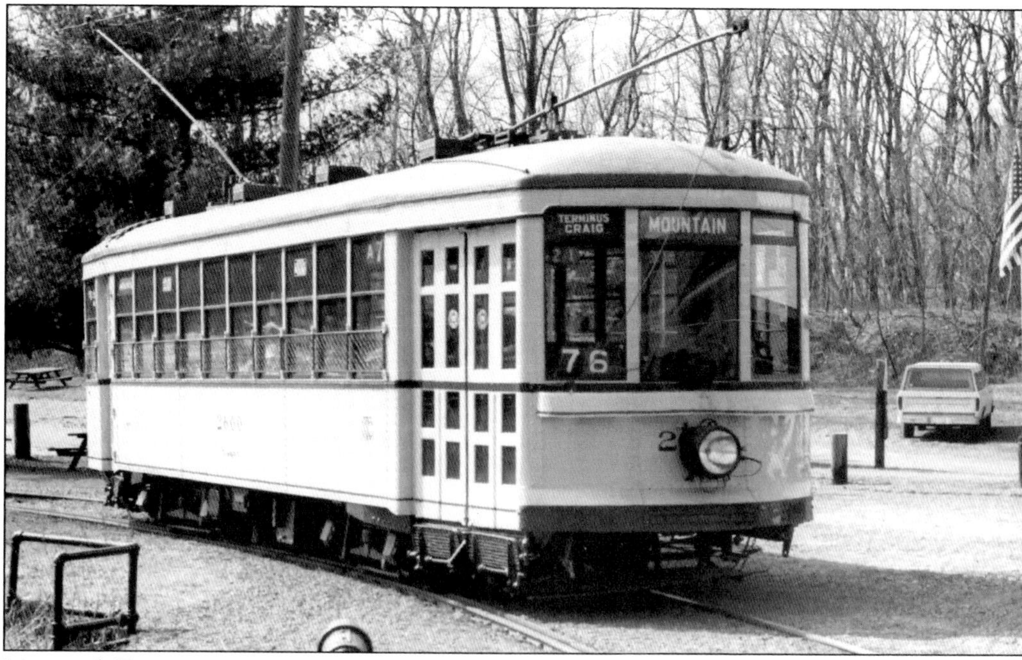

Montreal Tramways car No. 2600 operates in regular service at the Connecticut Trolley Museum. Built in 1926 by the Canadian Car Company, it ran in Montreal until 1960. (Courtesy Connecticut Electric Railway Association Archives.)

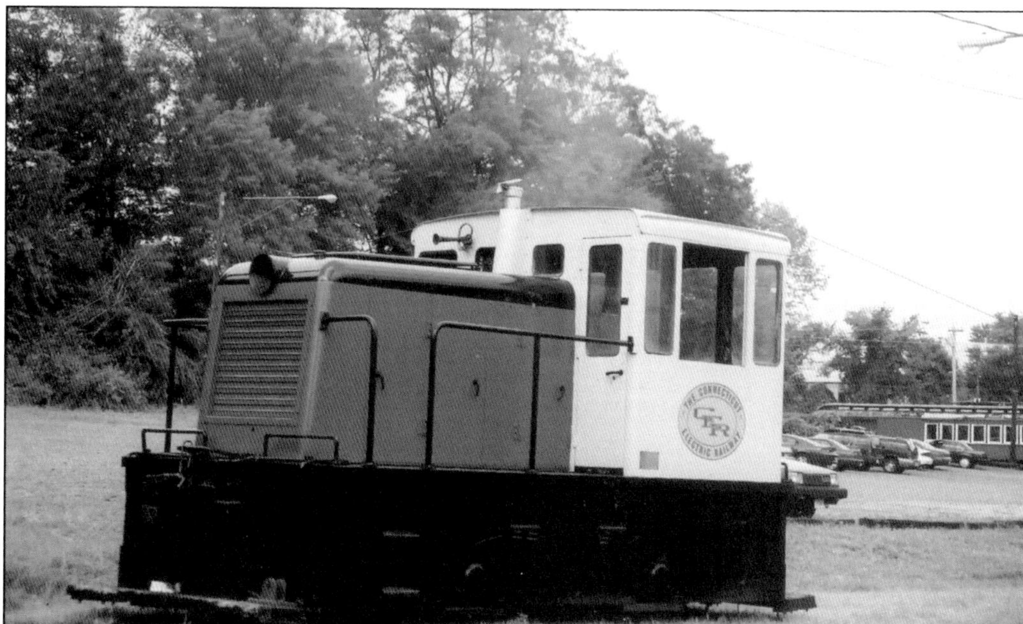

The General Electric Company built this 25-ton diesel engine for the Hartford Electric Light Company in 1949. It served at the South Meadows station in Hartford until it was retired and donated to the Connecticut Trolley Museum in 1988. Today the museum uses engine No. 1 to switch streetcars around the carshop and to rescue streetcars out on the line in the event of a power failure. (Courtesy Connecticut Electric Railway Association Archives.)

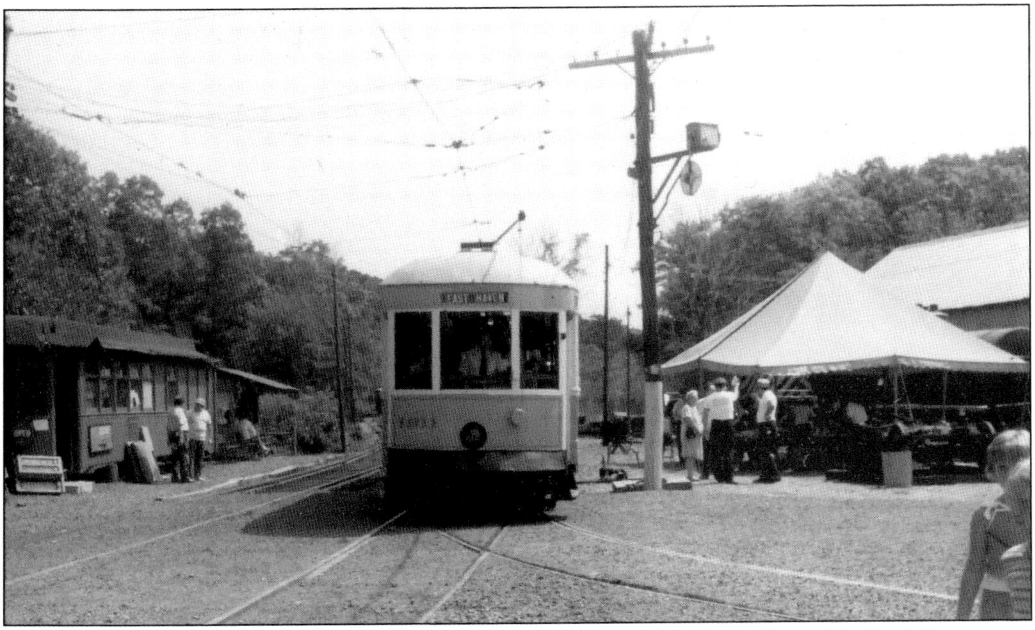

Connecticut Company car No. 1911 was still running at the Shore Line Trolley Museum in East Haven in the 1980s. It was the only car of the series that was saved after the Connecticut Company discontinued streetcar service in New Haven in 1948. The Connecticut Company once owned 50 of these large double-truck suburban cars, which ran on longer trips out of Bridgeport, Hartford, New Haven, and Waterbury. (Courtesy Branford Electric Railway Association.)

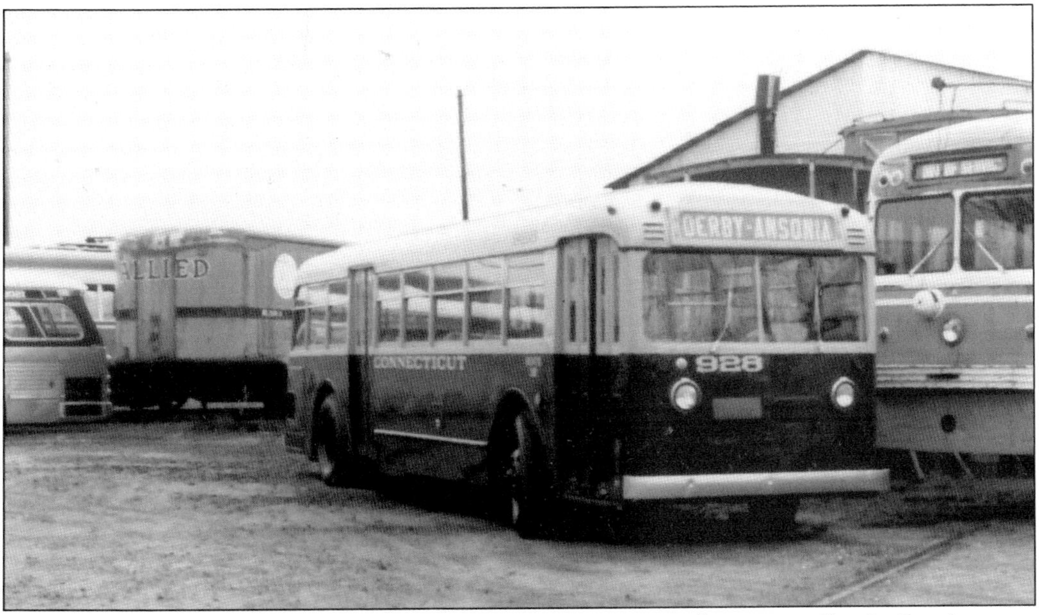

Former Connecticut Company Yellow Coach No. 928 was originally preserved by the Smithsonian Institution. After sitting in a warehouse for many years, it was given to the Shore Line Trolley Museum for display in the 1980s. While buses like this helped replace the streetcars all over the country, museums are now starting to appreciate their historical value. This bus was built in 1939. (Courtesy Branford Electric Railway Association.)